One Family: Indivisible
A Spiritual Memoir

Steven Greenebaum

For information, contact
MSI Press
1760-F Airline Highway, #203
Hollister, CA 95023

Library of Congress Control Number 2019941932

ISBN: 978-1-933455-46-4

To all who have striven and who will strive to embrace and unite humanity. May we learn to celebrate and respect our diversity rather than fear it.

Contents

Preface

Humanity is astonishingly diverse, and that reality can be at the same moment both beautiful and disconcerting. Throughout history we have divided ourselves into groupings of "us" and "them." And once we create the "other," we come to fear and even hate "them." Isn't there some way to acknowledge our differences without dividing and subdividing ourselves into competing tribes, ever-hostile to one another? I believe this question to be the great and overarching challenge to humanity in the twenty-first century. Grappling with it has been the calling of my life.

I deeply believe that one of our greatest challenges as a species has been and continues to be how to hold with respect our almost endless diversity while at the same time recognizing our common humanity. How can we come together? Where do we even begin?

How, for example, do we address the crippling scourge of patriarchy that has demeaned so many of our spiritual paths? How do we acknowledge the beauty of our races while actively rejecting racism? These are two of the questions that I have wrestled with and continue to wrestle with, and there are many others. But the fact that there are no easy answers in no way gets us off the hook. I believe we must not only pose the questions, but are called to try to solve them. I cannot know at this moment how far I have gotten, but I have spent my life climbing that mountain.

This book chronicles that climb, and by its very nature must be deeply personal. But before I begin, it's only fair and responsible for me to be candid about how I'm approaching it, and why. For that reason, the brief introduction that follows will discuss how *One Family: Indivisible* came together.

What do I hope the reader takes from this book? First, that as divided as we are, it truly doesn't have to be that way. There *is* a way up the mountain that can bring us to unity, and the sight from the mountaintop is breathtakingly beautiful. There is no one "right" path, but I want to share mine as an example of how the summit can be reached. Second, I want to share Interfaith as a faith—a spiritual reply to the "us and them" divisiveness that seems to be ripping us further and further apart. I am Jewish. I haven't left my spiritual path. But I have embraced Interfaith as a faith: a faith that all of our spiritual paths *can* lead us up the mountain. I haven't left my path, and neither need you—as a Christian, Buddhist, Baha'i, Atheist, or any other believer or non-believer —leave your path behind to embrace Interfaith.

How did I get there? How might you get there? That is what this book is all about.

In all honesty, the theological revelations that form the foundation of the faith of Interfaith, as well as the possible ramifications for our human family, aren't discussed until Part Three. But it took a lifetime to get there, so please do bear with the first hundred sixty pages.

No life is a straight line. There are detours, high points and tragedies, and sometimes we'll hit a brick wall. Then what? I've hit some pretty mean brick walls in my life, but then, who hasn't? The question isn't, how do we avoid brick walls, but rather, how do we find a way to continue? I have tried to find an answer by remembering that the pursuit of justice and unity is a course setting. For sure, from time to time storms will blow us off our desired course—way off! But if justice and unity are truly the stars by which we steer, eventually we will find our way back.

Despite all of our differences, we are one family—the human family. What I would share with you is my spiritual odyssey in pursuit of a way for us to live with and indeed celebrate our diversity. One family: indivisible.

Introduction

This is a spiritual memoir, not an autobiography. I will, in good faith, include everything I can remember that reflects on my spiritual journey—whether it reflects flatteringly upon me or not. By the same token, things that seem to me to have no spiritual relevance will not be included, whether they reflect flatteringly on me or not. I realize all this is subject both to memory and my own sense of what's important. There's no escaping that.

When I talk about other people, the reader should know that if I call someone Joe Smith, then the person's name is Joe Smith. If I refer to a person as "someone I'll call Joe Smith," it means that the person is real, but for reasons of privacy I'm not going to use their actual name. What I can pledge is that what I say is what I remember—no tweaks or embellishments.

Speaking of memory, I have an important admission to make. From the time I was a child, two things have had a deep influence on what I remember. The first is that I have a mind for concepts, not details. In studying history, I can quickly grasp the "why" of even the most complex events but have a much harder time remembering the specifics and most especially the timing of the events. As a simple example, I can tell you why there was a "Tea Party" in Boston. But other than it came before 1776, I don't remember the date or who was involved. When I was studying first my own language and then other languages, grammar was something I could grasp quickly. But vocabulary building has always been extremely difficult for me, and spelling next to impossible.

The second memory admission is perhaps the strangest. When I was a kid and people told me they could close their eyes and "see" something, I always assumed this was just a way of speaking. When people described vivid dreams, I always assumed they were just telling a good story. I no longer remember when, but it finally occurred to me that my mind works differently. If I look at someone and then close my eyes, I can no longer envision that person—even someone who is very important to me, that I have known for years. My mind's eye doesn't exist. When I dream, it's like a radio drama. I don't see things, I can only hear them. All this to say that when I remember something from my past, I can remember the facts of it and the sounds of it, but I have no ability to see it. None.

This is so foreign to most people's life experience that it bears emphasizing. I have no visual memory—of anything.[1] When, later on, I say that my mother looked straight at me when she said something to me, it's not because I can see her looking at me. It is because the incident was so emotionally charged that my mother looking eyeball to eyeball at me at that moment is burned into my factual memory. Still later, when I speak of one of my teachers with his head in his hands weeping as we entered the classroom, I can't see it. I remember the fact of it because this is not something a student normally encounters when entering class. From time to time, my lack of any visual memory has gotten me into trouble, particularly with people who were offended when I didn't recognize them.

So, as Walter Cronkite used to say, that's the way it is. When I say, "I think I was around seven when," it's not that I'm being coy. It's that I think I was around seven. But I might have been six, or eight or even five or nine. I don't know. Unless I have a document to ground my dating, I can only guess (I did find some early report cards as well as my college transcript, and that's helped with some dates). And unless what I saw was so emotionally powerful or specifically important that I memorized it, I won't be talking about how something looked.

What follows then is how and why a child born into a Jewish family, who still walks the path of Judaism, grew up to become an Interfaith minister who calls all of humanity his family.

---

1   I have only recently learned that I'm not alone in this (though it would have been strange if I had been). There's even a word for it! It's called aphantasia. See http://www.bbc.com/news/health-34039054.

Part One: Childhood and Youth

Steven Greenebaum

Chapter One

What are the forces that shape us, that make us who we are? Which events merely nudge us and which truly alter our lives? Mine has been a sometimes explosive, frequently difficult life—often made even more so by my own decisions. But things started wonderfully. I had two parents who loved me. My sister, three years older than me, was for as long as I could remember my advocate and protector. I never knew my grandfathers but had two grandmothers who doted on me—Nana, my mother's mother, and Grandma Helen, my father's. Life was safe and life was good.

My world wasn't perfect. I was always quite small for my age, and had both environmental and food allergies. The environmental allergies especially meant I was sick quite a lot, but I was born into a middle-class family that could afford a good pediatrician, so there was little reason for complaint. Besides, when you're a child you think whatever you're going through is normal, so I assumed everyone had allergies.

Not that I was pleased with it. I don't remember the incident, but my mom told me many years later that early in my childhood I'd rebelled against the rigid limitations my food allergies demanded. Evidently, as only a pouty child can, I accused my mother of being mean and unfair and demanded that I have a cookie chock-full of ingredients that weren't good for me. Mom told me that, driven to tears, she gave up and told me that if I wanted to get sick it was my decision. She had turned my life over to me, and it worked like a charm. I took responsibility for my own life in so many ways, and in this case never nagged or grouched again over what I was or wasn't allowed to eat. I made the decision, and I chose health. Mom was huge in my life, and mostly in a very positive way.

My grandmothers also influenced me, though they were quite different. Nana was fun to be with. She told great stories. But while she lived in a lovely house just down the street, I didn't like going there. The reason was Lilly, Nana's maid.

Lilly treated Nana like royalty, and I didn't like it. It felt creepy. When Nana had guests, Lilly wore a black outfit with a white apron and some kind of white hat. It looked stupid and demeaning, though I wouldn't yet have known that word. I felt hugely uncomfortable and wanted to talk to Mom about it. But Nana was her mother, so I said nothing.

Grandma Helen lived a short drive away from us in an apartment complex. She was hard to be around, and seemed so fussy. Grandma Helen was loving, but so many things seemed to worry her. I was very glad that she didn't have a maid, but surprised that she chose to live in a small apartment in a ten-story complex rather than a house. Money was not yet a part of my world.

As for my immediate family, we had a house, for which I was grateful. We also had no maid, for which I was also grateful. Mom kept the house. Dad did stuff outside the house but was always home for dinner.

One of the great joys of my childhood was that our family made a big deal out of coming together for dinner. We might not be at the same place at the same time for breakfast, and certainly not for lunch, but at dinner we all gathered. More than that, conversation flowed. We talked history, politics, and the world, as well as whatever was going on in our individual lives.

I learned so much, about people, about life and most especially about politics and history just from paying attention at the dinner table. Both my sister and I were encouraged to take part. If I said something dumb, I was told it was dumb in a gentle enough way that I wasn't discouraged from speaking up but also in a detailed enough way that I was encouraged to think before speaking. And when I did think before speaking I was listened to. How I looked forward to dinner! It was the best time of the day.

There are innumerable events, moments, thoughts, and people that shape a life, but for me there are five that were truly pivotal. Two of them occurred when I was quite young, and it is time to discuss the first.

One thing I always felt as a child was safe. My parents and indeed my grandparents and my sister all helped to make me feel warm, loved, and totally secure. That all disappeared at dinner one evening in one, horrible, life-changing moment. I'm guessing I was about six, maybe seven—whatever the age is when a child's mind begins to register what people are actually talking about.

Something may have happened in the news that day, but for whatever reason, the Holocaust was discussed at dinner. I'm sure the topic must have come up before, but this was the first time that it registered. With all children, I think you can tell them things when they are quite young and those things simply don't compute. Then one day it suddenly makes sense. For me, this was that day. Six million Jews, exterminated. Two out of three in Europe (where's Europe?). One out of three on the planet! Gone. Murdered. Stepped on like so many ants. And I'm Jewish. I'm Jewish!

To be honest, at that age, six million was just a number—it was a big number to be sure, but only a number. But my immediate family was my father, my mother, and my sister. One out of three Jews murdered meant one of them—gone. Two out of three meant that only one would be left alive. That I could comprehend.

It was devastating. The terror of the Holocaust was made clear. One out of three on Earth, two out of three in Europe murdered for the "crime" of being Jewish. I don't know how to describe this other than to say that completely, to my roots, I was terrified as I have never been terrified before or since.

I not only knew that I was Jewish but also that all my neighbors were Jewish (though why this was I didn't learn for years). I was not yet old enough to know what being "Jewish" meant, but whatever it meant, whatever being Jewish was, I was Jewish. This was clear. I was Jewish. One out of three people like me, whatever "like me" meant, had been gassed, or shot, or hung, or tortured and starved to death. One out of three. My father, my mother or my sister. One out of three!! "How could this happen?" I asked.

"It happened because some people hate Jews."

"Why?? What did we do to them?"

"Nothing."

"Is there something bad about being Jewish?"

"No."

"Then why?"

Some people, particularly Christians, hate Jews. A Christian bigshot[2] helped to make it possible.

But that was across the ocean (as in Europe). We lived in the United States. And the war was over.

"Then we're safe?"

---

2   Dad may have even said "Pope," but the name didn't register. All I remember was that it was a "bigshot." I'm pretty certain now that Dad was referring to the Pope's Concordat with Hitler.

"From Hitler, yes," Dad told us. "But there are people in the United States, again, mostly Christians, even in our city, who hate Jews and want to hurt them. It's called anti-Semitism."

I think that this was when it first registered that there had been things like pogroms, where Jews had been tortured and murdered, and ghettos, where Jews were enclosed to keep them separate from "civil" society. Maybe Dad explained these to me to explain what "anti-Semitism" meant.

It was shattering. I don't know if I can possibly convey just how shattering it was. I don't think I fully understood death yet. But it wasn't death so much as realizing that there were people who hated me, *hated* me, wanted to kill me sight unseen, never having met me. They didn't know me, but they hated me. And they always would, no matter what I said or did.

That night, that moment, everything changed. My world was no longer safe. They hated me. They hated my parents. They hated my sister. They hated Nana and Grandma Helen. How many Christians were there? Did they all hate me? What was I to do? What did it mean? What if America produced a Hitler?

Then Mom talked to me. I don't remember if she said this at the dinner table or not. Perhaps, seeing how distraught I was after dinner, she talked to me alone. I don't remember, but I will never forget what she said.

She looked straight at me. I knew that whatever she was going to tell me would be important.

"Do you like that some people hate you?" Mom asked me.

"No," I whispered.

"Do you like what it feels like to be hated?"

"No."

"Then, don't ever hate."

I will carry that moment with me as long as I live. Mom's words became central to my life. As time passed, it also pounded at my mind that the Holocaust had happened in Europe, not the United States, and I was born afterward, albeit only a few years. Yet, learning that because I was Jewish some people hated me and that the world was not safe for Jews had a profound impact on me.

As I grew, I began to ponder what it must be like for a black child that very first time that she or he comprehends that slavery happened *here*— not in Europe, it happened *here*. And that after slavery was outlawed, Jim Crow happened *here*—not in Europe, it happened *here*. And that racism is still alive and well in the United States. Some people despise, fear and even hate people of color, all people of color, without ever having met them.

What a wrenching, devastating effect that must have. How can it be anything but life-changing?

I cannot know and do not pretend to know what it is like, especially in that first moment, for a black child to realize that his or her life isn't safe in America, that too many, many too many in this "land of the free" consider people of color to be "other." But I do feel I have at least an inkling of what it must be like, and it makes me shudder.

Chapter Two

Smaller events early on also affected my spiritual growth. Two experiences especially from before we moved (and therefore before age eight) remain with me.

The first was wonderful. One day it was raining hard on my side of the street, but the rain stopped more or less in the middle of the street. I had a friend, Bobby, who lived on the other side. It blew my mind! I could run in and out of the downpour simply by running across the street! How was that possible? Suddenly, something I had never thought about before, weather, took on a fascination for me. Some sixty years later, I still remember the incredible joy of that experience. It's a big universe out there. It's a very big universe! Wow!

The second event was far less fun. I was very small for my age[3] and some of the local kids liked to pick on me. I should be clear. This was a different era. They only punched me in the stomach, arms, or thighs. Never once can I remember being bloodied. No one ever pulled a gun or a knife— let alone threatened me with one. Again, I lived in a Jewish neighborhood so there was no anti-Semitism involved. That said, being picked on was no great joy. I still vividly recall the day that a bunch of kids shoved me to the ground and started punching me—and Bobby, my *friend* Bobby, was present. He didn't run, yet he didn't try to help me. Instead, he joined in with all the other bullies and gave me some pretty hard punches.

After the other kids ran off, Bobby stayed with me. He told me how sorry he was, and he pleaded with me not to "tell" on him. He told me he

---

3   I remember being stuck at 67 pounds for about three years, while all my friends were growing. There was a time when my greatest ambition in life was to be 6-feet tall!

had no choice, that he had to fit in. He knew it wasn't right, but he had no choice. I was fascinated.

Bobby and I remained friends. It never happened again, and I never told on him. But the fact that he would feel compelled to join a bunch of bullies in doing something he knew was wrong to anyone, let alone a friend, seemed important for me to remember. For as long as I can recall, I've always been eager for "life lessons." "What can I learn from this?" is something I ask myself after virtually every experience. What I learned here was the power of the mob—and how little I could trust anyone.

Then came 1955, the year we moved to our new house. From the second to sixth grade I went to Canyon Elementary School. I was a kid. I made new friends. I had fun. But I was also depressed and without anchor. When I was alone, my thoughts drifted back to the Holocaust. Early on I developed a cold, unyielding question that I would ask myself about every person I met. If the Jew-haters took over our government, if the Nazis came for the Jews in America, would this person turn me in or would they have the strength and honor to help or even hide me? It's a question no kid should ever have to be asking himself. And in all honesty, it meant that I had very few people I would let close to me. Indeed, for many years I let no one close. Bobby was just another example of why I believed I should be very, very careful about letting anyone get too close. And at this point I held a strong prejudice and fear of anything and everything to do with Christianity.

These feelings took form in the very first poem I remember writing:

Love won't await you.
There's only death.
If you're looking for joy here,
Don't hold your breath.

Ok. Not a happy kid. But I did continue to learn from what I watched and read. Just before we moved, Dad had, to the great excitement of our family, brought home our first television set. The first show I remember watching was Disney's *Davy Crockett*, but it was the second (or third?) time I saw it that had more of a spiritual impact on me—specifically, Davy Crockett treating Native Americans as human beings and standing up for them and against President Andrew Jackson, who was trying to steal their lands. That felt important.

Watching the movie *The Desert Fox* with my family, though, was different. No movie I have ever seen has had more of an impact on me than this one. It's a movie about World War II. There's a moment in the movie that became hugely important to me and how I approach life. To be honest, the war story didn't interest me. Nor was I impressed by Field Marshal Rommel's part in the plot against Hitler. For me, the pivotal moment came early in the movie. Rommel has been ill and in hospital. He's flown back to Africa, because without his guidance the troops are losing battles. Rommel flies in, still not feeling well. He gets an update on where things stand, he examines the maps and he thinks about it. Then, he's decisive. "We'll do this, this and this," he says. "It's never been done before. If it works, we'll take them by surprise. If it doesn't work, we'll know not to do it again."

Wow. I didn't care about the rest of the picture. This was perfect. This was important. *This* was how to approach life. Learn as much as you can, make a decision, and then move on. If it works, it works. If it doesn't work, don't do it again. Don't stay up all night worrying about it. Make a decision. Make the best decision you can. Learn from it, and move on.

It made so much sense! I inhaled it and made it part of who I am. As I reflect on it, it complemented my tendency to want to turn the page after any experience, good or bad. Though this occurred when I was young enough that perhaps it marks the beginning of that trait.

Another movie I saw a few years later had a similar lifelong impact, though this one was less life-changing than life-affirming. It was a welcome confirmation of something I already deeply believed. In effect, it gave me permission to be who I was, which is a great and powerful gift. The movie was a western called *The Big Country*.

My father and I had some lifelong conflicts. In the beginning I idolized my dad, but as I grew he and I began to have major differences. In the end, I went pretty much in a wholly different direction than my father. But as a kid, when I realized that who I was didn't please him, it bothered me. I refused to let it change me, but it bothered me. A lot! And one of the first places where our roads diverged was in the role that physical force should play in our lives.

I seem to have leapt from the womb a bona fide pacifist. My belief that fighting was stupid and pointless made my life pretty miserable when I was a child. What could be more inviting to a bully than a small kid who won't defend himself because he believes fighting is wrong? I was picked on all through grade school and into junior high.

11

Looking back, I must have been hugely difficult to raise. How does a kid get born with what appears to be a fully formed and ingrained sense of right and wrong? I remember vividly the time my father called me into the den.[4] Stewie, a kid who lived across the street, had yet again broken some streetlights by throwing rocks at them. Why didn't I ever throw rocks at streetlights? my father wanted to know. "But it's wrong," I said. "Isn't it wrong to break something that doesn't belong to you?"

My father's reply chilled me. All these years later, I can still hear his horrifying words in my head: "Why can't I have a normal son?"

As tough as that was, even more difficult was my firm belief that fighting was not only dumb but also pointless. It didn't solve anything! Dad and I had had more than a few "discussions" about this. Dad was a staunch Republican. He believed that the communists were coming for us and that only the strong would survive. We had to be as nasty as they were. We would prove our superiority by beating the commies at their own game. I disagreed.

Then came *The Big Country*. I cherish that movie. Gregory Peck starred. And for one of the few times in his career, Charlton Heston was a costar. Heston doesn't like Peck from the beginning, and keeps trying to pick a fight. But Peck refuses to fight him as well as refusing other "offers" to prove his manhood. Finally, when Peck realizes the woman he came to marry (that Heston also loves) is not who he thought she was, he decides to leave. But before he leaves he meets with Heston, and as the sun rises the two of them have a truly epic fistfight. Afterward, they are both on their knees, panting and exhausted. Peck says to Heston, "Tell me, what did we prove?" The answer was clear. They'd proven nothing.

I leapt up and pointed at the television. "That's what I'm talking about," I told my father. "That's what I'm talking about."

I didn't always rebel. It was clear I was not the son my father had hoped for. My dad was desperate for his disappointing son to participate in sports so I gave in and participated in some form of Little League. I was put in right field, where I would learn later all the klutzes were placed. I spent every game hoping the ball wouldn't come my direction, and making a fool of myself when it did. When I was at bat, I invariably struck out. My eye-hand coordination sucked madly, but if I went to Little League, it satisfied Dad. So I went.

Another thing I did for Dad was join the Cub Scouts. He seemed to feel it would help to "make a man" of me. I never liked Cub Scouts, and found

4   My favorite room in the house. It's where Dad kept his books. Row upon row of books!

"earning" badges unfulfilling. Still, two things impressed me. The first was that Dad took an interest in Scouting and indeed, before I knew it he was Scoutmaster! I was having trouble with badges, and Dad just walked in and ended up running things. Yikes! But far more important was a moment at some Scouting event. We were supposed to blow up balloons until they burst. There were two rounds in this contest. The top finishers in round one would compete against each other in round two. The prize was a plastic gumball machine. I wanted it.

I had a pin hidden in my hand. I mean, I wanted that gumball machine! I got the balloon pretty well blown up when I heard someone else's balloon pop and knew it was now or never if I wanted to make it to round two. I used the pin and popped my balloon. I knew it was wrong, but I wanted to win.

There were a few minutes between rounds one and two. Dad took me aside. Not only will I never forget what he told me, but also the care and compassion he used in *how* he told me. "Steven, a lot of kids want to win, you know that." It was a simple, non-accusatory statement.

"Sure."

"It's good to want to win," Dad continued, "but I sure hope no one cheats. Cheating is wrong, it's always wrong, even if you don't get caught. And it's really embarrassing if you do get caught."

Message received. Loud and clear, The gentle way the message was given was appreciated. It seemed clear that Dad knew I had cheated, yet he didn't embarrass me or punish me. Instead, he helped me to understand that no matter how tempting cheating can be, it is wrong. I tossed away the pin and lost the competition, but I felt a lot better about myself than I would have if I had kept the pin and won. I also knew that, despite our growing differences, my dad was cool. That seemed another important lesson. Don't be too quick to judge people!

Looking back, I think it must have been in moments like this that I earned my parents' trust. I learned from them, and they learned that they could reason with me—well, most of the time.

I was allowed a lot of freedom. When I said I was through with Scouting after Cub Scouts, my decision was respected. No Webelos, no Boy Scouts. More important to me, my judgement was trusted—within limits.

My grade school was only a few blocks from the ocean. The one sport where I wasn't a washout was swimming, and indeed I participated happily and successfully in the Junior Lifeguards. I knew how to swim, and my parents trusted me. Indeed, in 1956 the family took a trip to Hawaii, where at eight years old I happily learned to surf! When we got home, I realized surfboards were expensive so I learned to body surf. It was a gas.

So, at least by the fifth grade, when the weather was good I was allowed to walk with friends from the school to the beach with no parental supervision. I promised (and kept my promise) to take up position in front of the lifeguard tower and then would body surf for an hour or so before my mom (or someone else's mom) picked us up and took us home to do our homework.

Yet another hugely positive thing was the encouragement of reading I received from both parents, but particularly my dad. When I was too young to read, both Mom and Dad read to me almost every day. Before I could read real books I was given something called "Classics Illustrated." These were comic books based on the classics of literature. Then, when I was old enough, my parents got me a subscription to a children's "book of the month club." I believe it was called "Landmark Books." Television (particularly *The Mickey Mouse Club*) was fun, but books were where it was at. Not that all my reading was serious. I also read every edition of *Mad Magazine* I could get a hold of, but other than *Mad* and the occasional Batman comic, my interests lay elsewhere. Happily, my sister, three years older than I, started bringing home books from her school that she knew I'd like. When I was still in junior high, Kathy, who was in high school, brought me home books from her library.

Speaking of my sister Kathy, she was my guardian angel in those years. Not only could she act as the perfect interpreter when I was unable to put the right words together to communicate with Mom or Dad, but even more important, she was also my protector. I don't recall a specific incident, but more like a series of times when bullies would be after me and Kathy would ride up on her bicycle to save her little brother from a pummeling. And she must have been pretty fierce, because when she approached the bullies would scatter.

I don't remember the dates, but at some point during these years another important person entered my life. Her name was Lila Foster. Lila came to work for us in the new house. She was black. And unlike my mom, Lila didn't answer questions by saying, "Ask your father." I loved her, and we had some amazing conversations. Whenever it worked out, she and I would meet in her room (there was a "maid's room" in our new house). I asked her about Lilly, and why would anyone dress like she did and act like she did. Lila was gentle but firm. She told me not to judge Lilly: "We all have to live and we all do different things to live." But when I told Lila I still thought it was wrong and that no one should treat someone else like they were better, she gave me a huge hug. I didn't understand it at the time, but I think that was the moment we truly bonded.

I no longer remember much about our talks, only that we talked a lot. Mom was becoming more and more ill and taking to bed, and when she wasn't in bed, she didn't seem to have the energy she used to. Lila was like a second mother or third grandmother to me and a wonderful source of wisdom. I never understood why she left. I couldn't bring myself to ask her or my parents why she was leaving. I wish I had, but I didn't. Maybe I was afraid. Whatever, I was deeply saddened when she left. Lila did leave me a forwarding address and for a while we kept in touch.

This was my life up to the watershed of the family trip to Europe, my second life-changing event and my entry to Paul Revere Junior High School. The next three years were powerful.

Steven Greenebaum

Chapter Three

The second life-altering event of my childhood occurred about the time I was in the sixth grade. By then I had attended religious school for several years and had been introduced to the idea of God, as well as the knowledge that some people believed in God and some people didn't.

We moved in 1955 when I was seven. We'd first lived in the Jewish section of Los Angeles, the Fairfax area near downtown. Now we were in a somewhat more mixed neighborhood near the ocean. I wouldn't learn of "restricted covenants" (agreements not to sell to Blacks or Jews) for several more years. Nor would I learn for years that a primary motivation for our moving was to get me, my allergies, and my breathing difficulties away from the ever-increasing smog of Los Angeles and near the cleaner ocean air. One thing I did learn was that we were just one block away from a world-famous golf course. It was the Riviera Country Club and Jews weren't allowed to join.[5] We'd moved out of our exclusively Jewish neighborhood, and just a block away from a club that specifically excluded Jews. Ok, then.

I think I was about 12 when what follows happened. I was by myself, either playing or reading. All of a sudden a voice was speaking to me. I was startled, to say the least. It was an inner voice, but I knew what it sounded like when I talked to myself and this was different. It had never happened before and stopped me in my tracks.

"They are killing each other in my name. Stop it."

---

5   Perhaps, and I certainly hope that restriction has long since changed. Meanwhile, if this is a world that is foreign to you, I'd recommend the movie "Gentleman's Agreement."

Oh, swell! What the heck was THAT?

I kept waiting for more, but that was it. My first reaction was that I must have imagined it. It couldn't be God, but if not God, then who? But God? Good grief, I was a kid! Hello, God? Kid here. Were you trying to reach an adult and got the wrong number??

I tried to forget it, but couldn't. I also felt there was no one I could talk to about it. I already knew that my parents didn't seem to take religion particularly seriously. My father had bluntly explained that he and my mom had joined Temple Leo Baeck primarily to be sure my sister and I would be educated about Judaism. He explained that too many Jews had gone to their deaths in the Holocaust not knowing their heritage. He wasn't a particularly pious Jew, and we didn't attend temple often, but in case the Holocaust ever came to America, it was important for his children to know who they were. So, my rather secular Dad wasn't someone I felt I could talk to about religious matters.

By this time, I had also learned something else that I found exceedingly annoying. Mom deferred to Dad on everything spiritual. Indeed, it bugged me that Mom seemed to defer to Dad on almost everything, period. Every once in a while she would spontaneously volunteer something on her own, and when she did it was worth listening to. My experience of Mom was that she was intelligent, kind and profound. Despite this, if I asked her a question, her response was invariably, "You need to ask your father." This was my introduction to patriarchy, and I loathed it. It made no sense for Mom to defer to Dad or anyone else. None!

What it meant at this moment was there was no one I felt I could talk to. I certainly wasn't going to talk to any of my friends. "Hey, I think I just heard from God" is not a conversation I wanted to have with other kids. I thought about my sister, but I was her little brother. I didn't feel comfortable sharing this with her either.

So, what to do? I thought about it a long while though by now I have no idea what for me at that age "a long while" was in real time. Hours? Days perhaps? I know I thought about it. I thought about it a lot. "They are killing each other in my name. Stop it." That had to be God. Who or what else could it be? So, I sucked it up and decided to accept the charge.

One thing, though. I was a kid. Just a kid.

"Ok" I thought/prayed. "I'll do my best." I knew I'd need guidance—a lot of guidance. So, I prayed for guidance. "You want me to do this. Ok. You know I'm a kid, right? Help me out here. Guide me. Please, tell me what to do."

I heard nothing. Not a whisper. Nothing. Silence. What the ...?????
I got depressed, but then I got mad—really mad. I was furious. What kind of god charges a kid to do something and then can't be bothered to help?!

Now I pondered something new. Can a person say "No" to God? What if God called on you and you thought about it and said, "No thanks, God. Find someone else."? Could a person do that? Could *I* do that? In the end, I decided it was the only answer. If God was going to call on a kid and ask something this huge and then offer no guidance or advice—well, God could go—look elsewhere.

I decided to move on. One thing that I learned early in life—and I have no idea where it came from unless it was inspired by watching *The Desert Fox*—was the desire never to dwell on anything. Just turn the page and move on. Not that I was always successful in doing this. There were times that I thought I'd moved on when I hadn't. There were other times when I should have confronted something but instead turned the page, and the "something" festered. Most of the time though, it has worked well for me. I have dwelt neither on my successes nor my failures. Both are quickly and equally moved to the rearview mirror. Yesterday's gone. It's a new day. What's next?[6]

That was that—or so I thought. It wasn't until years later that I could look back and realize how completely my life changed after that day. I never truly turned that page. Or rather, I turned the page on asking for guidance and moved ahead without it. Up to that point, education had been okay but it had never seemed all that important to me, let alone urgent. Now it became paramount. As I entered junior high (seventh grade), I wanted to read everything I could get my hands on. I wanted to learn everything I possibly could. I didn't understand why I was so driven, nor did I ask myself why. The question didn't occur to me. Whatever it was that I was going to do with my life, it was clear to me that I needed to know everything I possibly could. In that sense, I did get the guidance I needed, assuming that the guidance was to take my education seriously and apply myself, but that's something for angels to argue about. Whatever the reason, I became focused on learning.

Indeed, it was in junior high that I developed a lifelong approach to education: "Help me, or get out of my way." I had no patience with teachers

---

6   I fondly remember the first time on the TV series The West Wing when President Bartlett says, "What's next?" at a meeting. Instant bonding. Yes, that's pretty much how I've lived my life. Consider something. Try to look at all the angles. Give it my best shot. Then, move on. What's next? And don't look back.

who (from my extremely earnest perspective) wasted my time. It seemed to me that grades reflected how much I agreed with the teacher rather than what I had actually learned. To my parent's consternation, as B's and C's poured in, I told them I didn't care about grades. I cared about learning. Grades were my teachers' subjective opinions. This from a kid in junior high! My father, particularly, was upset. For him, good grades were a badge of honor. But despite this, once he realized I wouldn't budge, he supported me. To their credit, both Mom and Dad supported me in my approach to learning even if they didn't like or understand it. I think they could see my mind was a sponge and took solace in that, but from time to time Dad would grumble, and sometimes loudly, about not being able to brag about his son.

It bothered me that I continued to be a disappointment to my father. It didn't stop me, and it didn't change me. I would be lying, though, if I said it didn't bother and sometimes haunts me.

Still, one thought drove me mercilessly forward. A child is powerless. As a child I cannot change the world. What I can do is learn as much as possible during these precious years when my only job is getting an education. I didn't have to work on the side (a luxury not available to a child of impoverished parents). So, I could and did dedicate myself to learning.

At virtually the same time I read a young person's edition of *The Count of Monte Cristo*. It may have been an assigned reading, or maybe a *Classics Illustrated* version. Either way, I was amazed that no one else seemed to get from the story what I did. The adventure was okay. I found the revenge aspect petty. What fascinated me was that Dantès, having been so terribly wronged and then escaping from prison and finding his fortune, didn't simply march out to seek his revenge. He spent ten years preparing. Ten years! THAT was the great lesson of *The Count of Monte Cristo*. Learn. Prepare. Don't be impatient. Ok. Got it.

As I entered junior high, I devoted myself to learning. THAT was my job. As a child I felt I couldn't do much to change the world,[7] but I could prepare myself so that when I became an adult I would not only know what to do but how to do it. This was going to be my chance to prepare so I could get it right.

At the time, I connected no dots. Looking back, I realize that my whole approach to education, not to mention my life, changed when I encountered what I later learned to call "a still, small voice." It would be nearly another 40 years before I again heard that voice.

7   The inspiring and wonderful Malala Yousafzai would prove me wrong, but not until 2012.

For all intents and purposes, my childhood ended at that point, 1960, age 12. I was about to enter junior high and my full-time job of becoming educated. But first we went to Europe. My parents later admitted to me that this was the last possible moment we could afford to make such a trip because they believed it was the last possible moment that they could house my sister and me in the same room in hotels. I was 12 and my sister 15. A year later would be too late!

On the way to Europe, we stopped in New York. New York! That was where Lila had moved! I wrote to her and gave her the information my parents gave me. And bless her, Lila was not only able to get time off from wherever she was working but found a way to come meet us at the airport! Unfortunately, the plane was late—very late. Lila couldn't wait, and I never heard from her again. That was a huge blow. It hurt far more than I felt I could allow anyone to know.

The highlight of visiting New York was seeing *The Sound of Music* on Broadway. I didn't understand it all, but it was glorious. From a 12-year-old's perspective, it was the triumph of music over the Nazis. Yes, "Climb every mountain." Another truly fun highlight came later on our visit to Tivoli Gardens in Copenhagen. I no longer remember much about it, but I do remember that I thought it beat Disneyland, which was quite an accomplishment.

The spiritual highlight of the trip came one early afternoon in southern France when for some reason everyone else in the family was resting. I went for a walk and met a man. I was able to communicate with him with hand gestures. He showed me an alley and then pointed out a church. Somehow, he was able to impart to me that I should come back at sunset. With gestures, he made me understand that the Sun would cast its light down the alley and that the church was built for that. The light and the shadows on the church would be spectacular. I promised I would return, but Mom and Dad had other plans. That was disappointing, but I turned the page.

Still, both that the Frenchman would be so excited about how sunlight played on the church and that he would want to share this with this American 12-year-old he'd never met before, touched me. It touched me so deeply that more than 50 years later it still warms my heart and brings a smile to my face.

I know there was much more to the trip. But except that I met a wonderful diversity of people and that all of them were warm and friendly, I don't remember much. Evidently, people enjoy an inquisitive 12-year-old, and I got along with everyone. Or at least, that's what I remember. Whatever, I returned home ready to get down to the work of learning.

Chapter Four

The next three years were among the most exciting and dynamic of my life. In junior high I was amazingly lucky in my teachers. Mrs. Pasella introduced me to the wonders of singing in choir. Mrs. Martin got me excited about math and then handed me off to Mr. Farnsworth, who introduced me to the wondrous logic that is algebra. Wow! Mrs. Windward beckoned me into the world of creative writing. Mrs. Nagel introduced me to the magic of plays and particularly a guy called Shakespeare. Mr. Swingler taught me not only to love science but also how to write a research paper. Mr. Merriman helped me to feel less of a klutz and gave me much needed encouragement in physical education. I owe a huge debt to all of these teachers. They helped my mind and spirit to bloom. It was a mental "big bang." The world exploded open.

Mom must have seen how much my education meant to me. She roused herself to take up my cause. I was a B and C student. So, how she succeeded I haven't a clue, but she went to the powers that be and demanded that her son be included in what were called "Advanced Placement" or AP classes. She confessed to me years later that she'd met a lot of resistance. Mom had to agree that if it turned out I was in over my head and on the verge of flunking out she would not only accept my being dropped from the AP program but also get me special tutoring. Only then did the guidance counselor she talked to give a reluctant "ok."

All the while, Mom was retreating more and more from the world and much too frequently taking to bed. Still, she had taken it upon herself to get me into better classes, and the experiment had worked. My grades stayed pretty much B and C, but I was now in classes that opened up huge new vistas for me.

One class that I was quite literally ordered to take was typing. All the way through grade school I had received Cs or Ds in handwriting. Again, with hindsight, my eye-hand coordination was and remained terrible. When I was told to "visualize" something as simple as how an "a" should look, I couldn't. I truly can't visualize. The one D that I recall getting in junior high was in art. I couldn't draw anything to save my life! But typing was mechanical, and it was once I learned to type that the world of words exploded open.

Of course, my hormones were also beginning to kick in. I had huge crushes on both Mrs. Nagel and Mrs. Pasella. They were both the personification of professional. What intrigues me is that over time Mrs. Nagel became a friend, indeed, a lifelong friend, whereas Mrs. Pasella faded from memory as soon as I left junior high. Nonetheless, when drama and choir came into conflict as competing "electives," I chose Mrs. Pasella and choir, and not because I preferred singing!

Still, one thing that I should have learned in junior high completely eluded me. I developed no social skills. None. If I wasn't studying for my classes I was reading one of the books that my sister brought home from high school. I would daydream from time to time about my beautiful teachers, but I never talked to girls. I had no idea what to say. For that matter, I had no male friends, either. I found it exceptionally hard to trust anyone and pretty much kept to myself.

The bullies remained, though and about this time I began to grapple with an exceedingly difficult conundrum. Whether I was at school or walking in my own neighborhood, the bullies never seemed to let up. I was tired of being the local punching bag. I was also tired of hurting. I was tired as well of hearing the nonstop teasing and laughter that accompanied my being punched, pushed around and shoved to the ground.

Still, I believed violence was wrong. The very essence of who I was told me that hitting people was wrong. That was the conundrum. The fact that I didn't like being hurt told me that I shouldn't be hurting anyone else—even the bullies who took every opportunity to make my life exceedingly miserable. What was the solution? Everything has a solution, right? There *had* to be a solution! But what?!

"Don't be a coward!" my father told me. "Fight!" Coward? That's what he thought of me? Dad wanted me to take boxing lessons, and when I wouldn't, he offered to teach me. Dad seemed to love slapping me on my face. He wouldn't throw a real punch. To be clear, my father had no inter-est in hurting me. He just wanted to get me mad enough to throw a punch. While I would try to block his slaps, I wouldn't fight back, and finally Dad gave me up as a lost cause.

Somehow I couldn't let go of the question. I would not throw a punch. I did not want to hurt anyone, but I also *really* wanted the bullies to stop. Asking them to stop hadn't worked, so what could I do? It puzzled and confused me. There had to be an answer. Surely, there was an answer be-yond just hitting someone.

At last, someone must have told me about judo—or maybe I read about it. Judo is not about throwing a punch. Judo is not about hitting or hurting anyone. Judo is about self-defense. You block your opponent's attempt to hurt you and toss your opponent to the ground. Even better, you actually use the force of the person's punch against them. Literally, the harder a person comes at you, the harder they fall when you throw them. How cool was that! It was as if someone was thinking of me when judo was invented. I asked my parents for permission to take lessons and got their wholehearted approval.[8]

It took a while. It was at least six months of lessons, perhaps longer. I waited patiently to be confident of my abilities before I let anyone know about the lessons I was taking. Then, I was ready. I knew it. As only a child can, I drew a mental line in the sand. No matter who it was, no matter where or when it happened, the next time one of the school bullies picked on me, he was going to be in for a surprise. The unfortunate bully's name was Dan.

You may be aware that the boy's locker room, at least in my day, had a cement floor. There was a narrow wooden bench bolted to the floor and metal lockers on either side of the bench. The pathway in between was exceedingly narrow. This was quite possibly the worst and most dangerous place a young boy could choose to get into a fight. But again, I'd drawn my mental line in the sand. Dan came up to me while I was at my gym locker and once again tried to punch me. His punch never landed. I intercept-ed it, grabbed his arm, knocked him off his feet and threw him, hard. He bounced off the bench and then against the lockers and onto the cement floor. Just watching him fall and then gingerly pick himself up, I realized that I was lucky, very lucky, that I hadn't seriously hurt him.

---

8   I was definitely no "Karate Kid." But when I saw the movie years later I did feel a certain identification.

Lesson learned. Choosing to defend yourself isn't enough. I needed to choose my battles carefully. I could actually hurt a person even in the simple act of protecting myself.

The second lesson learned truly amazed me. Word must have spread around the school immediately. No bully ever picked on me again. Ever. I also began to realize that how I held myself must somehow be different. It occurred to me that simply having the confidence in my own ability to protect myself had to be something visible. Yet if that were true, then my lack of confidence and apprehension about being picked on had also been visible. This, I realized, must have been what had so galled my father. I was asking to be picked on by how I held myself. I went on to take karate, not because I ever wanted to use it (nor did I), but in the belief that the better I could defend myself, and knew it, the less likely it would be that I would ever have to.

It worked. Through junior high and then high school, no bully ever came near me again. I still believe that violence is wrong. Happily, not once in my life have I ever thrown a punch in anger. But neither since that day in the boy's locker room have I had to block a punch.

All of this was part of the package of confidence—mental, physical, and spiritual—that began to develop within me. My confidence in myself grew to a point that my last year in junior high I was able to confront an exceedingly difficult problem with a teacher in a way that set a pattern for me for the rest of my life.

The teacher's name was Mr. Faucet. He was the exception to my run of outstanding teachers. Mr. Faucet was the opposite. He was both a lousy teacher and a bully. He routinely ridiculed his students if they didn't give him the right answer. He nagged at us, mocked us and drove several students to tears. I wanted to confront him, to tell him how wrong and brutal he was. But I didn't dare. He was the teacher!

I didn't know what to do. Surely someone should do something. There were some big kids in class—smarter than I was, braver than I was. Why doesn't someone *do* something? I kept asking myself. Then it occurred to me. This was the first time that I can remember asking myself "Why doesn't someone do something?" and having it come back to me in my own mind: "You're someone. Why don't *you* do something?"

Me? Ok, then. I had to step up, but I figured I'd better ask my parents first. I explained the situation to Mom and Dad. I told them that enough was enough. I wanted to face Mr. Faucet and tell him to stop. I wanted to tell him that he was a bully, I knew that talking back to a teacher might get me suspended. It would certainly get me in trouble. My father gave me a beautiful, gentle answer. For me, it turned out to be perfect.

"I wouldn't recommend it," he told me. "I think there must be a better way, but if you feel you need to confront him, your mother and I will support you."

Looking back, this was hugely empowering. My parents and particularly my father did not say, "This is too big for you. We'll handle it." That would have robbed me of power and confidence. Nor did they say, "Know your place. You can't talk back to your teacher." Rather, I got some low-key advice ("I wouldn't recommend it") but then was trusted to find the right solution and assured that *whatever* I did I would have my parents' support. What a gift that was! What an amazing gift! "I think there must be a better way." Hmm. Ok. A better way?

I went to see Mrs. Nagel, who had by now evolved from a crush to a confidante and a source of wisdom. She listened carefully to me, which was also a beautiful gift. She cautioned me to wait, and then went to speak to our Principal, Mr. Ferguson. The next day Mrs. Nagel reported back to me and explained that Mr. Faucet had what's called "tenure." He couldn't be fired. Mrs. Nagel's advice was not to let him get to me, that sometimes the best thing to do is to just wait it out. That's what I did, and Mr. Faucet disappeared the next semester. It turned out that, having tenure, he was being bounced from school to school.

I took a lot of lessons from this. One was that sometimes a battle is better declined, a hard lesson, that in truth I didn't fully learn—not for many years. Another lesson was that I'm somebody. If I ever again asked myself the question "Why doesn't somebody do something?" I was required to ask of myself why *I'm* not doing something. This may seem simple enough, but from then on it has guided my life and some of my most important decisions.

Steven Greenebaum

Chapter Five

Lack of trust and how to deal with bullies were not the only spiritual challenges that followed me from grade school to junior high. Another challenge was my health. Most of us may recall the poem *The Night before Christmas* and the lines, "Away to the window I flew like a flash, tore open the shutters and threw up the sash." As it turned out, I woke up morning after morning with a queasy stomach. Frequently I would quote a part of that line as I leapt from the breakfast table and headed for the bathroom. "Tore open the shutters ..." I would say. Everyone understood there was no time for me to ask permission to be excused.

I was a kid and accepted vomiting breakfast most mornings as a part of growing up. But my parents were concerned, and looking back I can certainly see why. One reason I still remember this so vividly is that I was deeply offended by what my parents did about it. They took me to my beloved pediatrician, Dr. Herbert Kehr, and prodded by my parents, Herb asked me if I was afraid of something happening to me at school. I was confused. No, I told him, I was loving school. Was I sure, Herb asked me more than once. My parents were concerned, he told me. That truly offended me. I was used to telling the truth. More than that, I was used to being believed.

Today I can be a lot more sympathetic toward my parents. I was, after all, the constant target of bullies. That I might be afraid to go to school would not be illogical, and my parents were very reasonably concerned.

But I was telling the truth. I wasn't afraid. Did I *like* being bullied? No! Did I like being hurt? No! These "no's" were what had prompted my interest in judo. But I was not afraid. By this point in my life, I felt indestructible.

It's only looking back that I realize this stemmed from how my mind had processed the Shoah.

Hitler had tried to kill all the Jews, but he'd failed. I transitioned from my fear, indeed terror, of anti-Semitism to a feeling that if Hitler couldn't kill me, then who could? Certainly no mindless bully could come close to Hitler. Bullies were like mosquitoes. No fun, to be sure. By all means, avoid them when you can. And with judo, I soon learned how to brush the bullies away. A punch in the stomach isn't Auschwitz. Teasing and taunting weren't Bergen-Belsen. In ways that I couldn't possibly have imagined at the time, I had become free and fearless. Not that I ceased to be exceedingly wary of my fellow humans. Too many people, including Jews, had been complicit with Hitler for me not to be wary. So, I continued to be careful—careful but not fearful. My trust issues remained, but whatever life held for me, there was nothing to fear.

This brings me to the weekly classes in Judaism that I attended at Leo Baeck Temple. Part of what I learned seemed important and very relevant. These things are a large part of why I remain Jewish today, although I did have a problem or two.

Like many, I had trouble with the idea of God. Nagging at me was my experience from several years before. I'd said "No thanks" to God, but still... And there were the riveting arguments we were taught that had taken place in the concentration camps during the Shoah.[9] If God had a covenant with the Jewish people, God had pretty well walked away from it while Hitler was around. Not only was there Hitler, there were also events like the Spanish Inquisition and its Grand Inquisitor, Torquemada. There were also the stories we were told of the Crusades where the Christian knights blooded their swords on the local Jewish population before heading to what they termed the "Holy Land" to kill Muslims.

So, where the hell was God? A loving God? Yeah, right!

The Noah story was one teacher's attempt at excusing God's absence. According to this teacher, God had destroyed a rotting human world with the great flood and then let the flood recede, promising Noah no more interference. From now on, humanity was on its own. God was going to root for us but not interfere. I didn't buy it. It seemed to me that God could never seem to make up his mind (and in those days, the God I was taught was definitely a He). Nor was God alone in inconsistency. There was our alleged heroic forefather, Abraham.

---

9   Though in those days it was still referred to as The Holocaust. I prefer Shoah, which means catastrophe, to Holocaust, which means burnt offering.

Abraham really got under my skin. On the one hand, when God is going to destroy Sodom and Gomorrah, Abraham stands up for people he has never even met. "What if there are fifty righteous? Will you destroy the righteous with the wicked?"[10] Abraham challenges God, stating that a just God doesn't act like that. And once God says ok, Abraham slowly works the number down from fifty to ten. This was cool. Score one for Abraham.

But then God "tests" Abraham[11] and, as far as I was concerned, Abraham fails miserably. God tells Abraham to kill his only son as a sacrifice, and without so much as a whimper of protest, Abraham agrees. Except for the timely intervention of an angel, Abraham would have plunged a knife into the heart of his own son. It was bad enough that God would ask this. But what kind of lunatic will stand up to God for strangers yet not even try to protect his own son? Why on earth should I or anyone have even the slightest respect for this monster?

The question did not endear me to my teacher. I was told that the point of the story was that there shouldn't be human sacrifice. The angel stopped Abraham. Ok. Fine. But for me that begged the question, what kind of father could Abraham be, if he were willing to murder his own son? And what kind of insecure, mean-spirited God would put Abraham to that sort of test? This stuck in my craw for years, indeed decades. I wasn't able to come up with a satisfactory answer until I wrote a paper in seminary, and by then I was in my late fifties.

But happily, at least in terms of my relationship with God, at some point in Sunday school we examined the book of *Exodus.* That's when things came together. Moses floating down the river, the miracles, the battles—all of that I shrugged off. What grabbed and held my attention was after the exodus when the newly freed children of Israel camp at the foot of Sinai and Moses walks to the top alone to speak with God.[12] When Moses doesn't come back down immediately, the people lose faith, melt their looted gold from Egypt, and make a golden calf. They begin to worship the calf and not God. Atop Sinai, God loses it and wants to destroy them all. Moses doesn't say, "Yes, God, of course, God, whatever you say, God." Moses says, "No, a just God doesn't act this way." And God puts aside his anger.

My mind flashed back to *Genesis*, and Abraham saying virtually the same thing when told God is going to wipe out Sodom and Gomorrah.

---

10 *Genesis* 18:23
11 *Genesis* 22
12 *Exodus* 32

Despite the insanity of Abraham being willing to murder his own son, I felt my religion was teaching me that justice was crucial. I felt that the point of Scripture was not simply that it was ok to argue even with God if you felt God was being unjust, but indeed arguing was a moral obligation. As important, it followed that I wasn't expected to follow blindly what I was told even if I thought it was God telling me. Always, always the crucial question to ask before taking any action was not "Does God want this?" but rather, "Will my actions be just?" Then, my mind went to the story of Jacob, and his long struggle with an angel and the folk etymology of his new name of Israel: "He who wrestles with God." This was huge. This was important. This was a God who looked to how I acted, not what I believed. And my actions must be just. This was a God who expected me to wrestle with what was just, even if it meant wrestling with Him. Count me in.

Of course, my religious training wasn't all as simple as that. I was also being taught something that I rebelled against from the very beginning. I was told to be "proud" of being Jewish. Many years later I would come to have much more compassion for those who were asking us to be proud. Very often a minority, particularly one that has received the backhand of history, feels it important to make a statement. "I'm proud of who I am." "Black, and proud of it." "Gay, and proud of it." "A woman, and proud of it." "Jewish, and proud of it." For me, being black, or gay, or female, or Jewish, or straight, or white is a fact. It's just a fact, nothing more. I personally don't believe in pride under any circumstance. Proud of a fact?

Today, I recognize that this need for pride is a reaction to our culture. "You're a lesser person (by whatever the twisted reasoning spouted). Be ashamed." Faced with this, the natural reaction when a person decides not to take it anymore is of course, "No, I'm not ashamed; I'm proud." For me, even before I could articulate it, both pride and shame seemed simply two sides of the same corrupted coin. I've never liked either. In our culture, I can understand an expression of pride as a reaction to being told to be ashamed. If Jews had been told they were the filth of the Earth and Jewish children were being told to be ashamed of being Jewish, as Europe had told them over and over and too many to this day were telling them "even" in America, then it made sense that my teacher's reaction would be, "No, don't be ashamed of being a Jew. Be proud."

I wasn't so nuanced in my thinking back then. All I could do was rebel against the "Be proud" teachings thrust upon me. "Look at how many Jewish doctors there are. Be proud." I was happy they were doctors if that's what they wanted to be. Good grief, how could I take pride in someone else being a doctor? Or the one that still stands out for me these many years later. One of my teachers told the class I was in that in Columbus' day Jews frequently acted as interpreters. Thinking he was landing in India, Columbus would most likely have sent his interpreter ahead. Therefore, the first European to set foot on the New World was probably Jewish. Be proud!

It seemed like incredibly tortured logic. Even if it were true,[13] how was this something to be proud of? It made no sense. It seemed stupid. I felt neither proud nor ashamed of my heritage. How could it be a source of pride or shame: I had nothing to do with it! And being fearless, and frankly not knowing when to stay silent, I spoke up.

It took me years to figure this out, to come up with a philosophy and rationale to back up the essence of me that disdains both pride and shame. I do recall resolving never to be ruled by either one. I will let no man (patriarchy again!) shame me. I will not be proud. I will never be proud. Pride is wrong. Pride is evil.

Kids can think in such stark terms. When I heard the expression, "Pride goeth before a fall," my reaction was, "Well, of course." When I was told by someone that pride was a sin, my reaction was, "Tell me something I don't know." Again, I was pretty much without nuance in those days. Things were right, or they were wrong. Both pride and shame were wrong. End of discussion.

I felt the same way when I got a similar message at home. "Take pride in what you do," my father tried to teach me. No, thank you. I will do my best. If I do my best, and it doesn't work out—well then, remembering Rommel, I'll know not to do it again and try another way. If I do my best, and it does work out I'll certainly be pleased, but I won't be proud. As I grew, it became ever-clearer to me why our spiritual paths consistently warn us against pride.

So when my parents told me they were proud of me, I grimaced. But one time in particular, when my mother told me she was proud of me, sticks in my mind.

I was old enough to be let loose at a playground, but not old enough to be left totally alone. I was playing with a couple of kids, one of whom I knew and the other newly met. Other than that we played together for some time, I really don't remember anything about the incident other than what happened when I went back to where Mom was waiting to take me home. "I'm so proud of you," Mom told me, "for playing with them."

---

13   Sorry, Leif Erikson.

What? That made no sense. Mom pointed out to me that one of the kids I had played with was an "Oriental" and the other a "Negro."

What? I was playing with a couple of kids. We'd had fun. What was she talking about? It still made no sense.

This was when I first began to understand that we humans divide ourselves. I knew that if Mom was proud of me for doing something, then it was something unusual, something special. But what was unusual or special about playing with other kids? What we looked like? Good grief, was it what we *look* like? This was my introduction to the concept of race. I didn't like it, and was angry at Mom for shoving it in front of me to see. The anger lasted for weeks. My horror at our propensity to divide ourselves has lasted a lifetime.

I had thought that Lilly's job requirements were demeaning. It had never once occurred to me to think it had anything to do with her skin color. Lila's skin was darker than mine. It never occurred to me that that meant anything. I would have loved Lila regardless of race or ethnicity. She was a loving and wise human being. That's what drew me to her. What else mattered?

I'd lived in either totally or primarily Jewish neighborhoods all my life. My exposure to Asian-American, African-American, Mexican-American or any other than Jewish-American children had been pretty much limited to Little League or the playground. But when I had seen kids from other ethnicities, they'd always just seemed like kids. If they didn't try to bully me and wanted to play—what else was important?

Now, for the first time in my life, I was forced to understand that some people thought "race" was important. Clearly Mom thought that what I would later learn to call prejudice was wrong, which was why she was happy I played with the other kids. But just as clearly she recognized the importance of division by what we look like or she never would have mentioned it in the first place! I've never gotten over my disgust with how prone we are as a species to divide ourselves: by race, gender, ethnicity, religion, economic status. If there was a genesis to this disgust and my repudiation of our divisions, it was in this moment of revelation.

Now it was off to high school.

Chapter Six

Ok, truth. For me, high school was a form of hell. There was nothing I could relate to. Mentally I could easily have gone directly to college, but my emotional maturity was still stuck in junior high. I remained shy and untrusting. For my education I had only three excellent teachers over three long years: Mr. Drury, who encouraged and guided me in creative writing; Mr. Chasman, whose iron-fisted approach to English finally succeeded in breaking me of spelling ad lib and got me to use a dictionary; and Mr. Weinstein, who taught AP World History without polemic and really helped to open up the world for me.

But outside of school, life was good. One reason was that my health had improved. Simply moving closer to the coast hadn't been enough. My folks started me on allergy shots (I think once a week). It took a while to connect the two (at least it did for me), but after about a year on allergy shots I stopped throwing up most mornings.[14] This was freeing, spiritually as well as physically.

Another reason life was good was my Uncle Jerry. Uncle Jerry was my father's brother. Dad had all sorts of ideas about how a man should act, and one of his beliefs was that "real men" don't hug. If my dad liked something I did, he firmly shook my hand. The only other times Dad would touch me would be, depending upon the offense, to slap my face or spank me. Again, Mom never punished me. It was always, "Wait 'til your father comes

---

14   As it turned out, my allergies clogged my sinuses, which would drain overnight. A lot of mucus would collect in my stomach and as soon as I ate anything the next morning, my stomach rebelled. It wasn't until I left college and couldn't afford allergy shots that it occurred to me how lucky I had been to have parents who could afford them, and what that implied for kids whose parents lived in poverty.

home." This is all I knew of what was expected of "real men" until Uncle Jerry came onto the scene.

Uncle Jerry was a bear of a man, and he loved to hug. He hugged everybody, including me—big, expressive bear hugs. I hadn't been exposed to him much when I was younger, as he and his family lived in Iowa. But as my father's business grew and prospered, he asked Uncle Jerry to move the family out and come to work for him.

I learned to love hugging, though early in my adult life it would get me into trouble from time to time. Still at a junior high level socially, I hadn't learned boundaries. If I liked someone, or just felt good, I would give that person a big hug. Some of my male friends thought I was really weird. Some of my female friends thought I was coming on to them. I respect people and their boundaries in so many ways. But it took me much, much longer than it should have to learn to respect boundaries when it comes to hugging. I regret that. I know that, particularly in my twenties and early thirties, I deeply offended some people and made others exceedingly uncomfortable. These days I am cautious about giving a hug, though every few years I still make a mistake. But caution would appear to be the best choice given the alternative.

All this said, the joy and warmth of being hugged by Uncle Jerry was as manna to a starving child. I will always be so grateful to him for his alternate example of how "real men" act.

Of course, not all touching is created equal. This was something I found out firsthand the summer after I turned sixteen when I went looking for a summer job with my freshly minted driver's license. I answered an ad from a men's clothing store. There the two men who interviewed me ran their hands up and down my thigh several times as they "explained" an inseam. One caressed my crotch and smilingly told me that the "fit" there was extremely important in the clothing business. Both of them seemed to be having a great time, but I wasn't. I had led a sheltered enough life to have no idea what was going on, but I knew I didn't like it. I told them I wasn't interested in the job and walked out.

The issue of fighting also reared its head yet again. Dad felt sure that my embrace of judo meant that I was becoming "more of a man." But I had drawn a very firm line. For me, if someone's fist is flying at my face, or the face of someone I love, I have the right, even the obligation to keep that fist from landing. For me, this was what judo was all about. But I still abhorred violence. My father's belief that "Might makes right" made me cringe. The pitcher Sandy Koufax entered the picture because he had, whatever year this was, recently refused to pitch a game in the World Series because it fell on the crucial Jewish holy day, Yom Kippur. He became my example as well as my hero.

"What if I say Sandy Koufax is the greatest pitcher in baseball and you disagree? If I beat you up, does that make me right? And if you say Juan Marichal is the greatest pitcher and you beat me up, does that make you right? It doesn't, does it? Fighting proves nothing!" Dad was flummoxed and, at least for a while, it ended the discussion.

These issues aside, for me the great joy of my high school years came outside of school when I delved into a study of the ancient Greeks. My interest had been piqued as a child by a TV program on Socrates.[15] Now I discovered Homer and particularly *The Iliad*. For me, the hero of the story was Hector, not Achilles. Hector was the one who saw his duty, kissed his wife and child goodbye and went off to do what he most feared—face Achilles. Achilles was for me a disquieting example of how pride destroys a person. What I loved about the whole story was that Homer was Greek, yet he hadn't turned the Trojans into fools or "the enemy." The Trojans were as human (and therefore not only as wise but also as foolish) as the Greeks. And the Greek gods were fascinating. The god of war, Ares, was a blowhard and a buffoon, the cause of mindless terror. What a jerk! How perfect that the Greeks saw their god of war in that way. But it was the goddess, Athena, who grabbed both my attention and affection. Strong. Independent. My kind of girl! She was the goddess of wisdom and a stark contrast to the primping Aphrodite, who was only concerned with her looks.

My education continued from reading unrelated to school. From Homer, I moved on to Plato and then Aristotle. But of all the Greeks, it was the philosopher Democritus who truly amazed me. Simply by sitting and contemplating a rock, *a rock*, he had come to the conclusion not only that all matter must be made up of atoms but also that these "atoms" were constantly in motion. This was a mind! I also loved discovering in the work of Pythagoras the melding of music and math. What a perfect combination.

What attracted me more and more to the ancient Greeks was what I saw as a true harmony in their lives that I felt was so very much lacking in mine: a unity of heart and mind, music and science—a full-throated acknowledgement that *everything* was interconnected. The truth of it is that

---

15   In 1953, on the wonderful educational series You Are There hosted by Walter Cronkite, there was an episode on "The Death of Socrates." It was a mind-blowing half-hour introduction to the essence of Socrates' teaching and most important, that being true to who you are was the one thing absolutely worth dying for. More than sixty years later, the episode still echoes in my brain.

up to this moment, while I was enjoying my education, I remained adrift and alone. Wasn't there *anyone* who approached life as I thought it should be approached? Well, now it turned out there was a whole civilization that had felt that way. Well ok, they'd been dead for more than two thousand years, but at least they'd existed. I wasn't a *total freak.* This was oddly reassuring.

There were other spiritually significant moments. One came on Friday, November 22, 1963. I was in school when President Kennedy was shot. I remember walking into my English class and seeing Mr. Chasman, this towering strength of knowledge, sitting in front of the class with his head in his hands, weeping. We all just sat there for an hour, getting updates as they came over the intercom. I'm sure my other teachers reacted, but it was walking into Mr. Chasman's class and seeing him so completely devastated that is burned into my memory. That, even more than the facts of Kennedy's assassination, is what I remember of that day.

One glorious thing were my visits to Uncle Ike and Aunt Esther. They weren't actually related to us, and I have no idea how my parents knew them. But they were truly delightful people. Ike would regale us with tales of the building of the Panama Canal, and I wish I had taken notes. I am pretty sure that Ike was a part of the commissary—the feeding of the people building the canal. I loved Ike and Esther, and always looked forward to visiting them. But I mention Ike in particular now because of a stark lesson he taught me some years later.

Another adventure I had was in the children's choir at Temple. It was fun and I enjoyed it a lot. But then came the day when I had to walk. Our cantor was the choir director, and we were preparing a song for Chanukah. The "Ch" in Chanukah is pronounced with a rolling, guttural "cha," as if you were clearing your throat before saying "Ha." We rehearsed, over and over. But we still weren't doing it right. Finally our exasperated cantor cried out, "ChhHah, ChhHah, Chanukah. Now do it again!"

We were kids. He had just challenged a bunch of kids to really clear their throats and then voice "Hanukah." If you've ever dealt with kids, you know what happened next. We sang out: "CHHHHHHHHHHHHHHHHH-HHHHHHHHHanukah!"

Our cantor was furious. He cried out, and I can still hear his angry words these 50-plus years later, "Stop it! You are *not* here to have fun. You are here to sing! Anyone here to have fun can get up and leave!"

There was absolute silence. We were all shell-shocked. I thought to myself: Yes, we were there to sing, but we were also there because we thought singing was fun. Singing *should* be fun. Is no one going to call him on this? Why doesn't somebody do something?

It echoed in my head: You're somebody, why don't *you* do something? So I did. I felt it would be rude to talk back to the cantor, so I just picked up my stuff and walked out. I never sang in the choir again. My very surprised parents, bless them, listened to me tell them the story and backed me up. It's ok, they told me. You made a decision and we understand it. If you have any trouble we'll support you. But there was no trouble. I continued in Sunday school, but not in the choir.

The last year of Sunday school was particularly enlightening and wonderful for me. Half the time we were taught by our rabbi, Rabbi Beerman, and half the time by Mr. Schecter, who worked at the Anti-Defamation League. Both men were loving and gentle and lived lives that cleaved to justice.

This was the year we learned in depth about things like the Civil Rights struggle and the work of Dr. Martin Luther King Jr.. Particularly from Rabbi Beerman, we learned that to be Jewish meant to be committed to a life of justice, and that justice meant treating all of humanity fairly and equally. No life was more or less valuable than another.

What was even more crucial to me, and what has stayed with me even fifty years later, was that both of these men *lived* what they preached. From my perspective, and what I took from it, held close and continue to hold close to this day, Rabbi Beerman and Mr. Schecter were men who lived lives of justice, and found that Judaism helped them to practice that justice. It was justice that needed to be the core of my life. This was the lesson I felt reaffirmed by both of them. Judaism can help. And I thought, if this was what it meant to be Jewish, then YES!

Yet even though it was the least of my concerns in these years, I don't want to ignore high school completely. There were a few things that impacted me. I had a few friends, not many but more than I'd had in junior high. One friend was Charley. More about him later. Another friend was Mark. Mark and I did a lot together, including joining the debate club. Debate was helpful. It demands not only that a person develop an idea logically but also present it understandably. It also demands that a person be able to argue the merits of both sides of an issue—good life skills! I don't know what happened to Mark after high school. We simply went our separate ways.

Another important friend was Sharon. We had an intriguing friendship. She had a crush on me in the tenth grade, but I wasn't interested. I had a crush on her in the eleventh grade, but she wasn't interested. Then, in the twelfth grade, we actually became friends. Just friends, but good friends. We had many deep talks that I very much appreciated. But spiritually, I think the true importance of the friendship was that there was not the slightest wisp of romance about it. It was delightfully counter-cultural but hugely valuable, as it helped to model for me a pattern that would repeat itself: very close friendships with women that had everything to do with being open and honest and having each other's back, and nothing to do with romance. When I last saw Sharon she was trying to decide between getting married after graduation or going on to college. It's one of those questions I would love to know the answer to some day.

I did date—one person. Becky. Becky was a year older and I enjoyed seeing her a lot. We even continued to see each other after she went off to college—but only for a short while. She thought it was her fault that we broke up, but it wasn't. It was mine. In truth, I was far too emotionally immature to cope with a girlfriend. I liked her. I enjoyed being with her. But I had no idea what to do or how to act around her romantically. Knowing I was in over my head I cut things off. But I didn't handle it well.

Still, with college looming, and possibly the last four years of my life that would truly and solely be dedicated to my education, I wanted to pick my college carefully. Over time, I narrowed my choices down to three: Occidental College, Stanford University, and the University of California at Berkeley. I knew they'd all want to see my grades and my grades were pretty much by now a solid B (a three point). So, for the first time in my life I worked at getting good grades. I pulled down a solid A (a four point) the first semester of my senior year, and did well on my SAT score. Still, I was no great "catch" for any school and knew it. There was one thing that might have helped had it worked out—but it didn't.

I'd wondered, as my high school years progressed, why there weren't any teenage voices on the radio station I listened to and liked a lot: KMPC. Why doesn't someone do something? So, I wrote them and asked. To my surprise, I got a phone call soon after inviting me to come to KMPC and talk about it. I think it was from the news director, but I really don't recall. Obviously, I went.

He was clearly disappointed the moment he saw me. "How old are you?" he asked. And I told him. "Then you're in—high school?" Yes, I told him. He told me that based on my letter, he'd assumed I was in college. So, ok, I was there, let's talk. And so we did. I seemed to impress him, despite my age. He talked about starting a program called "Young America

Speaks" and having me anchor it. It sounded cool. I don't recall which year this was, but I do recall that it was almost summer. My family was going to Mexico for a few weeks. I asked for and received a courtesy card from KMPC—identifying me not so much as an employee, which I wasn't, at least not yet, but as a young person with the KMPC news department's confidence.

To my amazement, I was almost able to parlay that into an interview with the president of Mexico. But, as it happened, the rather high-ranking Mexican official I talked with said the president wouldn't be back from his own vacation for several days. Mom and Dad decided that we couldn't extend our vacation, so I missed it. But I did do some "man in the street" interviews (I'd been taking Spanish for some years) and was able to come up with what I thought were some interesting bits of information. This was the early 1960s. Communism was still seen as a big threat to the United States, and lots of people were worried about communism in Mexico. But the people I talked to had no interest in communism. What they were interested in was putting a meal on the table and not being stepped on by the millionaires who seemed to run the political machines. To my mind that wasn't communism, it was a desire for justice.

I wrote about this and it ended KMPC's interest in me. When they thought of "Young America Speaks" they were thinking of a show concerned with where rock music is going and such questions as, What about the long-hair movement? I was quickly but politely uninvited by KMPC and therefore had no special coup to list on my résumé for college. I'd both talked myself into and then out of my own radio show, all on my own. I thought that fascinating.

So, I mailed my applications. As it turned out, Stanford had no interest in me whatsoever. Cal Berkeley accepted me. Occidental was unsure and offered to put me on the wait list. Occidental was where I decided I wanted to go, so I held my breath and waited. In the meantime: a road trip and some serious reflection—about money!

Chapter Seven

How do we relate to money and what are the spiritual implications? This is not something most of us tend to think about. But our relationship with money affects our entire lives, and those relations tend to start early.

That summer before college I went on a trip with Charley, one of my high-school friends. We traveled in the car my father had given me for graduation: a used Chevy Corvair. Yes, this was the car that Ralph Nader had called "Unsafe at any speed," but I was just ever so grateful to have wheels. Charley and I tossed sleeping bags in the back and set out for our great adventure. It was fifty years ago, so I'm sure there is much that I've forgotten. But there were some important spiritual highlights and learnings that summer, the most profound of these cementing how I see our culture's obsession with the almighty dollar.

Traveling with Charley taught me a lot. I've already shared how learning of the Shoah deeply affected me. But I still had my grandmothers, my Uncle Jerry and my Uncle Hal (who was my mother's brother) as well as a bevy of cousins. The only casualty of World War II from our family that I knew of was my Uncle Bill, my mother's brother, who was killed in action. But Charley only had his parents. As I recall, his aunts, uncles, cousins and every other relative were all obliterated by Hitler's quest to exterminate Jews. Charley's folks had just gotten out in time. No one else in the family made it. That's putting things in perspective.

Charley's family also had a lot less money than mine. This crystalized as we traveled. My father's finances had frankly not been something I was concerned with. We had enough. More than that, I knew that things had gone well for my father since I was a kid. When I was in grade school there was a toll charge to call Grandma Helen—who lived near us, but not in the same town we did. To save money, on the days we were going to visit her dad would call, let the phone ring three times, and hang up. Grandma Helen knew that meant we were on our way. We no longer needed to do that. We were definitely on the "upper" side of middle class.

Charley wasn't. Not having much money saved as yet, I was not only happy to adopt Charley's approach to how we spent money on the trip, but also felt there was much I could learn from it. We got a summer pass and spent our nights almost entirely in national parks. This was the summer I fell in love with Mount Lassen, and I went back there every summer I could for years. I also learned that for me, home was the Pacific Ocean, not Los Angeles. Late in the trip Charley and I explored the Seattle area, again mostly in sleeping bags, and somehow I knew I would be coming back some day.

I learned that summer that living simply came naturally to me, which was also a good lesson. We had no tent. We'd just toss our sleeping bags down and sleep. At this point I don't remember much more than paying close attention to how much we spent on food. Lunch almost always came from a market. Frequently breakfast did as well. And we were careful where we ate dinner. I learned some good, frugal habits—but much more than that I also learned not to assume. Specifically, I learned never to assume how much money another person might or might not have; and if I'm with someone, to think before suggesting something that involves spending money.

My whole relationship with money was taking form in high school. Now it became a way of living. I was young enough that I still thought in terms of absolutes. I am, I hope and trust, rather more nuanced today. Nonetheless, my essential feelings haven't changed. Money seemed a necessary evil, but still an evil and one that had to be kept in its place.

Having gone to Palisades High School, I'd met a rather large number of pampered kids. They not only had money (thanks to very indulgent parents) but also seemed to have a rather unhealthy disdain of anyone who didn't. I was repelled.

Having money is important. There's no way around that. Money to a large extent determines what kind of health care a person receives. Money can determine not only whether you eat regularly but also whether or not you have books surrounding you in your house, if indeed your family has the money to own a house! And with my grades, I had no scholarships, so money determined whether or not I could go to college, and where. So money was an important tool, not to be sneered at. Still, it was only a tool and nothing more. It baffled me that so many held it in such high regard. For so much of a young person's life to depend on how much money a parent made seemed unjust and therefore wrong. To have the quality of your health care depend on your parent's wealth seemed equally unjust. Why should needed allergy shots, as but one example, depend on the ability of my parents to pay for them?

It was another benefit of being part of the debate club in high school that I had argued both sides of the question. Health care, capital punishment, religion in our schools; these were all topics I'd researched and debated as well, but nothing surprised me more than how accepting we all were of the triumph of the dollar.

Some people, I already saw, were enslaved by money. With sadness I came to realize that my father was such a person. We had more money now than we'd ever had in the past and yet instead of making Dad feel more comfortable, it seemed to make him want even more. Why? I asked myself. So many people had so much less. What would drive my father to want more when we already had plenty? Nor was it just my father.

We were taught in school, on television, everywhere we looked, to measure our success by how much money we could make. How much good we could do and how many people we might help came in a poor second, if that. Already in high school, I would listen to students talk about the jobs they wanted to get, not in terms of the satisfaction or joy of the job, but how much money it would bring in. This made me exceedingly uncomfortable. Would I become like that? What would it take, I pondered, *not* to become like that? This was important to me.

How to make and keep myself free of enslavement to money was a question I spent serious time on, starting in high school. I knew I would never need the amount of money my father did to live. But I also knew I needed some. To be free to be the person I wanted to be, I needed to be independent. That meant money in the bank—not a lot of it, but some.

This was one reason I started with summer jobs while still in high school. I didn't need the money. More to the point, I didn't spend the money I made. With very few exceptions, it all went into savings, into what I called in my mind the Steven Greenebaum Independence Fund. I knew there would be a time when I'd need money. If I didn't have enough, I would have to subordinate myself to the desires and instructions of whoever *did* have money.

Not that I wasn't incredibly lucky from the beginning. I knew how lucky I was. While I was in high school, my parents still bought my clothes. So I could afford to keep the money I earned. While in college, my parents paid my tuition and room and board, at least for the first few years, so again, I could afford to keep most of the money I earned. As I understood during my road trip with Charley, a lot of kids my age didn't have that luxury.

So, in a sense I found myself in the no-man's-land of the middle ground. I had friends who had lots of money and always had new cars, new clothes. They seemed to have no respect for budgeting or having anything other than possessing the best. I still recall an acquaintance in high school whose parents bought him a new sports car for his sixteenth birthday. Within a month he'd totaled it, so they just bought him another one. Whatever he wanted, his wealthy parents bought him. On the other hand I also had friends like Charley, who needed to be very careful about any and every purchase.

Me? I worked in the school cafeteria. I really don't remember, but think I was paid in food. If so, that meant I could pocket the money my folks had given me for lunch and deposit it in my Independence Fund. I worked summers. But living at home, I could again put the money away toward my future independence. I kept my life simple and saved every penny I could.

One summer I worked at my father's tile factory. I had taken Spanish for years, which now came in handy. But as the only non-Mexican-American working there I also learned that there is school Spanish and street Spanish. I insisted on receiving no favors and was happily granted my request. I enjoyed the men I met. Among many things, they taught me not only the joy of hard work, but the need to help each other. It was manual labor. My first taste. I also got my first taste of fear of my own government.

It started out simply enough—just a summer job. But this simple summer job truly opened my eyes and they would stay open. Study what we will, it's when we actually *see* something that really helps us to become aware and learn. One day several vehicles appeared. A lot of men were interviewed. One man with whom I'd bonded was Armando. They took Armando away. I never saw him again. It turned out he was "illegal." To my mind he was a hard worker and a caring man. If he didn't have the "right" papers, then good grief, help him get the right papers. Whatever his background and whatever language he spoke, Armando was a good man, a good human being. Why would Immigration come to arrest and deport him?

He certainly wasn't taking anybody's job. When I told my friends the nature of my work over the summer, the near universal reaction was "why?" That's such *menial* labor. Get a good job: one that makes good money and has some prospects." At that moment, and several times afterward, not only did I sympathize with the so-called illegals, I identified with them. All Armando ever wanted was to put in a hard day's work for a decent salary. For me, the United States needs more Armandos, not fewer.

I talked with my father about it. He expressed his sorrow for Armando. But he also said he hadn't known he was "illegal" and the law was the law. A stupid law, I told him. But the law, my father said. I began thinking that perhaps I should become a lawyer. Or should it be politics? What was more important, more worthwhile? Should I be defending people against stupid laws? Or should I be in politics trying to prevent stupid laws? These were the questions that were bouncing around in my head as I completed my senior year.

It wasn't simply Armando. In high school and in Sunday school, I learned more and more about the lack of respect and the lack of rights in our country for people who weren't "white." Medgar Evers was assassinated just before I entered high school. While I was in high school Governor George Wallace ordered troops to tear-gas and beat demonstrators who were peacefully marching for their rights. Segregation was very real. America was a mess. Choosing a career was not something to take lightly. How could I help? What could I do?

There was another factor. By now I was well aware that there were a lot of people who didn't consider Jews "white." That was fine by me. To the KKK and other white supremacists, as a Jew I was one of the "subhumans." Also fine. I was much happier being considered "subhuman" by the KKK than as one of "the anointed." I also realized that I "looked white." More than that, most people who weren't bigoted against Jews considered me "white." So, what was I? It seemed to me I was the man in the middle—not really a part of anything, yet in fact a part of everything.

Pondering these difficult questions helped me to focus. Whatever college I went to, I would major in political science. I'd need that regardless of whether I chose politics or the law. I felt I had direction. There was no assurance of success, but I did have a direction.

More and more, as I worked my way through high school, I'd found poetry a great help in connecting me with my feelings. This would continue in college but started several years before. Whenever I was bothered by something, or felt unsure about something, or just wanted to connect with myself, I would sit down and write, and the answer (usually) came in the poem. This time, the poem was one of confidence.

> I cannot say how I will die,
> But I decide how I shall live.
> I do not know what I will get,
> But mine the knowledge I can give.
>
> For love's a gift that's born within
> And shows the other pleasures pale.
> Though mist enclouds what fate may bring,
> The life is mine; I cannot fail.

I'd grown up a bit. I was ready for college. And when I got home from my travels there was a letter waiting for me. I had been admitted to Occidental. Oxy, here I come!

Chapter Eight

My four years at Occidental College were crucial to my mental and spiritual development, so I need to spend some time here. This was the first time I was truly living away from home, and my first lesson was deeply personal. At Oxy, during the very first quarter all freshmen were required to take what was called a "Physical Appraisal" class. I excelled in swimming and was asked by the coach to join the water polo team. I had no overwhelming desire to do so, but felt I had something to prove. I wanted to show my father that my not participating in sports was a choice, not fear of failure or because I lacked ability, nor because I feared being hurt. It seemed to me that the only way to prove it was to do with sports what I had done with scouting: participate, succeed, then voluntarily walk away. So I joined the team.

Water polo can be pretty ferocious—many called it football without padding. I certainly didn't excel at it, but I was able to hold my own. I can only remember one time when I had to be pulled from the pool after being simultaneously kicked in the head by one person and in the groin by another. I didn't pass out, which felt like a badge of honor. Take *that*, Dad! But something else happened which over time proved far more important. I began to get ear infection after ear infection. It wasn't enough to keep me from swimming, but it hurt. Still, I pushed my way through it. At the end of the season, the crowning achievement was that I lettered. *I'd* lettered in an intercollegiate sport. Case closed. Point proven.

There's no getting around the truth that my next actions were motivated by spite. I knew how much lettering meant to my father. I knew how much he wanted to see his son in a "letterman's jacket." Knowing that, I neither picked up the letter nor bought a jacket. I'd earned the letter, and that was all that mattered to me. Keeping my father from being able to take pride in it made me happy. I was being childish and petty. I knew it, even at the time, but did it anyway.

It was as my ears recovered from the rash of infections that I began to realize that the infections had done irreparable damage. I could no longer dive to any depth in a pool or the ocean without severe pain. Even more disturbing, my ears wouldn't seal to keep water out when I swam. Over time they got progressively worse, not better. Eventually, because of the pressure changes, I would not be able to fly in an airplane without a lot of pain and the risk of rupturing my eardrums. To this day I still can't. But for the moment the only thing I had to give up was any activity to do with water.

As I reflected on it, this seemed an important lesson. I wrote it down to memorialize it: "A man who must prove something to others, will never prove it to himself." I had let my need for my father's approval mess up my ears for life. For life! This was *not* my father's fault. It was mine. I had to own it. In feeling that I had to prove something to someone else, in this case my father, I'd lost control over my own life. I resolved never to let that happen again. There was only one person I *ever* needed to prove anything to and that was me—and the only way to be free to do that was to ignore as irrelevant both the approval and disapproval of everyone else.

It occurred to me that I was back to a lesson I'd thought I'd learned earlier but obviously hadn't. When I get up in the morning, *I* have to like the person staring back at me in the mirror. To be worried about whether *other* people liked me or didn't like me only made it more difficult for me to be true to myself. That was the first great lesson that finally sank in for good while I was at Oxy, but life at Occidental College was much more than that.

It seems ironic that my two main reasons for going to Oxy disappeared the very first year. One reason had been Oxy's strong political science department. I was a declared political science major. But it only took one class to convince me that this was a huge mistake. Every lecture made me feel like I needed a shower. Political science seemed to me all about how to win. "Winning isn't everything, it's the only thing" had become the model not only for sports but also politics. I still believed in and to this day am committed to "It's not whether you win or lose, but how you play the game." Political science was not a good match. Strike one.

My second reason for going to Oxy vanished nearly as quickly. Oxy had a two-year program called "The History of Western Civilization." In the brochures and course description this was exactly what I had been looking for: the Greek model, if you will, combining history, art, philosophy and music in a two-year class. In part, it did combine these things. I particularly remember Janson's *History of Art* and learned a lot from it. Yet overall, Civ was a hopeless mess. We would meet for massive lectures. Then once a week we would meet in small groups led by one of the professors. The small groups were meant to pull things together, but most of the professors I encountered were—unfortunate. The one exception was Professor Richard Trexler. If not for him, it would have been three strikes at Oxy.

Dick Trexler was an iconoclast. He was very left-wing, and while I had embraced a modestly liberal point of view in terms of social justice, I had gone off to college embracing my father's exceedingly right-wing worldview. In those days I considered myself a social liberal, a fiscal conservative and a staunch anti-communist: very much a part of the progressive wing of the Republican Party. Dick Trexler was so far left that he made most of his fellow liberal professors exceedingly uncomfortable. But he and I shared a crucial value that bonded us: that it's more important *that* you think than *what* you think. Dick far preferred talking with someone who disagreed with him but had reasons, than someone who agreed with him and didn't. I truly enjoyed talking with him.

Two specific incidents in particular bound me to Dick Trexler. One was in History of Civilization, when our final exam consisted of one the program's notorious "compare and contrast" questions. For me, these exams were always insultingly absurd. It was like being asked to write an essay comparing and contrasting Earth's orbit around the Sun with vanilla yogurt. Trexler made me feel comfortable enough that I wrote my entire bluebook[16] on the incredible stupidity of the question being asked. I received my first and only A-plus grade ever—which should tell you where Dick stood on the question. Not that he was an easy grader. Despite that A-plus on the final, I still received a B for the course.

The other incident was in one of the other Trexler classes I took. I don't remember which. But clearly Dick was tired of students mindlessly writing down everything that their teachers told them. So this day he started writing what amounted to gibberish on the blackboard, stuff that made no sense. It cracked me up, but everyone else was frantically scribbling what

---

16   If you're not familiar with them, bluebooks had, well, a blue cover! They were small, bound booklets of blank paper that were handed out for the final exam essay. With my horrid handwriting, I wrote in my bluebooks very slowly!

he was writing into their notes. Dick turned around. He noticed me laughing and gave me a quick smile. Then he sternly lectured the class. His point was, no matter who is talking to you, if it doesn't make sense, reject it—or at least question it! Think. Think!!

It so happened that in the spring quarter of my freshman year, I had two complementary and spiritually rewarding classes. One was Ancient History, taught by Trexler. The other was The Bible as Literature, taught by Donald Hobson. Ancient History allowed me not only to study the Greeks in greater detail, but also in historical context, as we studied ancient Egypt and Rome. I loved it.

Bible Lit, as we referred to it, was mind-expanding. It was my first chance to read Scripture cover to cover: *Genesis* to *Revelation*. Wow! As I read, one of the things that leapt out at me was how I had cherry-picked as crucial some of my favorite passages and completely ignored the passages that didn't call to me. As an example, I remembered and treasured God and Moses meeting at the top of Sinai and Moses prevailing in his arguments for mercy and justice.[17] Yet I'd conveniently forgotten that Moses had encouraged a slaughter of his own people just a few verses later.[18]

Not that I was alone in this, which was Professor Hobson's point. I began to understand how different people could draw rather contrasting versions of what they were reading based on what called to them. There was a fascinating book on the archeology and sociology of Scripture by Gottwald that introduced me to the various sources of the Hebrew Bible—not one source but various sources. This was exciting stuff! This was what I'd come to college for!

Happily for me, I was able to talk both Don and Dick into letting me do a single term paper for the two classes. Passover was already by far and away my favorite Jewish holy day. I wanted to throw myself into trying to research the exodus, and with their permission did so. So, I had the time and spent a lot of it in the library, digging for answers in every book I could lay my hands on. In the end, I wrote a 67-page term paper. I came to realize that if I assumed there was an exodus, then there were plenty of historical documents and archeological remains that came together to justify that claim. Simlarly, if I started out with a blank slate, then there were no historical documents and no archeological remains that would tell me that an exodus had occurred—not one! Spiritually as well as intellectually, this was mind-blowingly important.

---

17   Exodus 32:7–14

18   Exodus 32:25–29

The undeniable, inescapable truth for me was that the facts of our world *do not* shape our beliefs. The truth of it is, what we believe shapes how we interpret the facts of our world (or for some, why they deny the facts of our world). This was contrary to most of what I had been taught and what was still being taught. It was, for me at least, an answer to how so many of us could view the same world so differently. This would not be the only time that the pivotal importance of what we believe would occur to me, but it was the first time it was right there in front of my face. It gave me a better handle not only in evaluating my own beliefs and assumptions but in looking with greater compassion and respect on beliefs and assumptions that were contrary to mine. I wanted to believe in the *Exodus*. But the truth of it was, the *Exodus* only existed if I believed in it. If I didn't, it disappeared.

By the end of my freshman year, I concluded not only that I did not want to major in political science. I wanted to major in history. Not surprisingly, I asked Dick Trexler to be my advisor. He agreed.

I honestly don't remember what my summer job was, freshman year. But I do remember that I stayed at home, so I know I lived rent free and had two free meals a day. I was able to put a decent chunk of money in the Independence Fund. Then, a full and remarkable sophomore year beckoned me back.

Steven Greenebaum

Chapter Nine

My second year at Oxy was both mind-opening and exciting. One of the things I discovered was why I'd been admitted to Occidental, despite my less than stellar grade average. Occidental had been a Presbyterian college, and a very white one at that. Now Oxy wanted to "broaden" its demographics, so they let in a few Jews and a few people of color. Weird, but what the heck, it got me into Oxy. Yet it also meant that I was asked for "the Jewish perspective" rather frequently. I tried to explain that I couldn't give *"the"* Jewish perspective on anything. I could only give one particular Jew's perspective. Still, having to "explain" your spiritual path to others helps a person to better understand his or her path. It helped prepare me for challenges that would come later.

Taking history classes was also a joy, and particularly an independent study I took from Dick Trexler on the Greek historians. Each historian had both his own personality and his own way of looking at what he witnessed. Perspective! But truly magical for me was the explosion of music into my life thanks to a wonderful Oxy professor of music, Dr. Lauris Jones.

I was a musical illiterate. I'd enjoyed singing in choir in junior high and high school, and at temple—a least for a while. But that was it.

Still, I'd always had fun playing with melodies in my head. So when the economics class I wanted to take was canceled and I searched through the catalog to find another class, I happened upon Orchestration. Perfect! But to take the class without first taking the prerequisites of Harmony and Counterpoint, a student needed permission. So I went to see Dr. Jones—with the confession that I was majoring in history.

"You don't have to be a music major," he told me. "I've let people into my class who haven't taken all the prerequisites." When I told him I hadn't taken *any* of the prerequisites, he said, "Well, I've let people who have a lot of orchestra experience into the class." But I hadn't played in an orchestra. "Then *why* do you want to take the class?" he asked me, dumbfounded. I told him that I loved the different sounds of music and wanted to learn how to write for an orchestra. Somehow, that made sense to him, and Dr. Jones said "Ok."

It only took one day of class for me to know I was completely in over my head. I had at least seen treble and bass clefs in choir but by no means could I read music, and I'd never realized that there was such a thing as an alto clef. I went to Dr. Jones after class and told him I needed to drop, but this inspiring teacher refused to give me permission. He told me that according to Oxy's rules I could still drop a class without penalty after the second week. If I did all the homework for the class and still wanted to drop after two weeks he would let me. I'd asked to be in the class, he reminded me, and the least I could do was to put some effort into it.

So, I did. I spent hours in the music library, listening to recordings of the differing sounds made by the oboe and bassoon, the difference between the violin and viola. I also crash-studied the various clefs, and learned to pound out notes on the piano. By the end of the second week it was still hard, but beginning to be fun. So I hung on and by the end of the class I'd earned a solid B. This was my leap into music. And given how crucially important music would become to me, I remain so very grateful to Lauris Jones, first for letting me into Orchestration and then for not letting me out. It opened up the world of music to me.

Still another crucial event came thanks to another professor, Ben Freedman. Oxy was experimenting with a new program. They called it the College Scholar program—but it really was about intellectual freedom, not scholarship. This was fortunate as I was only a solid B student. Oxy allowed its regular students only one IS or independent study a year. But the College Scholar program eliminated that restriction and allowed a student to take as many independent studies as s/he wished; all they needed to do was approach a professor and say, "I want to study ...." whatever. If the professor agreed that the study was worthwhile, then you worked one on one with that professor and studied your subject.

Independent study was what I'd always wanted, what I'd dreamed of. It gave me the ability to pick my subjects and to branch my knowledge wherever I felt called to explore. By some miracle, Ben accepted me into the program. This was heaven!

Another exploration of the world beyond my sheltered upbringing was in meeting and talking with some of my fellow students. I met avowed homosexuals for the first time. I had managed to get to college with no idea that there was such a thing as sexual orientation.

I found homosexuality hard to grasp at first, but otherwise was unbothered by it. It seemed to me just one more example of how we're all different. But then in my ancient history class the textbook actually talked about "the dark side" of Sparta. Sparta was the most war-oriented of all the Greek city-states. But since women didn't go with the troops on Sparta's many campaigns, the warriors took young men with them for—relaxation. This was what the writer of this history of Sparta called "the dark side." It intrigued me that he didn't consider Sparta's love of war or embrace of slavery "the dark side," just this. Still, even the idea of homosexuality remained an intellectual exercise until sophomore year when I discovered that one of my friends was gay and we had some discussions.

I had and have no gay inclinations. The idea that some people were gay felt interesting, not threatening. It never occurred to me to make a judgement based on the two men who had interviewed me when I was sixteen, though I now realized that they were undoubtedly gay. Every community holds unfortunate people who abuse their positions. That my friend had faced discrimination because he was gay reminded me of my own Judaism and just how small-minded people can be. How different we all are has always been a source of fascination for me. The only time I can recall really being upset about homosexuality was when I really liked and was attracted to a girl I'd met at Oxy and it turned out she was gay. That sucked.

Another source of education for me was talking to some of Oxy's black students. Two, I remember, were refugees from South Africa and apartheid. They shared some terrible, indeed horrific stories. But as horrible as the hell they'd had to deal with was, at least it was taking place in another country. Then I made a friend, I think her name was Sheila, who shared with me some shocking and horrific stories of what she had experienced as a black woman, not simply in the United States but in the neighborhood around Oxy. The experiences she related to me helped me to bring what Dr. King was talking about and marching for out of the realm of abstract thought and into the real world of day-to-day injustice by a racist culture—just as a Chicana friend helped me better understand the why and need for what Cesar Chavez was talking about and marching for.

Massive change was needed. So much of this racist and sexist crap seemed to be systemic—a part of our culture, not just in the South but everywhere! How some people could treat others as lesser human beings was still beyond my comprehension. But that it was happening had become a clear and sickening fact.

I saw no difference from me in my black and Chicano friends, which pushed me even further away from my father. During one of the breaks in my sophomore year, I realized after a discussion with Dad that the white-sheeted haters of the KKK who lynched Negroes and made Jim Crow laws were not the only flavor of racist that existed. Dad was a racist. That both astounded me and hurt.

To be clear, my father would never have wished a black or a Chicano harm. Nor would he knowingly ever personally have done them harm. But he also thought them "lesser" beings. I was dumbfounded. My own father. My own father! He then tried to tell me that Dr. King was a communist, and that pretty well ended it. I loved my father. He was my father! But I ceased to like him very much. Our relationship became increasingly tense.

Not that it was all work and serious study. I had learned bridge, a glorious card game, when I was rather young. Back when I was living at home, my father and I would take on my sister and mother. Now that I was at Oxy, whenever there was a little spare time, I'd get together with three friends to play bridge. I was perversely pleased that the only "all-nighter" I ever pulled at Oxy was not studying for an exam, but playing bridge. I only did it once, but it was fun.

Still, the world around me was increasingly tense. The environment seemed headed for total disaster.[19] The smog in L.A. was so bad that I actually kept a "war surplus" gas mask in my dorm room, and there were days when my roommate would find me lying down on my bed in our room, wearing the gas mask and gasping for air. More ominously, the Vietnam War was continuing to escalate.

As a sophomore, I knew that my student deferment would end the moment I graduated—and it seemed that everyone was being drafted. I decided to enter the Reserve Officers' Training Corps (ROTC). I was growing more skeptical, but still embraced my father's worldview that losing in Vietnam would be the first domino falling—leading to Soviet world domination. I felt that if I was called, I needed to serve. My thought was that if as an officer I could get into "intelligence", perhaps I could fight communism without having to pick up a gun and kill anyone. To my utter astonishment,

19   *Silent Spring* had been published six years before, and it would be another two years before the EPA would be created.

I scored very high on some kind of written ROTC "leadership" test, finishing a close second, I was told, to one of Oxy's major jocks.

In the end, I decided at the last moment not to sign the papers that would have committed me to that path. This turned out to be a very fortunate decision. The year I graduated from Oxy was the year a "lottery" was set up based on a person's date of birth. As I recall, my birthday turned out to be number 361. I was never drafted. And by then my opinion about the "rightness" of the Vietnam War had changed considerably, sealed, if you will, by the tragic events at Kent State just a month before I graduated in June 1970.

A year of even more violence and deep tragedy, 1968 was a truly shattering year. Dr. King was assassinated. Bobby Kennedy was assassinated. How could this be happening? How could it possibly be happening?? I couldn't put a handle on who "they" were, but it seemed to me that "they" were murdering the people I not only cared about but to whom I looked for leadership.

In a way I have never recovered. I cannot, even to this day, see a flag at half-mast without my first thought being, "Who have they murdered now?" To this day, I cannot hear the song "Abraham, Martin and John" without weeping. Bobby and Martin were two men I deeply respected and looked up to with high regard and deep fondness. Both gone.

Heartbroken, and frustrated with what I considered to be God's refusal to help the world, I wrote a poem that would turn out to be important in shaping how I would live my life.

> I'm tired of waiting, God.
> Tired of crying and watching
> As my tears flow only to the sewers.
> I'm tired of praying, God.
> Tired of hoping that it's over
> While it's not and never shall be.
> When stops the hate?
> When ends the death?
> And the masks that change with minutes,
> And the stares that mark contempt,
> And the cows who watch it all
> With a vigilance unending
> And a mind uncomprehending.

The trees are green, God.
The sun the brightest yellow,
And the moon a pale friend at night.
A warm and loyal friend.

But the softness of the river
Is now slickened with its slime.
And the sweet air of the mountain tops,
The free and boundless air,
Is now sickened with the time.
As the ashes turn to ashes
And the dust fulfills the sky,
Just how much will I have witnessed
When at last it's time to die?
They tell me there is reason, Sir,
And logic to it all...
I'm tired of waiting.

What made the poem crucial to me was not the intense hurt I felt. I think I first called the poem "I'm Tired of Waiting," but the next year I changed the title to "A Call to Action." That became my motto. Don't wait. Don't wait for anyone. Not even God. Do. Act. And in that simple shift of title, the poem changed from one of despair to one of empowerment. So, my second year at Oxy was very much a mixed bag.

And during the summer, my education continued. For some context, the fact that most of my fellow students were against the war in Vietnam didn't bother me. My own support of the war was increasingly tenuous. What did bother me was that these angry students would belittle their parents as bourgeoisie and sell-outs to capitalism and make great fun of their parents' "jingoistic" support of the Vietnam War, and yet at the very same time happily and without any hesitation take their parents' money to pay for their clothes, their room and board and their education. This seemed to lack ethics and it bothered me a lot. I mention this because these feelings directly colored what happened when I arrived home for summer vacation after my sophomore year.

My car was crammed with, well, everything that I owned in this world. There was certainly no need of a trailer. "Everything I owned" fit nicely into the back seat and a small portion of the trunk. Arriving home late in the afternoon, I decided I would unload the car after dinner.

I have no memory of what happened at dinner. But whatever we were discussing and clearly disagreeing about, I do recall my father telling me that I wasn't at Oxy now. I was home. "You live under my roof," Dad told me, "you live by my rules."

"You're right, Dad," I replied. "You're absolutely right. It's only fair. If I live under your roof, you have every right to expect me to live by your rules. So I will never live under your roof again." I walked out to my car and drove back to Oxy (which fortunately was only about an hour's drive away). Technically, we didn't have to be out of our dorm rooms for another six days. So I had a week to find a job and a place to live. As it turned out, I quickly found a job in the cafeteria, clearing tables and washing dishes for Oxy's summer session students. And I found a cheap apartment nearby. I never again lived under my father's roof.

Dad and I were alike in at least one bad habit. We were both incredibly stubborn. I don't know what would have happened had no one intervened between these two bullheaded males.

Fortunately my sister entered into what amounted to shuttle negotiations between us. Kathy talked to me, then to my father, and then to me again. At last she was able to get us both into the same room. Our relationship was strained, but we could now talk to each other in a helpful conversation. Some important lines got drawn, and we both agreed to them. We agreed that I would not again live in the house, but that we would continue to talk—letters and phone calls. I would continue to come to the house to visit, and Dad agreed that under those circumstances, he would not question how I lived my life. We'd have meals together as a family from time to time. Dad also said he really wanted to continue to pay my tuition. I agreed, as long as it was also agreed that I'd pay for my own books and most important my room and board. In the end, our relationship had evolved but not been terminated. The important thing was that we were both still willing to talk. Without my sister's intercession, I doubt this would have happened.

Steven Greenebaum

Chapter Ten

I returned to classes in the fall feeling off balance. Even so, this was the year that everything seemed to blossom. Now that I was a "College Scholar," I took four more independent studies in addition to my regular classes: two in music and two in history. History was fun, but music was a completely new world that opened up for me like the most beautiful flower imaginable. Choral music seemed to grab me by the lapels and say, "Where have you been!?"

Because of this newfound love of choral music, I was not only singing in the college choir but also taking voice lessons. I also took "sight singing," which was a class in reading music. There was purpose behind this. Choir was nice, but the pinnacle of singing at Oxy was to sing in the Glee Clubs—which was entrance by audition only. I wanted to be prepared. The director of both the choir and the glee clubs was Dr. Howard Swan. The Occidental Glee Clubs were world famous, as was Dr. Swan. I took my first conducting class from Dr. Jones (choral and instrumental conducting) and him in the second quarter though again I was not a music major and hadn't met the prerequisites. So, this time around I took the class as a pass/fail and not for a grade.

One of the great unexpected joys of taking conducting was that I met in that class an amazing young woman named Faye. As it turned out, Faye and I would become lifelong friends. She was a wonderful conductor, a dynamite harpist, and a major league extrovert. I have always been very much an introvert. Still, we bonded, and the bond lasted forty years.

As I threw myself into music, I continued my joy of studying history—in particular, ancient Greece and early Rome. I was included in a special "honors" class and then invited to join the national honor society for history students: Phi Alpha Theta. Cool.

I made friends with a fellow history major named Paul. Paul had had polio when a child. He needed a lot of metal braces to get around and breathed through a hole in his trachea. We not only chatted history but also had some fun contemplating life as outsiders at Oxy. It was Paul who began referring to us as the Crip and the Jew, and I quickly took up the reference.

I think it was Dick Trexler who first called me "The Extrapolator." He was having fun, but it also felt at least somewhat on target. My joy, particularly in history, was looking at several differing pieces of an historical puzzle and coming up with some kind of theory that tied them all together. My big theory after studying Greece and Rome concerned democracy. It seemed relevant, as the Vietnam War was still raging and one of the rationales for it was that we were fighting for democracy. Some saw the United States as at least potentially the great "exporter" of democracy, not only to Asia but also South America. They insisted our battle with World Communism was all about democracy.

Forgive a quick digression, but I think this is important. As I studied and pondered it, it seemed to me people had really missed the boat. I pored over the example of the Greeks, and then how Rome had transitioned from democracy to dictatorship. It came to me that while Marx had been on the right track, in the end he'd blown it. Democracy, it seemed to me, was least of all a philosophy—no matter how attractive the idea of it might seem. There is no "righteousness" to democracy. Democracy, in point of fact, is a political solution to an economic conundrum: "If you have a lot of small businesses, how do you keep the extremely rich from annihilating their economic competition?" The answer is democracy.

As I studied, it became clear that a functioning democracy requires a strong middle class to succeed. Nor is it a "chicken or egg" question. Democracy cannot develop unless there is first a strong middle class. Why? The extremely rich can buy whatever government they need. The extremely poor are far more concerned with being fed and sheltered for the night than they are with the niceties of the ballot box. It's the middle class, not wealthy enough to buy the government but still needing a government that will listen to them, that must have democracy to have any chance of surviving.

Thus democracy, despite the politics and polemics, cannot be exported. It is not because a society or culture is too "immature." That's patronizing gibberish. As we saw just recently with the failure of democratic reforms after the so-called "Arab Spring," trying to impose democracy without first having a strong foundation of a middle class leads to chaos and tragedy. We might want to note that in ancient Rome democracy imploded when the insatiable super-wealthy wanted even more, and those without anything at long last rose up in violent revolt. The result was a dictatorship. A dictatorship was the only way the poor could possibly get what they needed: food and shelter. End of digression.

From a spiritual point of view, what this did for me was take democracy out of the equation of "right or wrong." A democratic form of government is all about economics, not spirituality or "good government." Democracy is not "spiritually or morally superior" to other forms of government. What democracy is is an absolute necessity of economics if there is a strong middle class (conversely: to kill democracy, destroy the middle class). It's one reason why democracy took such a strong hold in that "nation of shopkeepers" across the Atlantic.

I did well in history honors, but not as well in music. I'd done my preparation and with great hopes auditioned for the Glee Clubs. To my consternation and sadness, I wasn't good enough. I didn't make it. That hurt, and it wiped me out for a few days. Ok, so then I'm not going to be in the Glee Club. Move on. That summer between junior and senior year I decided to throw myself further into the study of Greece by actually studying Greek (and therefore, I hoped, be able to study the Greek historians without translations), but the only school I could find on the West Coast teaching Greek over the summer was Stanford.

I took a year's worth of Greek in one intensive summer class. What the incredibly hard class taught me first and foremost was that I was most definitely NOT a reincarnated Greek. Yet, the truly important and life-long lesson I learned that summer had nothing whatever to do with Greek. Going to Stanford meant no summer job. And with no on-campus dorm rooms available, I needed the cheapest apartment I could find. As it turned out, the cheap apartments were in East Palo Alto, which was largely a black ghetto. Living there taught me a lot.

The apartment I rented brought me into an endless battle with cockroaches. They were everywhere, but, what the heck, it was a cheap apartment.

What really grabbed my attention were the police. I'd been taught from the cradle that the police were my friends. Ever in trouble? Ask a policeman for help. Where I'd grown up this had certainly been true. If I saw a cop I waved, and he (no women on the beat back then) waved back.

In East Palo Alto, everything changed. I need to be absolutely clear here. I never once saw *any* police misconduct. Not once. I never saw a police officer hassle *anyone*. Not once. Yet, and this was what threw me, there was a palpable change just in how it all felt. If you've never experienced this, I don't know if there is any way to understand it. I don't know how else to describe it but that the police held themselves differently. When a police officer looked at me it felt like he was just waiting for me to step out of line. His hands always seemed like they were poised to draw his gun. I had trusted cops all my life. Now, in one summer living in East Palo Alto, I learned to fear them. I've never forgotten.

I could and did leave the ghetto behind after just one summer of being terrorized by the police. But what of those who can never leave? I can only imagine what it must be like to live in that kind of surrounding for a lifetime. Again, this is simply the day-to-day atmosphere. It was toxic and smothering. It seems to me that if we ever truly hope to make progress in our mutual regard for one another, we must not only deal with the very real existence of racism, but also the toxic atmosphere of policing in ghetto areas. I was never hassled, and I'm not a person of color. Still, in just one summer I learned both to fear and distrust the police.

There was, however, a positive highlight to the summer as well. I had no television, but neighbors I barely knew invited me over to watch Neil Armstrong land on the Moon. "One giant leap for mankind" indeed! We *were* capable of great deeds. Humanity could indeed rise to incredible heights—literally! We had landed on the Moon—on the friggin' Moon! How to hold a humanity capable of going to the Moon, yet also capable of mindless racism and brutality? This was an ongoing challenge, with no clear answer.

I returned to Oxy for my senior year newly sensitized to what many of my fellow American citizens have to live with every day. But that was pushed aside, at least temporarily, by some large, personal difficulties.

Over the summer, Dick Trexler had left Oxy. I'd had no warning. During this first quarter back I was not only assigned a new advisor, but also called into the office of Dr. John Rhodes, the chair of the department. Rhodes laid it out for me. Trexler had protected me, but my protection was gone and I was going to have to live by the rules of everyone else in the history department; namely, the rules of John Rhodes. A basic rule was that as a history major, I needed two areas of specialization. No sweat, I thought: "Greece and Rome."

No, I was told. Greece and Rome were both ancient history. Ok. Greece, Rome and Egypt. No. That was all ancient history. But, I argued, we're now talking about two different continents and nearly a thousand years of history! Too bad. But, I argued, some people can specialize in U.S. History before 1865 (the Civil War) and have their second area be U.S. History after 1865. That's one country on one continent, and just a few hundred years! And you're saying a thousand years of Egyptian, Greek and Roman history only counts as ONE area? Exactly, Rhodes told me. Ok. Then I'll specialize in Ancient History and Medieval History. No! Rhodes said. That's still effectively ancient history.

"I won't do it," I told Rhodes. "That's stupid and unfair." These are probably not the best choice of words when a student is talking to the department chair.

"You'll do it," Rhodes told me, "or you won't graduate."

I sat there silent for a while, then I looked at him. "You mean I won't graduate a history major."

"You're going to change majors, second quarter of your senior year? Good luck!" He laughed at me—not the wisest choice of words or actions from him. He'd thrown down the gauntlet. Ok. Gauntlet accepted. Now what? Yeah.—Ok. Now what?

So, I went back to my off-campus housing (it was actually cheaper than living on campus) and started thinking. I talked to Dr. Jones. He was ready to embrace me as a music major, but I'd need to take more classes (you know, like the prerequisites!). I wouldn't be able to graduate on time. What to do? What to do? I asked friends and got almost as many different suggestions as I had friends.

Dick Trexler was gone. Ben Freedman thought I had a difficult problem but could see no way out. I wrote two poems. The first I called simply, "Now What?"

Searching for a dream that may never find me.
Gaping at the world and all its choices.
Hearing what to do from all the voices—
Every voice a different key and harmony.

Ok. I shut myself in my room and pondered. There had to be choices. There are always choices. But I didn't see any. I thought about something that a well-meaning friend had offered as comfort or advice: "For every door that closes, another door opens." Ok. Where was that other open door? I didn't see one. But I'm not going to give in to Rhodes, and I am going to graduate on time. How? Good grief! How? I didn't know. So, I wrote the second poem. No title.

> The path ahead is blurred.
> I know not where it leads,
> How long it is,
> Or if it leads at all.
>
> To think, I might be stalking
> This phantom called a life;
> And yet only be stepping
> A muddled road to nowhere.
>
> Doubts abound—for who am I
> That I should dream,
> That I should hope,
> That I should win this game I've never sought to play?
>
> A savage world awaits.
> With bared teeth,
> With panting breath,
> With ever-clenched fists that know only taking.
>
> Yet I do not walk alone.
> For there are friends
> Who share my life;
> But not the road!
> It is mine and none dare tread it.
>
> And so the question seems to be:
> Am I of the road
> Or the road of me?

As I wondered what to do, it occurred to me that the saying needed to be changed. It wasn't "For every door that closes, another door opens." That invited passivity. That invited me to wait until, by some miracle, something happened. I remembered that I was called to action. Ok. How's this? "For every door that closes, there is a door that can be kicked open!" Where's the door I can kick open? There has to be one. Where is it?

I went to talk to Dr. Scott Littleton. Scott and I had become friendly. I had taken a couple of independent studies from him (starting with Greek myth but not stopping there). I found myth totally fascinating, and discovered that Scott shared that fascination. I came to Scott to see if he had any thoughts about what I might do. It turned out he did. More important, he was the chair of the Sociology and Anthropology department. "Have you thought about majoring in anthropology?" I hadn't before, but I did now.

For his part, Scott agreed to accept all the independent study classes I had taken as anthropology classes. Loved it! Still, there were two classes I absolutely had to take as an anthropology major. One was called "Man and Culture." It was the basic anthro class. The other was the senior seminar. But the senior seminar was only taught winter quarter and I had to take "Man and Culture" before then. Ok then, what if I studied over Christmas break and took "Man and Culture" by examination? Then I could take the senior seminar in the winter and graduate as scheduled after the spring quarter. Yes?

Scott agreed, with the proviso that since he didn't teach the class, it wouldn't be fair for him to grade me on "Man and Culture." The teacher who normally taught the class (whose name escapes me) would have to be satisfied. That was fair, so I agreed.

Needless to say, I studied like mad over the Christmas break. When I told my parents what I was doing, my father lost it. He was paying my tuition. He had a say in what I did and what I majored in. How dare I not consult him?

I told Dad that I agreed. I did. He was right. If he was paying for my tuition, he had a right to have a say in any decision I made about my major. Therefore, from now on I would pay all my expenses at Oxy.

Oxy was nowhere as expensive in 1969 as it is now. But it still wasn't cheap. Worse, I hadn't worked over the previous summer. So I raided the Greenebaum Independence Fund and put myself on a very strict budget. Fortunately, the apartment where I lived, while definitely a firetrap and way below code, was also dirt cheap. But food. For the next two quarters, my primary source of nourishment was one ten-pound bag of potatoes every week.

I passed the class I took by exam, and got an A in the senior seminar. And with Scott's guidance I dove more deeply into the magical world of mythology. As I did, I realized how important it was to me to continue and to deepen my study of myth. Philosophy was, or so it seemed to me, what we thought we *should* believe. Myth was what we actually *did* believe. If I wanted to understand humanity, I needed to study myth. As it turned out, I not only graduated on time but with honors in Anthropology. I decided not to go see John Rhodes and rub his face in it. It was enough to have graduated. More than that, I knew where I wanted to go to graduate school: UCLA. And I knew what I wanted my M.A. to be in: mythology.

Leaving Oxy brought mixed emotions. I felt I was on the right path, while at the same time not really knowing where it was that the path was taking me. Graduate school, I knew, was a way station not the destination. The poem I wrote as I awaited graduation day, my diploma and vindication, was not so much one of triumph but of confidence.

In a place I've yet to wander
Lies a path I've yet to take.
There's a meadow never sensed before,
And at least ten rules to break.
With a sky that craves exploring
And its promise to fulfill,
There's a task that calls enduring
From an endless wish and will.

If you see the need to know me,
Ask the jay who's decked in blue.
Seek a never-ending west wind
That's oblivious to hue.
Taste the apple known as freedom.
Bless the thorn that galls the brain.
For the glow that is creation
Runs impervious to rain.

A leaf in wind may self-delude.
The paradox may always be.
But fire or bliss—a golden fleece,
This dream that may never find me.

"If one door closes, another door can be kicked open" became my motto for living.

Chapter Eleven

College and a liberal arts education are becoming increasingly controversial. So many are asking, "Isn't job training more important?" While I can understand the economics of it, I got so much from college, both spiritually and intellectually, that I have to answer emphatically: "No."

I experienced several wonderful awakenings. The first was music. Choral music particularly called to me. There seemed something so very special about a diverse group of people woven together in common purpose. After graduation, I continued to take voice lessons. Even as I pursued the fascinating study of myth, I very much wanted singing to be a part of my life—perhaps professionally.

Still, I was starting late and knew it. There was a massive amount of work to be done if I wanted to be ready and able to have the option to choose singing as a creative path. The bonus was I just might be able to sing at night while pursuing a different path during the day.

A second awakening was my introduction to the incredible diversity and beauty of humanity's myths. What became so very clear to me was that all of us, *all* of us, ask the very same questions (at its most basic, "How did we get here?" and "How should we act?") and yet we come up with such divergent answers! This was fascinating, and engaging. Yes, I was Jewish. But there is so much more to humanity than Judaism! I had no desire whatever to leave Judaism (and never have). But I did very much want to sample and experience other ways of perceiving the sacred.

A third awakening came in the diversity of humanity that I met at Oxy. I had come from a rather cloistered Jewish background. In college I met mostly non-Jews, not to mention gays and people of color. And hello!

We're all human. Race, religion, gender, whatever—just divisions. Mindless divisions. Crazy divisions. Bottom line, we're all human—with dreams and prejudices, hopes and fears, astounding strengths and gaping weaknesses. All of us. Jews no better or worse than anyone else.

Also, and this was a huge joy, for really the first time in my life I made a lot of friends. I was at long last beginning to trust people—at least, a few. Several of the friends I made would become lifetime friends. Nancy, Elaine, Richard, Faye, Tom, Candy.

The last of my great awakenings came senior year when I realized just how much food had been available to me all my life and how little I actually needed to survive. I've already mentioned that my primary source of nourishment at that time was a ten-pound bag of potatoes a week. This was supplemented by a half-gallon of milk and some cereal. Neighbors in the apartment next to mine let me read their paper when they were through with it and, crucially, let me clip their coupons. I kept a stash of coupons for cereal. Reading the weekly supermarket ads, I learned where the cereal, milk and potatoes were the cheapest that week. Milk particularly was always on sale somewhere. My cereal for the week was determined by which cereal was both on sale and for which I had a coupon.[20]

I would later be forced to eat a cereal, milk and potato diet for nearly three years (and yes, for several years after I couldn't look at a potato, let alone eat one!). Senior year at Oxy was my introduction to it. I learned the important lesson that there is a big difference between going hungry and starving. I was hungry most of that time. I went to bed every night knowing that if there were more, I'd eat more. Still, I was never threatened with starvation. When I read that too many in America and indeed around the world go to bed hungry, I know what that feels like—and it's *not* fun. I made choices. At times, those choices would result in very little to eat. There are so many, *too many*, who face hunger not, *not* from their own choice but because we as a society make that choice for them. That is so very wrong. It is particularly wrong when it is our children who must go to bed still hungry, still hoping for just a little more.

It's my rather strong guess that this is why hunger issues remain so important to me. I support the local food bank. I'm involved in walks to raise awareness of hunger. If a person like me chooses to live with hunger

---

20   I also managed a glass of juice a day thanks to buying cans of frozen concentrated orange juice when on sale, and also one mug of coffee a day, reconstituted from whatever instant coffee was, like the cereal and orange juice I bought, on sale and for which I also had a coupon. Once I could afford it, I switched to ground coffee and a Melita and never looked back.

for a while, then it's a choice. That said, no one on this planet should ever be *forced* to go to bed hungry—let alone starve to death. I consider my experience with hunger an important if not crucial part of my education. Choices have consequences. That's not only reasonable but important to learn. While I was perfectly willing as well as able to live with the consequences of my choices, *no one* should ever face hunger, let alone starvation, simply because society can't be bothered to help.

One other thing I learned in college was that I had a hard time holding jobs. I've mentioned a few summer jobs. But there were others. Two in particular carried some spiritual importance—albeit in rather strange ways.

As I started out, having little job experience, I took what I could find. One summer job involved selling vacuum cleaners door to door. It paid well, but presented an ethical dilemma. I believe the product was called the Compact vacuum cleaner. Technically, we didn't "sell" the vacuum cleaner, we "placed" it. This was my first exposure to what's called a pyramid scheme. The vacuum was super expensive. But if a person gave us ten names of friends, and those ten people either bought the vacuum or gave us ten more friends' names, then the vacuum was free. In truth, it was a rip-off. We were given a patter, and phrases that would in effect shame people into signing the paper that obligated them to "placing" ten vacuums with friends or, more likely, buying a vacuum they couldn't afford: "Don't you have ten friends?" and, "The offer is only good for tonight, I need your answer now."

The vacuum was exceptionally good. That wasn't the rip-off. But the idea of "placing" this expensive machine was terrible. Would anyone actually fall for it? I was curious. To my amazement, everyone I visited trusted me completely. Without exception, everyone I went to asked me, "Should I do this?" And I told every one of them who asked, "I wouldn't. I was taught never to be pressured into doing something without thinking it over first." I didn't sell/place one vacuum, and after I think three weeks I was fired. But I felt I'd saved quite a few people quite a bit of money.

One Christmas season I worked at the Beverly Hills Robinson's, a very plush store. It was a fascinating experience, as a lot of movie stars shopped there. I particularly remember interacting with three. Earl Holliman, a few years away from *Police Woman* but still well known to me, was a gentleman, a "salt of the earth" fellow even amidst the pushing and shoving of the Christmas rush. Diahann Carroll, whom I believe at the time was making a huge splash on television with her hit show *Julia*, was one of the sweetest people I've ever met, willing to wait patiently to be served and then both generous and gentle with me when I misunderstood her the first time she asked for something.

Then there was Barbara Stanwyck, who just before our Christmas Eve closing tried to push her way through a line of people in front of her, all of them desperate to buy their gifts and get home. I told her, "I'll be with you just as soon as I help these folks who are ahead of you." She was unimpressed and demanded to be served immediately. I repeated that I would get to her as soon as I had served the people who were ahead of her and then turned away. She didn't take it well. Neither did my floor supervisor, who told me I would never work at Robinson's again. I didn't. I took two lessons home with me. First, that Hollywood people were like everyone else—some lovely, some not. The second was that no job was worth compromising who I am. I don't need new clothes every year, and if need be, I can always eat potatoes.

Not everything got ironed out, of course. The one place I really remained behind the pack all four years of college was in my efforts at dating. That someone as good and wise as my mom always put Dad first still stuck in my craw. Patriarchy not only felt very wrong to me but literally turned my stomach. Looking back, one of the surest things to send me running from any relationship was dating a woman who seemed to be putting my interests ahead of hers. I saw what it did to Mom. I never wanted to be responsible for doing that to another human being. Ever!

Still, I left Occidental College incredibly glad that I had gone there. And while I in truth had no idea where my life was headed, the two things I knew were that music and mythology were going to be huge. Among other things, that meant I would be heading for UCLA to pursue a Masters in Mythology.

Chapter Twelve

I don't recall what my summer job was between Oxy and grad school at UCLA, but I'm pretty sure I squeezed in a few days at my favorite place to relax and unwind: Lassen National Park. During the day I would hike alone, just me and the wilderness—heaven for an introvert. At night I was welcomed by the college kids who worked there to join them for cookouts, chats and singing. This was the "in" crowd. There were official offerings such as nature talks for the "guests" at the park, but for some reason I never really understood I was always accepted as one of the gang. So I got some delightful unloadings about difficult park guests, and in particular the visitors who came to the park expecting their cabins to have all the amenities of home including a dishwasher and television.

One of the lessons learned at Lassen came one summer when I must have gone late in the season. I was invited to the "goodbye" party for one of the rangers, who I assume must have gotten another job. I'd met him during the day. He was a terrific guy—warm, friendly, knowledgeable. At the start of the party he was still a lot of fun. But then, for the first time in my sheltered life, I learned that a person can be perfectly delightful sober but mean and even dangerous when drunk. He went out of his mind. We had to tackle and incapacitate the guy before he hurt someone. It was mind-bending for me. Dr. Jekyll and Mr. Hyde. I'd heard of it and read about it, but it's something quite different to actually see it happen in front of you.

It's hard to exaggerate how much I loved Lassen and how completely I felt connected to it. There was a time when I felt I knew every corner of every trail. There were some truly off-the-beaten-path trails that felt like my own private heaven. I was connected to nature, to the Earth, to the cosmos, to God.

I'm not sure, but I think it was that summer between Oxy and UCLA that something very personal and difficult happened. I had my campground. I was munching on something—breakfast, lunch, I don't remember. And my jaw locked. I had opened my mouth wide to bite into something and the jaw locked open. Wide open. I couldn't close it. This was not only acutely painful but scary. I really don't remember what happened after that, except that as soon as I got home I saw my doctor, who sent me to a specialist. The conclusion: my jaw hinges were "hyper-mobile." I'd evidently lost most of the connective cartilage in one jaw and a good 50% in the other. I was given some drugs to keep my muscles relaxed while things healed. Meanwhile, I was told that it was my singing, and more specifically my singing exercises, that had done me in.

It was a body blow. I loved singing. I knew I was going to study mythology, but I also intended to continue with my voice lessons. I checked with my voice teacher to be sure, but she confirmed I was toast as a professional singer. If I laid off the singing for a while, I would surely be able to sing again—although no longer for hours at a time, and certainly my vocal exercises, all of which accented a wide-open mouth, were off the table. The choice of being a singer was gone.

Ok, then. Turn the page. If there was a way to fight this that was one thing, but there wasn't. So after several deeply down days I let it go. Something I learned at the bridge table seemed to help me in this. I knew a lot of people who complained about their luck. For a while, I'd been one of them. But whatever cards are dealt to you are the cards you have. The best players, the people who really excelled at bridge, took the cards they were dealt and made the most of them. That seemed to me an important life lesson. Whatever cards I'm dealt are my cards—and "unfair" or not, no amount of complaining will change that. The only constructive question is, "What can I do with the hand I have?" I made a conscious effort to make this a part of who I am. It complemented my lesson from Rommel.

Singing aside, I also had to learn to eat differently. Anything super chewy was now off limits. No caramels, no gum, no taffy. Ever! If I wanted to eat an apple, I needed to cut it up first. But these were all simple adjustments. With singing off the table, it was time to throw myself into grad school and the study of myth.

I usually tell people that I have an M.A. in mythology, but that's not strictly true. While I spent my time studying myth I have an M.A. in folklore and mythology. My particular joy was experiencing what is called "comparative mythology." Joseph Campbell is famous for his thoughts on how so many differing myths are related, but I was particularly intrigued by the work of the French mythologist Georges Dumézil. His palette was Indo-European myth, with the idea that the myths of India and Ireland, as two far-flung examples, came from the very same source.

What was both fascinating and enlightening was to see how a people could start with the same sacred stories, myths, but then over time and with very different cultural experiences end up with what appeared to be very different stories! As but one example, the Germans made their god of war the head of their pantheon, while the Greeks made their god of war a laughing stock. I was pleased that one of my first papers in grad school on the subject was respected enough to be included in a book on Indo-European myth that would be published a few years hence.[21]

What I had no way of knowing at the time was that that paper was also going to save my bacon. While most of my professors at UCLA were very helpful, there was also Dr. Robert Georges. We were oil and water. My "help me or get out of my way" approach to education seemed to unhinge him. I only had to take one class from Bob Georges, the graduate bibliography class required of all folklore and mythology students, but that was enough.

We didn't meld well from the first day of class. But everything came off the wheels when Georges gave us an assignment that seemed a total waste of time. There was a large set of books that he thought important. Ok. He wanted us to become familiar with them and know how to use them for research. No sweat. The assignment was to look up a large number of subjects (ten, fifteen, twenty, I really don't remember) and then prove that we'd found them by saying what volume and page number they were on. What?

This was the equivalent of asking students to go to the encyclopedia, look up 15 subjects and then, to prove that they'd really looked them up, report on what volume and page they'd found them on—in *graduate school!*

I spoke to Georges privately about this being at best a high-school assignment. He didn't take it well. As it turned out, while not the chair, Georges was "the power" in the department. In the end, I got a C in his class, as I recall my only grade not an A. In grad school, a C isn't passing. That meant trouble. Professor Jaan Puhvel had shepherded me through the process and I had just received a full fellowship for my continued study.

---

21   *Myth in Indo-European Antiquity* edited by Gerald Larson, 1974. My paper compared the relationship between a mythic figure in India and what I believe is its direct cousin in Iran.

This was extremely handy as the Greenebaum Independence Fund was dwindling dangerously low. I learned from the department secretary that Georges had tried to get me dropped from the program. Puhvel, the department's mythology specialist, argued that it wouldn't look very good if I was dropped and then a year or so later one of my papers was published in an important book—and the book was going to be published. Georges settled for having my fellowship revoked. Realistically, without that paper my career in mythology would have been over.

Ok. I had no fellowship, which meant I had no way to continue at UCLA even if they hadn't officially kicked me out. What to do? For every door that closes, a door can be kicked open. What was the door I needed to kick open?

Without the fellowship, I would very soon be running on empty. So I immediately gave up my apartment. For about ten days I was able to sleep in the tenth-floor mythology library before being evicted. But by then I had things figured out.

I applied for and received a leave of absence from the folklore and mythology department. I would need to go to work for at least a year to make and save enough money to finish my degree without a fellowship. And as long as I was going to have to go to work full time, why stay in Los Angeles? I decided to move to Washington for a year. But the problem was, with little money left, I'd need a place to sleep until I had a job. That dictated that I move to Yakima, in central Washington. I had two friends from college, Candy and Tom, who had married and were moving there. They said I could stay on their floor until I found a job. Cool.

The only problem was that they were *moving* to Yakima. They weren't there yet. So for several weeks I was homeless. I slept in my car about half the time. I was also able to bum a few nights off of a variety of friends (no more than two nights at any one friend's apartment as I wanted to *keep* them as friends!), which made up the other half. Meanwhile, there was that small necessity called eating. Cathy Gedowski was one of the main librarians at the graduate library. She adopted me, bless her, and took to making large, very nourishing sandwiches for me. That was lunch. Breakfast was at a place called Norms, which specialized in their "49er" breakfast. It's been a while, but as I recall it was an egg, two strips of bacon and toast, all for 49 cents! Dinner, to be honest, became optional. Sometimes I ate and sometimes I didn't (usually if I was able to bum a night from friends, they fed me, and if I was in my car, I fasted).

It was no great adventure being homeless. But I recognized even at the time that there was a difference between being homeless for several weeks and being homeless for months or years. And also, while I learned that sleeping in my car was not all that difficult, it certainly wasn't much fun. Still, I had been spared living only in my car. I was able to unroll my sleeping bag from time to time on the comfortable floor of a friend's apartment. But it reinforced for me that I could adapt to almost anything.

The experience also reinforced for me the difference between accepting the consequences of my decisions, whether those decisions resulted in my not eating well or being homeless, and systemic issues of poverty that had nothing to do with personal decisions and everything to do with a society that granted some privilege from birth and stripped others of even their most basic rights of health, shelter and education because of gender, color, religion or other cultural prejudice. Then Tom and Candy moved to Yakima and I moved up right behind them. I had been careful to save enough so that I could pay for my gas and even have a few bucks left over for an emergency.

I spent a brief but important year in Yakima. Except for a summer in East Palo Alto I'd never lived outside of the Los Angeles area, let alone out of state. Yakima was almost dead center of the state of Washington, and far from anything like the big-city atmosphere I was used to. I had three very specific goals in mind. The first was to replenish my virtually annihilated Greenebaum Independence Fund. The second was, for the first time in my life, to hold down a regular job for more than just a summer. The last goal was to start my first novel.

I'd begun to ponder just what I was going to do with my life once I had a Masters in Mythology. Certainly teaching was a possibility. But writing had begun to call to me. This call had taken on a bit of gentle urgency when I stumbled upon some compelling Roman history and realized that for whatever reason, no one had as yet written about it—at least not in English. But while I landed in Yakima full of ideas and desires, one thing quickly took precedence. A job!

I was staying with my friends Tom and Candy, and fruitlessly searching the want ads. Nothing. Nothing. Nothing! But, "For every door that closes, there's a door that can be kicked open." Ok. Where?

There's a community college in Yakima: Yakima Valley College, or YVC. I didn't have my M.A. yet. But how many people know anything about mythology? Might I possibly get a job there as an instructor? I quickly discovered that without an M.A. there was no place for me at YVC as a regular instructor. But there was something called the Evening College. These classes were not as rigorous, and I was told that if I could submit a résumé and present a good lesson plan I would be allowed to teach. This wasn't what I had hoped for, and certainly wasn't going to pay as well as a regular teaching job. But this was the door that I'd kicked open, so I walked through it.

I'd never written a curriculum plan for a course. Now I did. When I presented it, two amazing things happened. First, my class was accepted. I had a job! Second, I was stopped on the way out by the dean of students. My résumé had stated that I had gone to Occidental.

"I was at Oxy," the dean of students said. "Whatever brought you to Yakima?" I decided on a very short-form answer. I said I was there to write a novel.

"You write? We need a public information officer. The job's been open for months! It's full-time, during the day, so you could still teach at night."

Another interview later, and suddenly I was very much employed. Public information during the day (and no, I had no idea whatsoever what the job entailed except that it meant I would be writing), and teaching at night. And as it turned out that I only taught mythology once, the rest of the year I had my nights available to write my Roman novel.

I got the cheapest apartment I could find, which turned out to be on top of a termite exterminator's shop. There was a giant sign that read "Pest Control" right outside my door (and an intriguing smell from the walls every time a new batch of pest killer was brewed below). Having found housing, I set about learning what I was supposed to do as the public information officer at YVC.

In short, I handled all publicity for the college. Besides answering any media questions and writing news releases about college events (both of which I learned to do on the fly), it meant I was responsible for all the college brochures and the college catalog. Yikes, there was a lot to learn! The first several months I was among the first people to arrive at the college and the last to leave. I worked ten and sometimes twelve-hour days. But I figured out what I was supposed to do and managed it. In the end I rewrote all the brochures for the various departments (they were very much out of date) and rewrote the descriptive side of the college catalog. I also arranged for a public service spot once a week on local public television (either one or two minutes long), and ended up producing, writing and "starring" in it. Happily, everyone seemed very pleased with my work.

I also wrote about 400 pages of my Roman novel. It was only a start, a torso if you will, but I liked it. I was confident that this was the story I was meant to tell. I just couldn't be impatient.

While I didn't really make any lasting new friends at YVC, my friendship with Tom and Candy flourished. I particularly remember a Passover dinner we shared. It was a wonderful evening and a wonderful dinner. I splurged and spared no expense.

I say splurged because I lived mostly on potatoes, though, as with Passover I would buy some good food to share when I invited my friends over for dinner. It worked. Within one year I had very much refilled my bank account.

To be honest, I also got a bit testy. When I was working 10-12-hour days, making sure I was doing my job, no one complained. February or March of the following year, things were running smoothly. There were times when there was nothing to do, and I wanted to leave a little early. "WHAT?!?" This was when I learned a little about at least some people's way of doing business. I owed them eight hours a day for my salary. If I chose to give more than that without getting overtime, that was my business, but I still owed them eight full hours. I was forbidden to leave even half an hour early.

I decided to leave YVC once I had a full bank account again. So, the following summer I moved back to Los Angeles, immediately ended my leave of absence, and again took up my M.A. in Mythology.

Finishing the M.A. turned out to be pretty straightforward. Happily, there were no more classes that I needed to take from Robert Georges.

I also wrote a paper based on an experiment I tried with one of my sister's classes.

My sister was teaching. I think it was a high-school class. I was looking for some way to get a better grasp of how myths develop and how they grow. So, I took a chance and, with my sister's permission, ran her class through an experiment. All the kids were just old enough to be alive when JFK was assassinated. I stood in front of them and began the experiment.

Who was John F. Kennedy? Most of them knew he had been president.

What happened to end his presidency? Most of them knew he had been assassinated.

Who assassinated President Kennedy? About 2/3 knew it was Lee Harvey Oswald. The other third thought it was Sirhan Sirhan, the man who assassinated President Kennedy's brother, Bobby. These students had merged the two assassinations. Fascinating!

What happened to Lee Harvey Oswald? Again, about 2/3 knew he had been killed by Jack Ruby. The other third didn't know.

Last, what happened to Jack Ruby? Here's where it really got interesting. Almost all thought he had been tried and convicted for murdering Oswald. Some thought he had been executed while others thought he was in jail for life.

The thing to remember is that they lived in the age of television. No Internet, but TV was everywhere, as it still is. Yet, a significant number of the students thought that Sirhan Sirhan had murdered John Kennedy. If this sounds reasonable (and it is), then remember that many of us kick and scream over discrepancies we sometimes find in differing passages in Scripture. Most of our Scripture existed for years if not centuries only in oral form before at last being written down, and these kids had mixed up two events that they had actually seen on television.

Then, there was what happened to Jack Ruby. In point of fact, he died awaiting trial. He was never tried, let alone convicted. But as the response from the students showed, we don't like unfinished stories. I always had a hunch that it depended on whether the student believed in capital punishment or not, but whatever, most of them had finished in their own imaginations their story of justice. Jack Ruby received justice. Either he was in prison or he'd been executed.

For me, this was both exciting and instructive. This is how we as human beings create stories—even in the age of television. Imagine how stories must have grown about Moses, or Jesus, or the Buddha, or Muhammad. This was and I believe is the essence of mythmaking; it's how our minds process information, particularly important information, crucial information like the assassination of a president.

Beyond this fascinating revelation, another way our minds process information was becoming apparent to me. I had two Christian friends who liked having me come to speak with their Sunday school classes and introduce them to Judaism. One class was particularly memorable. The kids listened politely. It was their questions that fascinated me.

"Are you from Israel?" one child asked.

"No," I said. "I'm from Los Angeles."

"Oh. When did you move there?"

"I was born there." I replied.

For these kids, the United States was a Christian nation. It was surprising to them that a Jew would actually have been born in the U.S. But it was the next question that truly floored me.

"Do Jews have human sacrifice?" No, I explained, and I talked about Abraham being guided toward sacrificing a ram rather than his son. This taught me not only the power of ignorance but also that ignorance is *not* hate. These kids were incredibly ignorant about Judaism, but they weren't bigots. Ignorance can develop into hate, but it doesn't have to. Maybe it was my practice explaining Judaism at Oxy, but I learned not to be defensive, not to get angry and not to assume bigotry. Not that I haven't met bigots along the way. I have. Still, I have learned not to assume bigotry until proven otherwise.

I want to be honest about what happened next. Though it's difficult and exceedingly humbling, I need to admit that from here until about the mid-1980s, much of what happened, and particularly what happened when, is exceedingly jumbled. I really can't put dates on things. It's one of the most important parts of my life, yet I have to fight through a massive haze to retrieve any of it. I apologize. I'll extract the bits and pieces that I can. It comes from an admittedly bruised memory, but I will be as accurate and honest as is possible.

Part Two: Into the World

Chapter Thirteen

I met the woman I will call Maria at the local Norms diner. I ate there now about three, maybe four times a week. They used to advertise that it was cheaper than eating at home, and if not strictly true it was close enough. Being as thrifty as possible, I sat at the counter. I'd been told that a person should tip 15 percent if you took up a table, but it was perfectly acceptable to tip 10 percent at the counter. So that's where I ate.

I was eating my breakfast when an attractive woman sat down next to me. I gave her a quick glance but was very careful not to stare. I didn't want to be rude. But then....

"Excuse me," she said. "Would you pass the salt?"

I picked up the salt shaker that was in front of me and turned to give it to her. That's when I noticed there was a salt shaker right in front of her. She saw me looking.

"Yours is better," she told me.

My grin was a mile wide. The ice wasn't just broken, it was pulverized. We chatted for a while, then made a date for breakfast the next day. From there our discussions progressed and we began to spend more and more time together. At one point, totally baffled, I asked her, why me? She told me about watching me one morning when I'd paid my bill. I was given too much change back, and returned the extra money. It seemed like no big deal to me but it seemed to have impressed Maria. I was never so glad for being honest!

We became friends. And then good friends. She was Chicana. Who cared? I also learned she was Catholic. That was fascinating. We started talking about religion. I shared not only that I was Jewish but also some of the things I felt I was finding out about religion and myth. She shared her Catholicism, but in a way that totally disarmed me. She never once tried to convert me or tell me that I was wrong. And we both learned that Catholicism and Judaism share one binding similarity: both are heavily rooted in guilt-tripping!

Neither one of us had much money, but neither of us was bothered by it. For both of us, life was about living, not spending. Success was in giving, not receiving. If ever two people were meant for each other.... I began fixing her dinner and she began fixing me dinner. We rarely went out—except to Norms.

I recall one day when we were walking, and she turned to me. "So, are you ever going to kiss me?"

Ok, then! Remember that she was a practicing Catholic and I an extremely inexperienced Jew. We necked some and enjoyed it a lot. It never went further than that. Still, we were becoming close. Very close. We had created our own private world. One of her friends knew of me. That was it. None of my friends knew of her. Most particularly, our parents didn't know about us and for that there was a reason.

While I don't think my parents would have been particularly pleased at my becoming serious about a Catholic girl, I doubt they would have objected too strenuously. I knew how my father felt about and treated Chicanos, though. For Maria's part, she didn't think her parents would be all that pleased at my not being Chicano, but her father definitely would not have approved of a Jewish boyfriend. It was by no means Romeo and Juliet, but we did want to be careful.

After about a year, I asked her if she might consider marrying me. She replied with a laugh that she'd been considering it for well over a month. But this was one place she had wanted me to come to unprompted, no matter how long it took!

So, it was time to think. Could we do it? Now that we were serious, she wanted us to talk to her priest. I don't recall his name. Let's call him Father Jaime. He and I had some good talks, and he too blew me away. We shared our common belief that the need for justice in the world knew no religious, ethnic or racial bounds. He shared that he regretted so very much the unfortunate bad blood between our religions. This was not what I had expected. Moreover, over time I came to suspect that Father Jaime would really have preferred fighting injustice with Che Guevara over being a priest. He was a man of action, and somewhat restless.

At this point, we had an important question for him; or rather, Maria had an important question, and I, too, needed to know the answer. If Maria and I got married, did we have to raise our kids Catholic? Father Jaime looked at her sternly. "Yes, you *must* raise your children Catholic." Then, bless him, he turned to me with a huge smile, "Of course, they don't have to be *only* Catholic." Oh, my! I was just bowled over.

With Father Jaime's blessing we began to plan our future. I had taken a class in screenwriting at UCLA,. I was about to get my M.A. in Mythology. Maria, for her part, was finishing her senior year. She had marched with Cesar Chavez. There was a journalist who had been killed, I think fairly recently, trying, as I recall, to expose the prejudice and discrimination that the Mexican-American population (Maria and others preferred the word Chicano) faced. Maria was trying to decide if her work in graduate school should aim her toward a career in law or journalism. She was still flip-flopping pretty regularly, but it would definitely be one or the other.

So, how would we live our lives? How would we raise our children? We came up with a plan. We would get married. Our parents would have their problems but we both believed that, grumble as they might, eventually they would all come around. Meanwhile, I would pursue screenwriting, as there was good money to be made there. While I made money, Maria would have and nurse two or three children (two if one was a boy and one a girl, and three if the first two were the same gender). Even though Maria was Catholic, we agreed we'd stop at three.

I would make as much money as possible while Maria nursed the kids. But as soon as the youngest was old enough to go to preschool, raising the kids would become my job. As a writer, I could stay at home. Maria would by then have decided whether she would pursue law or journalism and with the money we'd saved she'd go back to school. At some point she'd have her career, the kids would be going to school virtually full time and I could leave screenwriting and at last get back to my beloved novel about Rome.

As for the kids, they would be raised knowing that Dad was Jewish and Mom was Catholic. Jews and Catholics looked at God differently, but Mom respected Dad and Dad respected Mom—and the kids would be expected to learn about both religions. Then, when they were sixteen or so, if they decided on Mom's path, Dad would be perfectly happy. And if they decided on Dad's path, Mom would be perfectly happy. And if they decided on a completely different path, both Mom and Dad would be happy (well, ok, not quite so happy). We would strive to teach them that love and justice were the basis of both of our religions, and as long as our children embraced love and justice, how they embraced it was up to them.

That was the plan, and it felt like a good one. We decided that we were finally about ready to tell our parents and set a date. Then one day Maria didn't show up at my apartment. I didn't think much of it. Something must have come up. Then, she was hours late, and I started becoming annoyed. Good grief, couldn't she find a telephone and call? The next day, exasperated, I called our one mutual friend.

No, she couldn't call me, I was told. She'd been killed in a traffic accident.

Killed. She was gone. No warning. Just—gone. One day she was there and the next—gone. What now? Dear God, what now? There was this overwhelming feeling of emptiness.

I couldn't go to her funeral Mass. Her parents didn't know me, and I didn't want to add to their grief at such a horrible time. The one friend she'd shared with me informed me she really didn't want to be friends anymore. I needed to respect that. But—such emptiness, such overwhelming emptiness. I've called her Maria because to this day I have no idea if her family ever knew about me, and I very much want to respect their privacy. That much I can do.

It was strange. At first, more than anything else I felt baffled. Confused. Then I wept endlessly and felt hugely sorry for myself. I'd lost everything. Everything of value—gone in an instant. What do I do now? What's the point of anything? Then I got incredibly furious with myself. She's dead, and I'm feeling sorry for me? What kind of a selfish, self-centered asshole thinks of himself at a time like this? What do I do now? I have any number of things I can do now. What can Maria do now? Nothing! She's gone. Forever.

We had argued about—well, discussed with intensity—the question of heaven more than once. I had always held the prejudiced opinion that humanity had created heaven so that we wouldn't have to face our own death. Now I found myself hoping, praying, that heaven did indeed exist. Not for me, but for her. Please, please let there be a heaven!

I don't remember how long I remained in this state of suspended life until, at some point I realized that I was completely drained. What now? I couldn't just sit there, wondering what the hell had happened. I wasn't prepared to take my own life, and if I were going to live, I had to do something. What?! I decided I would turn the page. That's it. I had to turn the page. I would move on. I would put this behind me and move on. I didn't speak

Maria's name out loud again for 20 years. I became emotionally numb. But I still had to pick up the pieces and do something. Something.

Before I'd met Maria, I had started writing a musical with the only friend I'd kept from my high school days. Ron and I had an idea for a story based on Murphy's Law. We had conceived of the story and had embarked on writing the book together, while I would write the music and lyrics. One of the truly lovely aspects of this was that I had shown a draft of the work to my friends Don and Vicki Nagel. That's the same Mrs. Nagel, my teacher and, at one time, crush from my junior high days. Now, she was Vicki, and she and her husband had become good friends. *Murphy's Law* brought out the twinkle, particularly in Don.

Unfortunately, Ron lived in Oakland, while I lived in West Los Angeles, and then Santa Monica. So, our work progressed slowly. Then, I got involved with Maria and work slowed down even more, almost grinding to a halt. Then, with Maria's death, I lost interest. A lighthearted look at how things go wrong in life just didn't seem engaging. In the end it remained unfinished, and Ron and I never did anything with it. But for a while I pushed myself. It was something to do.

I did come up with one more song that I called "A Credo for Living." It was supposed to be the main character's response to the trials of life. It was much too serious for the musical we were working on, but perhaps I wrote it hoping in my own mind that I could live up to it someday. It was only a hope, because at that moment I couldn't possibly live up to the optimism of the song.

When my life confounds me, and there's nowhere to run,
Total gloom surrounds me, and the end has begun.
My world's completely collapsed.
The future seems totaled and lapsed.
Flat on my rear,
I shed a tear,
Then down a beer
And FIGHT!

I can't run from losing, or I'd run all the time.
If the staff I'm using breaks, I still have to climb.
I've never been able to hide.
No patience to wait out the tide.
You choose a game, that's worth a throw.

Then win or lose, you'll always know
You've really won
At life.

(Chorus)
Damn the ship
Full ahead on the torpedoes.
We'll get 'em.
Giant bear,
Pull their hair
Because mosquitoes
Always win.
Sound the bell!
Leave your shell upon the seashore.
Give 'em hell,
That's what they're there for.
Half the fun is in the fight.
And it's your right.

This reflected in large part the me of my youth. It would be years before I could truly make that song who I was again. But I think having it out there helped. It gave me something to shoot for, and, with all due lack of modesty, it did turn out to be a pretty good song.

Chapter Fourteen

I don't clearly remember what happened after I got my M.A.. I've tried to arrange the bits and pieces that I do remember into some kind of logical order. But that said, all timing is approximate. I do know that inertia set in. So, I set about becoming a screenwriter. I didn't really want it, but looking back I think this may have been my way of holding on to the past just a bit.

Starting with a script that I ended up never selling, I got involved in researching the paranormal. At some point I actually taught a class or two in it. It was interesting work, but when I found out that the person I had been working with had lied to me and others about his education and credentials, everything he had said was called into question. I moved on.

I do know that I attempted to find solace doing the one thing she[22] and I had never done. I slept with I don't know how many different women. In retrospect, given that the AIDS epidemic was just beginning, I was incredibly fortunate. I fathered no children and caught no venereal disease. But at last it occurred even to my fried mind that this just wasn't working.

At some point, I taught mythology. I think I was at Occidental College, at least for a while. I also got involved with Common Cause at some point. Somehow I actually ended up running the publicity for Common Cause in my area, and built up a pretty good committee. I recall getting permission from Will Rogers Jr. to use some of his father's quotes in the cause of good government, but nothing came of it. I lost interest and left, and noticed that as soon as I did everything that I'd built up fell apart. It had all been my energy and I hadn't brought anyone along with me, so when I left, it died. Thoughtless. Unprofessional. And at this point in my life, typical.

---

22   I didn't say Maria's name aloud or even allow it in my mind again for over 20 years.

My spiritual education wasn't completely stunted. At some point, I rented a townhouse and had a very nice neighbor I'll call Jeff. We were never good friends, but we were quite friendly and did chat from time to time. I remember one day in particular when Jeff was very excited. He had a very special night planned with his girlfriend. I really don't recall if it was just a special night, or if he had planned to "pop the question." Whatever, he was abuzz with excitement. Then, the next morning, I saw him and he was really down in the dumps. He'd taken his girl to a very special place for dinner, but a bigoted, anti-Semitic waitress had ruined everything. The special night had turned to dust. The waitress ignored them. Then she was sullen when at last she did wait on them. Then, when told she'd gotten the order wrong, she angrily snatched the wrong dish from the table. Her insulting behavior continued all evening.

The puzzlement I had was Jeff's characterization of the waitress as anti-Semitic. Jeff didn't look particularly Jewish. I'd seen his girlfriend once or twice. Neither of them wore jewelry that identified them as Jewish. So, how did Jeff know the waitress hated Jews? "Why else" would she act that way? Jeff grumbled. Well, there were a multitude of possible reasons. Maybe she was just having a bad day. Maybe something horrible had happened to her just before coming to work. Maybe she'd had a fight with her boyfriend or husband. There were an endless number of maybes, but the odds that she hated Jews and somehow instinctively knew that Jeff and his girlfriend were Jewish seemed pretty far down the list.

It's one thing to be able to face this as a Jew. There is a certain "look" that many people associate with being Jewish. Still, if you don't have that "look," and you don't wear jewelry that identifies you as Jewish, and if you don't tell a person that you're Jewish, then there's no way for a stranger to know. A person of color never has that luxury of doubt. If you're a person of color, there is no way ever to know, unless a person actually calls you racially charged names, if the person acting like a jerk toward you is simply having a bad day or is in fact racist. I vividly remember thinking that that has to be hard. It's lifelong. You never know.

I think I sold one script that year, maybe two. If I did, it wasn't under my name. During my rather brief career as a screenwriter I wrote two distinct types of scripts: scripts I liked, and scripts I threw together to pay the rent and put food on the table. The scripts I liked, I put my own name on. For scripts I ground out for food I used a pseudonym. Not once did I sell a script with my own name on it.

I remember during this time being puzzled that for some reason, no matter what happened during the day, so many nights I would simply sit in the dark and cry—for no reason! Stupid, I thought. Weak. I also noticed that I was one hugely angry person. A traffic light doesn't go my way and I started yelling at it. Any little thing goes wrong and I was furious. What the ...? I couldn't understand the why of that either. But at last it dawned on me that the life I was leading was not tenable. I was a young man, with perhaps another fifty or sixty years ahead of me. Another fifty or sixty years of this?? I realized I was in some kind of emotional quicksand, and already up to my neck.

I needed to claw my way out. Ok, how?? I realized that for me, at this moment, the only possible way out was through music. I went to the local community college and started studying the basics, the classes I had simply skipped in college. In so doing I made friends with one of the teachers there, Dr. James Smith. Jim and his wife Barbara became friends, and have remained friends to this day. I started singing in Jim's church choir, and music, choral music, became my lifeline. Married friends from Oxy, Dick and Mary, sang in Jim's choir. Singing just might be my salvation—my way to reconnect both with life and the sacred.

I don't know if I would have been able to make my next big decision on my own, but as it turned out, the decision was made for me. Dr. Swan, the choir director from Oxy, had been forcibly retired by Oxy's rather foolish "when you're 65 you're history" policy. He had gone to Cal State Fullerton to continue teaching, remaining there for several years because, well, he wasn't done sharing his knowledge yet. But then he announced that the following year would be his last. That pushed me out of my lethargy. If I were ever going to study with the incomparable Howard Swan, it was now or never.

There was one small impediment. I had no music degree! If I wanted to be accepted into the graduate program at Fullerton, located south of Los Angeles, I would have to take and pass the GRE (Graduate Record Exam) for music. So I took it, and I passed. My classes at community college had indeed done the trick. Impediment gone, I scooped up everything I owned and moved to Fullerton. Time to dip back into the replenished Independence Fund.

In large part, this move to Fullerton was to fulfill my dream of truly getting involved in choral music. Singing in Jim's choir was fun, but I knew I didn't have the voice to make it as a soloist, nor with my "hyper-mobile" jaw could I ever do the work needed to sing well enough. Even as a "mere" singer in the choir, long rehearsals were quite painful. If I wanted to be involved in choral music, there was one way and only one way and that was as a conductor. But more than that, another part of me knew or at least believed that this was my second chance at a life. I might not have another. If anything could pull me back into the land of the living, it was choral music. I wanted to go for it. I needed to go for it.

> Pull yourself up.
> You're of little use to anyone
> And no use to yourself
> With your chin draped upon the floor
> Complacent in self-pity.
>
> Pull yourself up.
> One, two, three.
> You've a lifetime to live
> And but one chance to live it.
> How much time will you spend
> Sprawled upon your rear—bewailing your despair?
>
> Pull yourself up.
> One, two, three.
> Crawling is an action
> Unbecoming to a human.
> It is no crime to weep,
> But one should weep while walking.
>
> Pull yourself up!
> One, three, five.
> The world will spin without you
> If you let it.
> Time never drags,
> Only man.

Chapter Fifteen

A second chance. Surely it was worth a shot. So I uprooted myself once again, this time heading to Orange County and a huge apartment complex a short drive from Cal State Fullerton. It would be a new experience: all music all the time.

As it turned out, I had to get past basic choral conducting before I could study with Dr. Swan. That meant classes from David Thorsen, and we didn't hit it off. I began to realize that one could divide powerful people into two very different groups: those who demand respect and those who command it. People who demand your respect need titles, ritual and that you bow to their power. But people who by their knowledge and abilities command respect are confident of their abilities, comfortable in their own skin and need no bowing. I seem to have done well with the latter group, but very poorly with the former. David Thorsen was a little man who demanded respect—and got none from me. It almost ended my choral career. Thorsen demanded that I not be allowed to take any more conducting classes, and as I recall he was the department chair.

Dr. Swan took me aside. We talked for a great deal of time and he figured out a way for me to continue my studies. I took other important classes in music history and theory, but from Dr. Howard Swan I audited classes. As an auditor, I needed no permission from the department chair. I learned a huge amount from Howard (he carefully ensured that I fully participated like any other student) and much more than simply how to wave my arms in front of a choir.

For me, one of the great learnings was that we never really liked each other. I would never have chosen Howard Swan as a dinner companion, nor, I'm sure, would he have chosen me. What we did have was a mutual respect. More than that, Howard strongly believed in his role as a teacher. He felt his job was to treat his students fairly and to give them everything he had. What truly impressed me was not only that he gave me everything he could, but that he actually went out of his way to help me. When, after he retired, I applied to Occidental to finish my degree and my studies, Howard Swan wrote me a strong letter of recommendation that I feel sure was instrumental in my being accepted. Again, he really didn't like me. Yet that didn't matter to him. What mattered to Howard was that I wanted to learn, and as a teacher this was what both called to him and motivated him. What a magnificent life lesson!

We did have at least one thing in common. Both of us were huge fans of the German composer Heinrich Schütz.[23] Both his music and his life called to me. I wrote two papers on Schütz: one as an undergraduate at Oxy and one at Fullerton. Both Schütz's music and his life touched my soul, and I've never heard as good a performance of my favorite Schütz choral work, his "German Magnificat," as was sung by the Oxy glee clubs, directed by Howard Swan, in 1970.[24]

I will always be grateful to Howard Swan, both as a teacher and a mentor. It wasn't so much that he believed in me. He believed in my right to be me. And more than that, he went out of his way to help me along the road. Howard had his faults. No doubt about that. Who doesn't!? But what a wonderful human being.

There were other spiritual doings while I was in Fullerton. For one thing, I recall yet another in a succession of wonderful Passover celebrations. My friends Jim and Barbara Smith drove down to join me, as did my sister. My father (and therefore also my mother) passed on coming. Some years before I had staked out my ground. I thought Passover to be hugely important, not simply as a celebration filled with piles of wonderful food, but as a deeply spiritual time to remember and reflect, both that freedom isn't cheap and also that everyone deserves to be free—no exceptions. For me, Passover was never a story of the "poor Jews" being enslaved by the "evil Egyptians" and the God of the Jews entering into the affairs of human-

---

23 Schütz lived from 1585–1672, dying thirteen years before Bach was born. He was THE great German choral composer—until Bach. And I still prefer Schütz. He studied with two of my favorite Late Renaissance composers: Monteverdi and Gabrieli.

24 It was recorded as part of the 1970 Home Concert, though I don't know if Oxy has ever made the recording available on a CD. Perhaps it will. The work of Heinrich Schütz deserves a renaissance.

ity to set His people free. Passover was the story of an oppressed people and how oppression must be resisted. Always. It was about slavery and how slavery is wrong. Always. It was about the need of all people to be free. No exceptions. THAT was something definitely worth celebrating.

For my father though, Passover was just a good excuse for a big party and some special foods. So, as soon as I could, I started holding my own Passover Seders (services). I invited Mom and Dad to come, but they declined. Mom started coming once she and Dad got divorced, but that would still be a few years down the road.

Another interesting learning came from my friendship with another Tom and his wife Pam. They were a lovely couple, very young, just out of college and just moved to California from the Midwest. They seemed rather lost in the big world of Cal State Fullerton and I gladly took them under my wing. Recall that this was my second M.A.. I was a good deal older than most of my classmates.

Tom and Pam were both truly sweet and caring, but Tom particularly was worried about my soul. He felt that as I hadn't acknowledged Jesus as my savior I was headed for an eternity in hell and he truly didn't want that for me. Through Tom and Pam I was introduced to a group I'd only heard about previously, "Jews for Jesus." And I was asked a question I'd never heard before: "Are you a completed Jew?" I thought of the perfect answer to that[25] but only several hours later. Tom also spent some time trying to convert me to the one right way of approaching God. It wasn't fun, but what made it tolerable and a teaching experience rather than an annoyance was the fact that Tom and Pam were sincere. They were two very caring human beings. I liked them both—a lot.

Then Howard Swan retired for good, and I certainly couldn't continue at Fullerton with David Thorsen. So, I applied to Oxy, this time for the M.A. program in music. I was admitted, but needed a full scholarship—so I put my studies off a year. Happily, a year later Oxy gave me a full scholarship. In the meantime, I had a year to fill.

I moved back to Santa Monica. I got a paper route to pay the bills, wrote a script to pad the Independence Fund and began singing in Jim Smith's choir again. For one of our concerts Jim decided to give me my first chance at conducting. I don't remember the piece, but toward the end, about a third of the choir marched out of the sanctuary, singing as we went. We then marched through the narthex and climbed the stairs to the balcony. During this time, we weren't singing and I couldn't hear the music

---

25 A casual glance to where my circumcision had taken place as a baby, followed by "Yep."

very well. Once we were in the balcony, we became Choir II. At the proper moment, we were supposed to sing a "reply" to what the choir downstairs was singing. My job, as a choir director in training, was to bring the balcony choir in at that proper moment.

I got lost. I tried to guess where we were in the music and thought I had. I gave everyone their cue to get a good breath and then brought about half the choir in. I say half the choir because some followed me, but about half the choir, perhaps more, just stared at me in utter disbelief. My timing was wrong. I was bringing everyone in too early. Once I realized that, we sputtered to a stop and then, thanks to someone in the choir who actually *knew* the correct moment, I brought the entire choir in, this time correctly. I don't know if I've ever blushed quite so deeply as I did then. Me, a choir director? Ok then, LOTS more to learn. Lots! Oy, gevalt!

Speaking of learning, there was another hard lesson that I learned about this time. You may recall my "uncle" Ike Goldman, whom along with his wife Esther I loved to visit as a kid. Well, I'd gotten distracted and busy. In the years that had passed Esther had died. Ike now lived in a retirement home. Dad took me to see him.

Ike had no idea who I was. I can still hear the horrifying words he spoke to me with shattering clarity. "Hello, sir. It's very good of you to visit me." Ike had no memory of me. I was a complete stranger, a stranger he treated with the utmost politeness, but a complete stranger nonetheless. I later learned the word *dementia*. But I also realized that my father saw him often enough that Ike still knew who *he* was. So this was my doing. I'd let my personal troubles allow Ike to slip away from me. I think I visited him at least once more to be sure. But he never remembered me. I had vanished from his life.

It was also somewhere along this general time period that Mom and Dad got divorced. The undoing of their marriage began as an act of love by my father. Mom was clearly ill, and the local doctors couldn't discover what was wrong. So Dad arranged for Mom to be admitted to the Mayo Clinic, and he flew back to be with her. At the clinic Mom underwent a huge battery of tests. I think she was there a week or so. But the result was the opinion that there was nothing "organically" wrong. In plain English, that meant the problem was psychological.

So, with Dad's full support, Mom entered therapy. That's when she began to understand why she was so unhappy and thus had been so ill for so long. Mom had a good brain and wanted to use it. There was a huge world out there and everything in her wanted to explore it. But instead she had stayed home and looked after the house and kids. Worse, she'd very much believed that it was wrong of her to want more. It was this inner conflict of wanting more but believing it was wrong that had torn her apart. But with therapy she began to change. When Mom at last began to believe in her own value as a thinking human being, real change happened within her. At first, this meant that she started to feel better and Dad rejoiced as we all did. But then the marriage began to have trouble. Dad wanted Mom to be well and happy, but he also wanted her to be the docile, deferring, "Yes, honey" woman he'd married. Mom was no longer that woman.

When Dad realized that Mom had become her own person, his response was to have an affair. Mom and Dad reconciled, at least for a year or two, but then divorced. In the meantime Mom had gone back to school and achieved her dream of a BA in psychology. She had finished college!

It was after the divorce that Mom and I at last became friends—not just mother and son, but friends. We talked all the time. And I learned so much—about her and about what we can do to ourselves and each other if we're not careful.

Mom had been born a generation too early. That was the tragedy of it. She was born just one generation too early. The person I'd always hoped she would be was in fact the person she had always wanted to be, but she'd felt it was wrong. She had believed that it was wrong for her to want her own life. She believed that it was a flaw in her that made her want to rebel against the patriarchal household that my father so cherished. Mom told me of the day, early in their marriage, when she didn't have dinner on the table at 6:00. Dad was furious. That's what Mom's job was: have the dinner ready and on the table *on time!* And rather than fight back, her reply had been, "Yes, darling. You're right. I'm so sorry. It won't happen again." And it didn't.

It became clear to me that Mom's being ill and depressed throughout my childhood and youth had been the result of this relentless inner struggle. But now, at last, Mom was free to be herself. Now, at last, she could live the life she had always dreamed of. And now, she got cancer. But Mom was not about to give up. She determinedly beat the cancer back not once, but twice. Twice she was declared "cancer free." In the meantime, I began my career in music.

Steven Greenebaum

Chapter Sixteen

Mom wasn't the only one starting a new life. My return to Oxy very much seemed like a second chance. I was pursuing my second M.A., this time one in music. I had a full scholarship. This meant I was able not only to attend classes but eat as well! Another joy was that I got to see my friend Scott Littleton as well as other Oxy professors I enjoyed. But while I had a scholarship, I also put myself on a strict budget. I drew up and adhered to strict budgets for well into the next decade.

In a very real sense, budgeting is as much a spiritual matter as it is an economic one. A budget reinforces and lays bare for us what our priorities are. For me, the highest priority was to be free to be who I am and to live as I choose. I had already learned that being myself could be costly. Realizing this, I carefully prioritized my budget. First came the Greenebaum Independence Fund. Second came enough to eat and a roof over my head. Third came helping others, both friends and people I had never met (charitable contributions). Those were the big three. After that came such things as clothes, a car and other stuff. In all honesty, this other stuff was never very high on my priorities. If there was extra money, I might buy some "thing." If there wasn't, I wouldn't. Right now, "things" were not on the horizon.

That the Independence Fund was my highest priority meant that I put at least 10 percent of whatever money I earned into my bank savings. I remembered a story that my father had told me years before. I had thrown off much of what Dad had tried to teach me, but not everything. In this I thought he was quite wise. The story, in its essence, stated that you should pay yourself 10 percent of what you earn, and treat it as a bill—never as an option. The idea of the story was that this was how a person could get rich. For me, it was my path to independence. I very much liked the freedom to be my (to be sure, sometimes obnoxious) self. So the Independence Fund got its deposit even if the deposit was very small and even when I was living on potatoes. First the Independence Fund, then food and shelter, then helping others. So, yes, if I had a little left over after feeding myself, dollars went to help others before a new shirt would be considered. I don't say this is the "right" way, but it has worked well for me.

Speaking of clothes, one change that I made at this time was in how I dressed. From the time I was in junior high school, I had worn polyester slacks. My beloved friend Faye, a flower child to her very soul, convinced me to switch to jeans. I quickly came to love jeans. Except for when I'm preaching or at some formal event, even to this day some forty years later, if I'm wearing pants, I'm wearing jeans—and no, not designer jeans. The only difference now is that these days when the jeans at last develop holes I recycle rather than patch them.

Still, the most fun I had in the year I spent back at Oxy was not in choral conducting but music composition. I worked with Professor Robert Gross, a delightful man with a permanent twinkle in his eyes, who was very helpful. I wrote something that was very dear to my heart: a "Cantata for Passover." My musical style was an unsteady blend of romanticism and the very late Renaissance. Bob Gross was very much a twentieth-century composer. But one of the things Bob reinforced for me was that you don't have to agree with someone to respect that person and, in my case, to be of help. Bob helped me to write my composition, rather than trying to get me to write his. My choral advisor was Thomas Somerville. My transcript says I had a conducting class from him, though in all honesty I don't remember it. What I remember most about Professor Somerville up to my Masters' Recital was that he was in no way a Bob Gross.

With 20/20 hindsight, I attempted far too much with my graduate recital. The first half was to be an idea I had that I thought would be both beautiful and fascinating. I would direct a choral mass, but not from the same composer. I would begin in the Renaissance (Kyrie) and end in the twentieth century (Agnus Dei). I still think it a lovely idea. But it required a lot of work and was only the first half of my recital. The second half was my "Cantata for Passover." This was a work for double choir and small orchestra. It too was a huge undertaking. To attempt them both in the same recital was exceedingly foolish—a mistake of the inexperienced.

Looking back, the recital was very deeply a homage to Maria. Her Mass for the first half, my Passover for the second half. In truth, it is only just at this moment, as I write this, that I have come to realize it.

Besides being too "big," the recital quickly picked up some other problems. For one thing, I had carefully figured out how many rehearsals I would need. Then, in the middle of the rehearsals, came the Oil Crisis of 1979 and huge lines at the gas pump. A lot of people missed rehearsals. They couldn't get gas for their cars! There was also the matter of having an accompanist for the rehearsals and the first half of the concert. The first person I asked and indeed the person I had counted on was my friend Mary. She was an accomplished accompanist.

You may recall that Dick and Mary were friends from Oxy that I had sung with in the church choir directed by Jim Smith. I asked Dick to sing in my recital choir. He wasn't interested. I pleaded. He held firm. I asked Mary to accompany the choir. She said only if I paid her and that she would not come cheaply. I was floored and deeply hurt, but there was no time to waste so I moved on. Part of moving on was eliminating both Dick and Mary from my list of friends. Looking back, that was and remains a character flaw on my part. I've done this three or four times in my life—just closed the door on a relationship and moved on. There really ought to be some place in the world between being a good friend and becoming a nonperson, but I couldn't find it. To my discredit, I don't think I looked very hard.

I couldn't find one accompanist so I made do with a patchwork of people, including one rehearsal with no accompanist at all. The organist at Oxy who had agreed to accompany for the concert, died suddenly. Jim Smith, overwhelmingly busy as he was, stepped in and saved the day. Meanwhile, for the orchestra I was able to assemble a strange combination of truly gifted musicians, including my friend Larry Sonderling who was playing for the L.A. Philharmonic, and a few musicians who, as it turned out, were not particularly gifted.

It wasn't until about two rehearsals out from the concert that I truly realized something was very wrong. That was late. Again, my inexperience showed. I should have seen it earlier. Now, given the difficulties we'd faced, I knew we just weren't ready. We needed, I guessed, two, maybe three additional rehearsals. Perhaps we could postpone the concert by two weeks, or maybe I could schedule two rehearsals a week for the next two weeks? Professor Somerville firmly said no. He said this was all part of the learning process. So, we plunged ahead.

It was an ok recital, nothing to write home about. Still, we'd pulled it off and both I and the choir were jubilant. A few days later Professor Somerville called me to his office and told me that the recital was terrible and I was not a conductor of any worth. He suggested that I forget the M.A. and quietly fade away to spare myself the embarrassment of being publicly humiliated by him. Then, he added that besides all that, my cantata was ghastly. If you've read the book this far, you know that, well, them's fightin' words.

I took what I'd been told and pondered it a while. It didn't make sense to me, so I did some digging. I first talked with some of the people who were professional musicians and either played in my chamber orchestra or sang in the choir for the recital or had been in the audience. No one had any ideas except a friend named Joel who wrote music scores for television. Joel, who was Jewish and knew I was too and that Somerville wasn't, assumed that Somerville was anti-Semitic. That didn't track for me. This despite a crack that Somerville had made at my final rehearsal, the only rehearsal he attended as a part of his duties as my instructor.

I had urged the choir to give the *Agnus Dei* all they had. It was written by Ralph Vaughan Williams right after the slaughter that was World War I. I still believe it is a heartfelt, indeed wrenching, prayer to God, begging for peace: "Dona nobis pacem—(Grant us peace)!" But Somerville corrected me in front of the choir, saying that Vaughan Williams was agnostic and therefore an Atheist and certainly no Christian—therefore, he couldn't possibly have been praying for peace. I tried to avoid a spat and told the choir that whatever they might think of Vaughan Williams' religious beliefs, this was an urgent prayer for peace and to sing it that way. After that experience, I knew that Somerville and I didn't think of religion in the same way, but to me by itself that didn't make him anti-Jewish. So I continued looking for an answer.

That's when I talked with the secretary for the music department and discovered that professors Somerville and Thorsen, my old nemesis at Fullerton, were friends. I couldn't be kept out of Oxy because Dr. Swan had recommended me. So Somerville had set out to be of no particular help and indeed, had recommended at least one person for my chamber orchestra that he knew wasn't up to it. How did I find all that out? you may ask. Back in the day, they were called secretaries; today, these invaluable folks are known as administrative assistants. Whichever, the bottom line is this: if you have a personal secretary/administrative assistant, that person knows you and just about everything you do. Everything. This was the second time that a personal secretary who thought her boss was acting in a less than ethical manner took me aside and let me in on the skinny. But the question now was, what to do about it?

First, whether the cantata I had written was good or bad wasn't the point. This was a conducting recital. So I assembled written statements from professional musicians who had either participated in the recital or were in the audience, giving their evaluation of my conducting. I then sat down with my masters' committee and we listened to a tape of the recital. The committee consisted of Professor Somerville, another person from the music department whom I don't recall, and Scott Littleton—as one member of the committee was to be a non-musician. Scott was decidedly in my corner. Tom Somerville was decidedly not. The third member of the committee, after listening to the tape, cautiously backed me up. I would get my degree.

A reasonable question might be where did I find the courage, the gumption, to challenge Oxy's one professor of choral music over my musi-cal abilities? A large part of the answer is, it's in my nature not to give up unless I know I have no cards left to play. A big reason that I knew I had cards to play was that by the time I had my recital, I was already employed by the First United Methodist Church of Monterey Park as their choir di-rector and was successfully leading their choir.

It had been an intriguing turn of events. After my studies in Fullerton and my embarrassment in Santa Monica, I decided the time had come to find out whether I had it in me to lead a church choir. There was one and only one way to find out. The first church I applied to wanted me to de-scribe (as a part of a written application) when I had let Jesus into my life. I didn't complete or submit the application. But there was no such question at Monterey Park. After I submitted my written application I was invited to come meet with the choir one Sunday. But when I arrived, the person who was supposed to lead the choir that morning (their interim choir director) wasn't there. In all honesty, I don't remember why. But regardless, I was handed the piece of music the choir was to sing in the service that morning and asked if I would direct it!

Ok then! Suck it up and give it a whirl! I said I'd do my best.

I sat down with the piece and read through it. It looked pretty straight-forward. So I rehearsed the choir and we sang it for the service. It was love at first sight. The choir really took to me, and I took to them. I was invited to meet with what I believe was called the Pastoral Relations Committee, which did the actual hiring. The minister, Fred Rogers,[26] was there. And before we got very far I told them I was Jewish. Fred smiled broadly and said, "That's wonderful. Perhaps, from time to time, you'll lead the choir in some Jewish music!"

Fred and I hit it off immediately. One of the things I loved about him was that this was a man who lived justice. He had been one of the Freedom Riders in the 1960s, literally risking his life marching in the segregated South for African-American rights at a time when it truly was dangerous to do so. Both black and white marchers had been beaten by members of the KKK and others. Some of the marchers had been lynched. Living his beliefs was who Fred was.

Thus, I knew going in and before Somerville had tried to destroy my confidence in myself that I was perfectly capable of leading a church choir successfully, but there was something else that I felt I needed to ponder. By now it had dawned on me that there was a certain unsettling consistency with my BA and now both M.A.s. Namely, the person in charge had tried to get rid of me. John Rhodes at Oxy, Bob Georges at UCLA, and Tom Somerville at Oxy were three very different people. The only person who was the same in all three cases was me. So, they weren't the problem. Something within me tended to bring out the angry fist of the powerful.

Since I had the time, I took a few weeks to do some soul-searching. In the end, I decided it would be prudent to try to be a little more intentional in how I addressed powerful people, but I was not going to try to change who I was. After all, that's one of the reasons the Independence Fund existed.

That settled, and with my M.A. in hand, I felt ready to begin my career in music.

---

26   No, not the Fred Rogers from PBS. He was a Presbyterian minister. This Fred Rogers was a Methodist minister.

Chapter Seventeen

My first two years at First United Methodist Church were heavenly. I learned a lot from Reverend Fred Rogers. One of the first things I learned was how tired he was. We worked closely, particularly in the beginning, as he had taken me under his wing to help me understand the parts of the Methodist service and where I fit in. I'd met older people before, but I'd never had a working relationship with someone approaching retirement. Fred had lived a long, good life, but also a demanding one, as his Freedom Rider days made clear. In a sense, one of the most enduring lessons Fred taught me was to realize that getting tired is not a sign of weakness.

I also enjoyed learning about Methodism. I had read the entirety of Christian Scripture for "Bible Lit" in college. But while Scripture told me a lot about Jesus, it dawned on me now that it had actually told me almost nothing about Christianity. Later, I'd learned at least a little about differentiating between the separate branches called Catholic and Protestant Christianity, but that was as far as it went. I knew about "branches" because I was well aware of the difference in practice between Reform, Conservative and Orthodox Judaism, and was soon to learn about yet another branch on the tree of Judaism that was quite new to me called Reconstructionist. Now I was learning about the branch of Christianity called Methodist.

I knew that we Jews all had the same Scripture,[27] and yet that unity of Scripture wasn't enough to bring anything even close to resembling unity

---

27   Even in our Scripture, I was aware of some differences. When I was confirmed, I received a copy of Scripture "According to the Masoretic Text." This is considered authoritative by most, but not all.

between us. It dawned on me now as I explored Christianity that it wasn't Scripture, but how we *interpreted* Scripture, that so divided us all. Jews drew firm, immovable lines between ourselves that quickly became full-blown and rather high walls of division. "We're Reform, *not* Conservative." "We're Orthodox, and the *only* true practitioners of Judaism." Now I was observing the same phenomenon in Christianity. No conclusions, not in my early thirties. Just a fascination.

I knew that Tom and Pam were Lutheran. Ok. Clearly, that's different from Methodist. I had become friends in grad school with people from many different branches of Christianity. But that there might be real differences between them had never occurred to me. At that point, they were all simply "Christians." As I chatted with Fred, I realized it was time to take a second look. I needed to open my mind.[28]

Fred never, not once, tried to convert me. I was his new choir director. I needed to know how the service worked and why, and what the role of the choir was. That was it. I hope it showed, because as I write this I realize I never actually told Fred just how much I appreciated what he taught me and most especially *how*. Over and over he made it clear that he was welcoming me, a Jew, into his family, and that he had no designs on changing me. He told me more than once that he hoped and expected to learn as much from me as I did from him. Whether that was true or said simply to put me at my ease, I so deeply appreciated it.

One slightly awkward moment came at communion. Fred made it clear there was no need for me to take communion. But it felt weird when the entire choir went up, yet the choir director stayed behind. I thought about it and after a few communions asked Fred if it would be respectful and ok for me to take communion simply to honor the memory of Jesus. Fred thought about it just a moment or two, then gave me a smile and his blessing.

Then, there was my first Christmas at the Methodist church. The place was packed. Fred looked out at the mass of humanity in front of him and spoke into his microphone. "It's so good to see all of you here today. I just thought I'd remind you that we're here every Sunday—not just at Christmas and Easter." He said it with a smile and there were lots of laughs and chuckles.... And you could have knocked me over with a feather. I'd lost count of how many times I had heard Rabbi Beerman at the beginning of the High Holy Days, the Rosh Hashanah service: "It's so good to see all

---

28   I see so many people making the same mistake as they approach Islam: lumping all Muslims together. I sympathize because I've been there. But it is a mistake. Islam, like every other spiritual tradition, has branches.

of you here this evening. I just thought I'd remind you that we're here every Friday evening—not just at Rosh Hashanah and Yom Kippur." People! We're all the same.[29]

Fred also introduced me to the minister of the church that was sharing space with First United Methodist. His name was Reverend Hidemi Ito. The church was Sage Methodist. Sage was a Japanese-American church. Hidemi was a nice man, but he spoke little English and I spoke no Japanese, so we didn't communicate much. A few members of Sage, like Rev. Ito, didn't speak much English either, but most spoke it quite well. I met and immediately took to Jeanne Taniguchi, who directed the Sage choir. From her I learned to my surprise that the people at Sage didn't mix much with the people at First Church, as many called it. The building was owned by First Church. Sage was a tenant, and there was some tension between the boards. That seemed very unfortunate and I puzzled over what I might do.

By the time I had my M.A. and had completed my first year, Rev. Ito was replaced by Rev. Wes Yamaka. Wes had been born and raised in the United States. He and I quickly became friends. I had an idea. I conspired first with Wes and Fred and as soon as I got their ok I sat down with Jeanne. I hoped we could strike a blow for unity amongst the Sage and First Church congregations by having our choirs sing together. Jeanne thought it a lovely idea—if I directed.

I remember vividly being taken aback at our first joint choir rehearsal. All the Sage members sat on one side of the room and the First Church folks all sat on the other. I let that go for just that first rehearsal before insisting that people sit by sections (soprano, alto, tenor and bass) rather than by church. They complied, and after a few more rehearsals, everyone began to loosen up. And our first time singing together proved to be so much fun that we did it at least a couple of times a year after that for as long as I was there.

A bit more about Wes Yamaka, as he became for me not just a lifelong friend but a mentor. I had taken what passed for California history in both junior high and high school. I'd also taken U.S. History in college. But I had never once heard of the internment of the Japanese-Americans during World War II until I talked with Wes. Like Fred, Wes was an activist for justice. He had participated in negotiations with the U.S. government that in the end resulted in both an acknowledgement of just how wrong the internment had been and also monetary reparations to the survivors.

29 Since then a Muslim friend has talked to me about people she calls "Ramadan Muslims."

Wes had been a youth when his family had been scooped up and im-
prisoned (technically, "interned") by order of the U.S. government. Pearl
Harbor had been attacked and anyone of Japanese ancestry was suspect.
U.S. citizens of Japanese ancestry—men, women and children—were not
only rounded up and interned but lost their businesses, their homes and
frequently their life savings as well as several years of their lives. I was
aghast, both that it had happened and that it wasn't being taught in our
history classes.

Wes also had a way with sermons that I found fascinating. He was the
only one talking, but his sermons always felt like conversations. Sometimes
they were profound conversations, sometimes not so profound, but they
were always interesting. Beyond all this, Wes was at heart an artist. I have
three of his amazing silk screens on my walls to this day. He had tried to
leave ministry to fulfill his dream of pursuing silk-screening as a profes-
sion. But his sense of duty brought him back to the church. There was a
deep need for Methodist ministers of Japanese ancestry.

One of the things that Wes and Fred both encouraged me in was actually bringing a little Judaism into the church. So at Fred's suggestion I organized a Passover Seder. I was both honored and very pleased that neither
of them wanted to co-opt the service. Fred in particular, who I worked
for, made it clear that he wanted his congregation to have an experience
of Judaism, not a Christianized version of the Passover. And it went off
beautifully.

There was such joy in this. It felt so right. I could have studied Methodism for years in books but never really learned the heart and soul of
this branch of the Christian tree without worshipping with my Methodist
friends, sharing their service. And now I'd had the chance to share with
them a Jewish service, albeit only one. Yet it hit me, why not be more intentional about this? Why not consciously set out to worship with people
of differing faiths, not in the search for who was "right," but to better understand our fellow human beings? It was broadening, not threatening, to
learn of our differing ways of approaching God, if indeed there was a God.
In worshipping together, there was also the potential for humanity to heal.
This seemed a beautiful and exciting prospect.

Building on that thought, I had a friend from my days at Cal State Fullerton studying with Dr. Swan. Her name was Mitzi Interlandi (her husband
was a rather famous editorial cartoonist). Mitzi led a Presbyterian choir in
Laguna Beach. Presbyterians. Another Christian branch! Mitzi and I conspired to put our two choirs together to perform some pretty spectacular

double-choir music—music that was beyond each of our choirs individually. We rehearsed our parts separately and then together, giving concerts in Laguna Beach and Monterey Park. It was a lot of fun—so much fun that I got in touch with another friend from the Fullerton days, I think his name was John. He conducted a Lutheran choir just a mile up the road from my Methodist choir. Sure enough, we did some joint choir events with the Lutherans as well.

Those first two years were absolutely wonderful. I got to know the choir, and what a wonderful assemblage of people they were. They became family. Several are still deeply valued friends to this day.

Nor was this my only musical activity. I wanted to do more serious music. I introduced the First Church choir to the music of Schütz, but that was a style of music we could only do every once in a while. So when there was an opening for a music director of a local community choir that specialized in Renaissance and Baroque choral music, I auditioned. It wasn't a good fit. I was too intense, or so a couple of their singers told me after the audition, when they told me how much they'd enjoyed singing for me and how disappointed they were I hadn't been chosen.

One door closes, another door can be kicked open. If I was going to direct a non-professional but still serious choir, I'd have to start one. Gulp. Ok then. I started making phone calls and the Choral Consort was born.

Starting the Choral Consort taught me a lot about some of my strengths and weaknesses. I'm a pretty good organizer. I'm good with details and getting things done on time. Where I'm horrifically weak is when it comes to publicity. I think this is a combination of not really liking publicity and, more emphatically, feeling exceedingly uncomfortable promoting anything that involves *me*. I did ok when working for Common Cause and Yakima Valley College because the work was short-term (only a year at either job) and I was publicizing something that had nothing to do with me. What this meant to the Choral Consort was that while we developed a small but devoted following, it remained small. Still, it was a great joy and we made some fine music!

I also landed a job as the High Holy Days choir director for a local Reconstructionist Jewish temple. I was there for two years. The first year was absolutely grand. I loved the people and the experience. I learned about a branch on the tree of Judaism that had been unfamiliar to me. I also did something I had avoided up to then: I learned to read (well, sound out more than read) Hebrew, so that I could know when to bring the choir in after a prayer. That first year the cantor was on sabbatical. A fellow I only remember as Mickie was the substitute. He was truly a "salt of the earth" kind of guy and a joy to work with. He really ran the show. The rabbi was only there to give the Rosh Hashanah and Yom Kippur sermons. Working with Mickie was an absolute delight. So, when I was asked to come back a second year and direct the choir, I immediately said "Yes!"

The second year was different. The cantor had returned. She was an excellent musician, but we didn't work well together. I don't think she was used to or interested in collaborating. But what truly sent me up the wall was her often-expressed opinion that Judaism was superior to all other religions, and particularly "those Christians." She made snide comments about Christians frequently and it didn't sit well with me. By this time I'd known a lot of Christians and a lot of Jews and had seen nothing that showed me that one religion was superior or inferior to the other. So after that second year, I didn't come back. If one believes in omens, this was an omen of some dark days ahead.

Fred Rogers retired, and in his place was a young minister I'll call Bill. At first Bill and I got along fine. Indeed, being much younger and just starting his career as a minister, Bill had a much lighter approach to life than Fred. Bill and Wes had a lot of fun clowning around. But after a few months of his being there, I asked Bill about a musical issue and he just shrugged it off: "Choir just provides the noise between my leading prayers and giving the sermon." At first, I thought he was joking, but he wasn't. Yikes. The work environment had very definitely changed.

Worse, Bill let it slip from time to time, always as a side comment to something else, that he was amazed that a Jew had been hired to direct a Methodist choir. At first, it was tossed off as a source of amusement and I didn't really think much of it, but after it happened a number of times, alarm bells went off.

Then came the time for Passover, and Wes told Bill that we had celebrated it the year before and I had agreed to lead it again. Bill put his foot down. Passover was a Jewish holiday. It didn't belong in a Methodist church. Since the Passover Seder was scheduled, Bill would allow it one last time, but he would run it, and it would be appreciated for what it was: Jesus' Last Supper. Afterward, Bill made it clear that he wouldn't fire me, but he was very uncomfortable with a Jew in charge of his choir and perhaps I might be happier working somewhere else. I loved my choir and didn't want to leave. But I did realize that this was the beginning of the end.

In the meantime, Mom had beaten her cancer twice and been declared by her doctors as "cancer free" twice. But now the cancer was back yet again, more virulent than ever. It was clear that this time she wasn't going to beat it, and I was devastated. A part of me selfishly felt bad for myself, because I'd really only gotten to know my mother these last couple of years. I wanted much more time with her. But mostly I felt bad for Mom because it seemed so flaming unfair! Finally, finally she had her life together and was truly enjoying it. She wasn't simply becoming, she had become her own person. She had bloomed. And now, now after only knowing for a few years how truly sweet life could be, it was all going to be snatched from her. That felt so very wrong, so unjust.

As I was struggling to deal with this, the beginnings of what would eventually become a complete rupture with my sister began. Every family has its dirty laundry. The details have no place here, but the lesson that anyone should take from it is that a death in the family can provide an immense amount of stress. That stress can crack fault lines you didn't even know existed.

Mom made a request of both my sister and me that blew me away. Mom's own mother had deteriorated greatly before she died. Mom's memory of her mother had been deeply scarred by watching Nana devolve into an incontinent, barely functioning, emaciated shadow of the woman she had once been. Mom didn't want that to happen to us. She didn't want a shadow of who she was to be how we remembered her for the rest of our lives. She became fixated on this. She told Kathy and me that when the time came she wanted to take her own life rather than deteriorate before our eyes, and she wanted our blessing. I was stunned and told her I needed to think about it.

By this time my relationship with Wes was deep. So I went to him with my dilemma. I didn't believe in suicide. I believed that a person should fight up to that last possible breath, and I also wanted every possible moment with my mother that I could get. I also believed in "Honor thy father and thy mother." If this was what my mother wanted to do, then I felt obliged to honor it. What should I do?

Wes refused to give me an answer. He listened very carefully. He made sure that I understood that he had listened very carefully. But then he just told me how much he appreciated that I had quite a dilemma on my hands. I had his love. I had his support. But what I did not have was his advice.

I was furious with Wes at the time, but came to realize that he was right. Whatever I decided to do, it was something I would have to live with. Therefore it was a decision only I could make. What Wes had reinforced in his own compassionate way was that there was no "right" answer applicable to all situations. This was my dilemma. And it was a very real dilemma. Therefore I had to come up with my own answer, an answer I could live with. In the end, I believed that honoring my mother's wishes was more important than imposing my wishes on her. So I told her I'd support her decision, though I hoped she wouldn't need to make it for a while. My sister also supported the decision.

Chapter Eighteen

Meanwhile, I wasn't selling scripts, money was running out, and I needed a secure source of income. One of the members of the First Church choir taught at a local high school and said they were in need of substitute teachers. I was warned by some that substitute teaching was a thankless task. But I was finishing up the last few dollars from a screenwriting assignment and did not want to tap my Independence Fund, so I applied to be a substitute.

Screenwriting was never a good fit for me. What I liked I couldn't sell, and what I could sell I didn't like—and this was just for television. I was going through agents like water through that proverbial sieve—and understandably so. No agent wants a writer who only writes when it's absolutely necessary and then gets into fights with producers over content. When my bank account reached near zero, I would write what I considered crap and then sell it under an assumed name, as I never, ever wanted to be connected to it. I even gave away the rights to what I wrote so that I'd be unreachable. No second or third checks for reruns. It was time to try something else.

I ended up loving my work as a substitute teacher. In no time I became the "go-to" sub for the English teachers. That was flattering, and also meant constant work. What was so much fun was that I wasn't asked simply to keep order for a few days while the regular teacher was away (the normal substitute task). I was actually trusted to teach. I was left a lesson plan, always understood what to do with it, and was able to keep things running smoothly. No downtime. The regular teachers appreciated that. And for me, it was a kick. I really enjoyed teaching. What made it even better was that I never had to grade anybody. I have never liked grades. I didn't like them when I was a student, and I liked them even less as a teacher.

But happily, as a sub it wasn't my job to say, "*You're* an A student, but *you're* not." No, my job was simply to teach, to reach out to each student where he or she lived and teach. I loved it! Yes, I had to keep track of who was absent and who was tardy, but I never had to grade anyone because of it. Then there was the matter of discipline. I'd been told that as the sub I'd have endless problems, but I had no problems whatsoever. I treated every student as an adult, and it worked. Ok, it worked in high school. I was sent once to sub at a junior high and the kids ate me alive. I told the district office NEVER to send me to sub at a junior high again.

So, I was paying the rent and having a good time. More than that, it was spiritually rewarding work. This was cool.

Then there was the time I was asked to sub for a rabbi! Two friends team-taught a class in comparative religion at their high school. But the rabbi they were counting on to speak about Judaism refused to come back. Evidently, he'd been asked some unfortunate questions and gotten upset. So I was asked with very little warning to come and pinch hit. My years of explaining Judaism to others paid off. The class went well. Yes, I was asked some pointed questions ("You seem like such a nice guy. Why did you kill Jesus?"), but I realized they came from ignorance, not malice. It surprised me that the rabbi had been unable to see that. I was asked back the following year and happily agreed.

I had some wonderful times visiting with Mom as well. Perhaps they were made all the sweeter by both of us knowing that it was all on borrowed time. Speaking of borrowed time, Mom wanted to be sure her affairs were in order. She asked me to be co-executor of her estate with my sister. I said yes. She asked me to take her two poodles after she was gone and care for them. Her two poodles?

When I was a very young child the family had had a dachshund. But I was allergic and "Julie Anna" had to be given away. Poodles, however, don't shed and that was the crucial thing. So, several years later the family got a poodle. Frosty. No allergy problems! Frosty died while I was in college. We buried him in our backyard, and Dad apologized for crying. A few years later Mom and Dad got two poodles, Pete and Phred (Phred named after the Doonesbury character). Both Mom and Dad felt that with no children in the house to play with, there should be two dogs so they could keep each other company. When Mom and Dad got divorced, Mom got the house and the dogs. After Mom died "the boys" would need a new home, and Mom did not want them ending up with strangers. I agreed to take them.

In the meantime, the Choral Consort was gaining traction and we had an enlightening experience. A family in Beverly Hills wanted to hire us to sing at their Christmas party. I was approached by the wife's personal secretary (the first time I had ever heard of a housewife having a personal secretary). But, I cautioned her, the Choral Consort sings classical music. I was told that that was why they wanted us. "You're sure?" "Yes." They wanted "A Renaissance Christmas" theme. Ok. We were a nonprofit. This was a way for our singers to actually take home more than the minimal "gas money" they received from each concert's gate. I consulted with the group, and everyone was enthusiastic. This would be my first brush with the super-wealthy.

We prepared and finely polished our best Renaissance Christmas music. We were ready and really excited. When we arrived at the house I must admit I was blown away. I won't try to describe it because I no longer remember anything other than that the three-story house was BIG! I guessed that it could comfortably hold three, maybe four families, and I mean comfortably. We were taken to the basement floor which, as I recall, included a huge gym. Ok. We warmed up and were ready.

There was buzz among the massive numbers of servants. Evidently, the big question of the evening was whether someone from the *L.A. Times* was going to be there. This was when I learned that there was actually a person at the *Times* whose job it was to track the rich and famous and write about them. You're kidding me, right? No.

This time of year, the coveted prize among the super-rich was to be recognized for throwing what would be called THE party of the season. That was why the Choral Consort had been hired—in the hopes that this house would be the only one to offer live Renaissance Christmas music. And, of course, there was the guest list. I don't know why Brooke Shields' name sticks in my mind, but she was there. I do know why Ricardo Montalbán's name sticks. More about that in a moment. But this was when I learned that we were a prop, nothing more. I remember thinking how obscene it was to have so much money—and yes, judgmental, I also thought how useless these people were. So much misery in the world and having their Christmas party judged "the best" by the *L.A. Times* gossip columnist was what made them feel important? Good flaming grief! Still, we had a job to do. We were hired to sing two sets, and it was time to begin.

We were led out from the lower floor up to where the party was and assembled on the stairs. I have to admit, we sang beautifully—or so I thought. But once we finished with the set we were hurriedly escorted away. Many of the guests were just staring at us, while others were ignoring us and deep in conversation. A few were clapping half-heartedly. I only recall one person clapping vigorously: Ricardo Montalbán. He had a huge smile on his face. He came over as we were being led out. We were moving fast so I'm not sure if he said "Well done!" or "Well sung!" but either way, it was nice. Here's to you and your memory, Ricardo Montalbán.

We were then told by the admittedly embarrassed personal secretary who had hired us that we wouldn't be required for the second set. I think but can no longer be sure that it was in an apology phone call a few days later that I was told that "the Missus" hadn't understood the difference between the Renaissance and the time of Charles Dickens. She had expected us to be dressed in *A Christmas Carol*-style outfits and to sing carols, not motets. Ok. So much for my brush with the rich and famous.

About the same time, things were deteriorating at First Church. I still loved the choir and to the best of my knowledge they still loved me. But Bill, having realized I wasn't simply going to quit, had taken it upon himself to make my life as miserable as possible. I was faced with a conundrum. At some point I was going to need to leave—that much was crystal clear. When I did leave, Bill would still be there and so would the choir. Should I let the choir know what was happening and risk their relationship with their minister? I concluded that that would be self-indulgent and decided to keep my own counsel. I even withheld my problems from Wes, as Wes and Bill seemed to be good friends and again, Wes would still need to work with Bill after I left.

Then I arrived late one day to visit Mom. She had had a close call and been hospitalized a week or so before, but then she'd been released and now was feeling much better. She and I had plans to do something we had never done before; in two weeks we would take a weekend vacation together, though I don't remember where. It would be a chance to get away and talk and talk. I was so very much looking forward to it, and I knew Mom was as well. But when I arrived at the house, my sister was there. She and Mom had spent the day together. Mom now told me she had decided she was going to end things tonight. What? Tonight??

What to do!?? Just two days earlier, Mom had been looking forward to at least another month of life. Now this? What had happened? What had my sister said? What to do? What do I do? Think, damn it! I had to make a decision and fast. It seemed to me that I could put up a fight and argue for Mom sticking to her plan of living at least another month. But if she truly had decided that this was her last night, did I really want her final memory to be of a verbal brawl? God, if you're there, for crying out loud, HELP ME!

I decided I couldn't risk destroying Mom's last night.

"Mom, please, look at me. Are you sure?" That was the most I felt I could do. She said she was and I let it go. We talked for a while, then Mom climbed into bed and took the pile of pills she had assembled. My sister and I went up to her one by one and kissed her goodbye. "Good night, sweet prince," Mom whispered to me, quoting from Hamlet. "Good night, Mom."

Once Mom went to sleep, my sister and I left. Mom had insisted on it. There was a maid living with her, so she wasn't left alone. My sister and I agreed to meet at the house the next morning. And when we did, Mom was still breathing. We couldn't wake her up, but she was still breathing. What now? We called Mom's doctor, who said she was probably dying but he didn't know how long it would take. We knew Mom did not want to die in a hospital, so with the doctor's permission we kept her at home and began our deathbed vigilance.

My mind was incapacitated, and I felt myself going under. I at least had the presence to realize that I was in over my head. In truth, I hadn't come close to recovering from Maria's death. I had no emotional reserves. None. I needed help. I felt like I was drowning. I called my friend Candy, who with her husband Tom and their children Megan and Paige still lived up in Washington. I explained the situation. Could she come be with me? Please!

Candy arranged for a friend of hers to come and stay with the children, as Tom worked full time. And Tom gave his blessing. Candy then flew down to stay with me. That's friendship. It was only afterward when I stopped to ponder it that I realized just how big a deal this was. For a husband to say to his wife, "Of course, go spend however long it takes to help your single male friend." For a mother to say to one of her own friends, "I need to leave for an unknown period of time. Please move into my house and take care of my young children."

Then, when Candy flew down, my sister got angry. How dare I turn to Candy and not her? But bless her, Candy was able to smooth things over, and the three of us stood a twenty-four-hour vigil. I think it took about ten days. Candy was the one watching when Mom died. She came out to let us know. Candy stayed with me and helped me remain at least marginally sane while we planned a memorial service at the house, and then stayed until the service was over. I was still a mess but no longer drowning, so Candy at last flew home to be with her family.

Now there was the question of Mom's estate and how to deal with it. Kathy and I met with Mom's estate attorney, Ira Bilson. Over the next year, we'd be dealing a lot with Ira and indeed, Ira and I became good friends. We kept in touch and saw each other whenever possible up until his death a few years ago. For now, it was all business. What we quickly learned was that while Mom had been diligent about some of the big things, she had let all the little things slide—particularly in the last months. There were piles of unpaid bills and a seemingly endless number of loose ends. Kathy was a practicing attorney and she couldn't spare the time. So, I put my life on hold, gave up my apartment and moved into Mom's house to try to put things in order.

Not that I had the slightest idea how to begin. Fortunately, my friend Richard from college was willing to put his accounting practice on hold. He flew down from Santa Cruz to help me sort through some of the basics and get organized. I never could have managed without Richard's sure hand in the beginning. He set everything up. He told me what needed to be done and in what order. Only when he was sure I could handle it all did he fly back to Santa Cruz and resume his practice.

Let me pause for a moment. This is a book about spirituality, and how we get to where we are going. What is the real meaning of life? What makes our lives truly worth the living? *Helping each other.* What had I possibly done to be so fortunate as to have friends like Richard, and Candy, and so many others who truly and without hesitation have been so giving during my life? I cannot begin to guess. But loving one another is what our lives, if they are truly to have meaning, is all about. This nonsense of "He who dies with the most toys wins" is for fools, or so I believe. To love and be loved, to somehow have friends who will drop everything to help you when you truly need it—there is nothing on this planet more important, more valuable, or more meaningful. I am not only continually bewildered by the love of my friends, but I am also endlessly grateful.

Chapter Nineteen

Being co-executor of my mom's estate took a toll on me, much larger than I realized at the time—so much so that I vowed never to handle an estate again. Some people get weird about money, particularly after someone has died. When the dust had at last cleared, it turned out that Mom had left my sister and me a pile of money. Some of it I had to keep. After all, I now had Mom's two dogs, which meant I needed to buy a house! I found one in Santa Monica, paid for half of it, and assumed the mortgage on the other half. Some of my inherited money went into the Independence Fund, but I felt acutely uncomfortable keeping too much of it. It was Mom's money, not mine. I wanted to do something useful with it so I gave about half of it away.

I wrote large checks to friends. I knew that Wes wanted to have his own silk-screen shop. It took some convincing to get him to take a good-sized contribution toward it, but in the end, as an act of friendship, he did. There were other friends with other needs. And there were a bunch of charities that I could help. I knew I couldn't give it all away. I now had a mortgage and two canine dependents. Also, Mom wouldn't have wanted me simply to "blow through it." Never since her death have I been homeless or had to resort to a potato diet. I'm pretty sure she'd be pleased with that.

Balance. Why shouldn't my life be a little better thanks to Mom's desire to leave me so much? On the other side, why should my life be hugely better when so many people still have so little? I'm not sure I've always achieved it, but that's what I was looking for. Balance.

Still, there was more than that going on inside me. Not that I recognized it at the time, but Mom's death caused some strong emotional earthquakes.

For one thing, I had finally had enough of Bill. A few months after Mom died, I resigned from my position at First Church. I told the choir simply that the time had come for me to move on. Everyone accepted that, or so it seemed, and in truth that hurt. I had expected a certain amount of protesting and people demanding to know why I was leaving. But maybe Bill had prepared the way so well that people figured it was indeed time for me to leave. Or maybe I had hidden my reasons for leaving so well that the choir itself felt hurt that I would leave for no stated good reason. Two friends I'd made there, Dennis and Maryel, remained strong and steadfast friends. But I grew apart from everyone else. I would again have good, indeed close, relations with some of the members of the choir, but not for many years.

The actual leave-taking also struck me. At First Church there was barely a ripple. But on my last Sunday as choir director Wes and Jeanne asked me to attend the Sage service. While nothing like this happened with Bill and First Church, at Sage Wes called me forward. I really don't remember most of it all these years later. I do know Wes thanked me for my service and for being a spiritual leader to both congregations. That felt so gratifying and truly blew me away. Then someone put flowers around my neck, everyone applauded, and I was invited to speak. But I just stood there. I remember Wes then saying that he had never before seen me speechless, and speechless I was. I was shaken to my foundation—grateful, but shaken.

There were two other incidents that truly stunned me, both regarding singers in my group the Choral Consort, and neither incident was positive. It wasn't just the events themselves but also my reactions to them that forced me to look deeply into myself, and not be at all happy with what I saw. I liked all of the Choral Consort singers. But there was a dedicated core that I was particularly fond of, and among that core were two singers. Let's call the first one Carol.

Carol was happily married. She was certainly attractive, but I didn't like her *that* way. Carol had a voice that was absolutely stunning, truly beautiful. It possessed a sweetness that at that moment in my life tugged deeply at my very raw emotions. If anyone ever sang like an angel, it was Carol. I very much hope she went on to a career in music, though I've never seen her name. The incident I refer to came as we were rehearsing for a concert. Carol had a solo, and she nailed it. It so connected with me that I threw my arms around her and gave her a big hug. Nothing more, but a definite hug. We continued with the rehearsal and sometime later she again just nailed her work. At the next break I gave her another hug. Her voice was so hauntingly beautiful! Then, at the end of the rehearsal, when I told the whole group how wonderful they were all sounding, I gave Carol a third hug—and I could feel her body stiffen.

Only when I got home did I realize how completely and unconscionably I'd crossed the line. I hadn't meant anything by it. But she had sung so beautifully, and I was a hugger. No. Face it. I wasn't a hugger, I was an abuser. I had trampled all over Carol's private space. Ick! What an idiot! I told myself. What a flaming, needy goon! Ok, my life was upside down at the moment, but what kind of excuse is that? What to *say*? What to say? I had no idea, so I compounded my transgression by saying nothing.

After the concert, it came as no surprise to me that Carol resigned from the Choral Consort—though she was exceedingly polite about it and simply mentioned scheduling "conflicts." But I understood what had really happened. So what had happened to me? How could I be so in need of a hug that I would cross this clear a boundary? "What on earth is wrong with you?" I asked myself. And I had no answer.

Then I truly hit rock bottom. There was another member of the choir who I liked a lot. Let's call her Anna. She called me one morning to tell me she had been raped by someone the night before. Raped. And she'd reached out to me for solace. I was very calm, told her how sorry I was that this had happened to her and asked if there was something I could do. After a moment or two she told me no, there was nothing I could do, but thanks for listening.

It was once she had hung up that it occurred to me that if there was nothing for me to do, why did she call me? Good grief, what was wrong with me? She didn't need me calm, she needed my compassion, my friendship and, most important, my presence. That's why she had called. I almost called her back, but I was so far gone that it remained "almost." I did nothing, and in doing nothing I failed her. I failed this sweet, wonderful young woman. There are no other words for it. My universe had so completely imploded that I could take from others, but I couldn't give. Candy and Richard had given me so much. And me? I was incapable of giving. What kind of a human being has nothing to give? I felt empty and useless.

Anna left the Choral Consort, and I think we limped on for several more rehearsals before I realized that my having nothing inside had crippled not just my ability to help Anna when she so desperately needed it, but my ability to lead. Who would want to follow? There was no way to do another concert, and I called it quits. The Choral Consort was finished. So was I.

This left only two things in my life still functioning. One of them was my screenwriting. I had written what's called a "treatment" (a lengthy, detailed synopsis) for a major motion picture. My agent loved it, and it turned out Columbia Pictures loved it too. I was called in to meet with a rather famous producer to iron out the details of how I'd turn the treatment into a screenplay. Ok fine. We met. I was told of the few changes that would be needed to make the picture the blockbuster that this producer anticipated it would be. It amounted to the same stuff that had so frequently caused me grief in the past. Namely, I was told I needed to add some sex and violence. I snapped.

"No," I told him. I held up the treatment. "This is the picture I envision. This is the picture that will be made or there will be no picture." This to an internationally recognized producer.

He seemed unfazed. I wonder now if he thought I was negotiating. He calmly mentioned the astounding amount of money the studio was willing to pay for the full screenplay that he was sure he could make into a blockbuster. When I still said No, he smiled at me and suggested that I think about it overnight and get back to him. The moment I got home my phone rang. It was my agent. He'd gotten a call from the producer and was not happy with me. I can't remember the figure anymore, but he would have received either 10 or 15 percent of whatever I got for the picture. Whichever, it was big bucks. I told him to stick it. He told me where I could stick both my treatment and my career and slammed the phone down.

Ok then. I'd ended my career in pictures. I'd resigned from First Church. I'd brought the Choral Consort down in flames, and in the process humiliated myself in how I had mistreated two people I truly valued. I was involved in other self-destructive behavior as well, but none so dramatic as these—at least none that I remember. Still, I had trashed my life so thoroughly that I knew something had to change. Something, but what?

I had to start over. That was it. Start over. It seemed the only answer if I was to have any chance of surviving.. But how does one start over? I mean, seriously, how does a person just start over? I climbed into my mind and pondered this.

In a way, I had an odd gift. Pete and Phred had gotten older. They weren't going to be around a lot longer. I had a responsibility to them and to Mom to see my obligation to them through. That gave me some enforced breathing room before I could make any decision. So I sat with these two love-filled fur-balls in my home that bordered Venice and Santa Monica and tried to make sense of my life.

Years later, I would learn that losing one's parent, particularly in such a difficult way, can turn a person's life inside out and, most particularly, spur major changes. For me this, trauma was magnified and compounded by my never coming to terms with the death of the woman I had expected to spend the rest of my life with. I had refused to acknowledge the pain and never given myself any chance to heal. But for now these insights were absent. All I understood was that I couldn't just give up. I had two charges that my mother had left me: Pete and Phred. It was my responsibility to care for them. I owed both them and Mom at least that much.

Their getting older proved interesting. Both were becoming arthritic. They couldn't jump on and off the couch like before. I could still take them for walks, but even the couple of steps up from the street level to the front door proved difficult. I had a friend, Greg, who was pretty handy with a hammer and saw and he made us some ramps so the dogs could remain independent. There was a doggie ramp from the floor to the couch, and another up the steps from the street level to the house. Then Phred died and it was just Pete and me.

In the meantime, I was still substitute teaching, mostly at Garfield High School in East Los Angeles. Even as the rest of my life was imploding, I was somehow still able to teach well enough that I was summoned for an interview with someone of importance, though I no longer remember who. There was going to be an opening in the English department. All the teachers I had worked with strongly recommended me for the position.

That was very flattering. But, I stammered, I don't have a teaching credential. I wasn't even an English major! I was told that everyone was aware of that, but I was a born teacher. The students didn't just like me, I was told, they respected and responded to me. My fellow teachers all strongly wanted me. There were ways around a credential with this kind of support. What did I say?

I said I needed to think about it. That was fine. So I went home and pondered. Was this my chance to start over? Think about it. Think!

It was definitely tempting. I really did enjoy teaching. I loved reaching out to interested minds, introducing them to ways of thinking, and guiding them along the way. And with very few exceptions I really enjoyed my fellow teachers—good, dedicated people, serving the future with good hearts and good will. Speaking of teachers, there was one about my age, single, very smart, very independent and very cute. I liked her.... Ok, I had a bit of a crush on her. Maybe? It's been ten years. Maybe?

As a full-time teacher, the freedom I had as a substitute would disappear. I was going to have to grade my students. It's hard to explain, but the idea of grading anyone, children or adults, is truly repugnant to me. Being given the power, let alone exercising that power, to say, "You're the best, but you're not as good," is truly at war with everything I am. I don't like it when others have that power, and I don't want it myself. It's the power to divide people and I would like to see it banished. But this was my chance to start over, wasn't it? Was it really that big a compromise to be able to do what I loved and teach? Yes. I felt appreciated and flattered to be asked. But to have to grade young people? I shuddered. I don't know if it makes sense, but it was a deal-breaker.

On top of this philosophical/ethical problem lay an emotional one.

Maria and I had talked about heaven. And though we'd argued about it, I very much hoped now that she was right. But if she were in heaven, and if by some miracle I made it there too, how could I face her if I now took up with someone else? My days of mindless promiscuity were stupid and degrading, but they were long since behind me and this was different. If I became involved with and married someone else, that was truly being unfaithful.

Then, something else made the decision absolute. I concluded that changing jobs wasn't enough. I needed to start over, and if I accepted a position at a school where I had already worked it wouldn't be starting over. If I were to have any chance of being successful, it seemed to me it needed to be a completely new start. I very gratefully but firmly declined the offer of a teaching position. I had always said I wanted to move up to the Seattle area "someday." Ok then, this was the time.

But I couldn't do it quite yet. Phred had died, but Pete was still alive and well. And to take an older, arthritic dog, used to the warm weather of Santa Monica, and move him up to the cold and damp Seattle weather would be cruel. I would take care of Pete as long as he lived. In the meantime, I would make some attempts to mend my soul and my heart. When the time came, I would sell the house and start over, not in Seattle, but in Edmonds, a few miles north of Seattle. I really liked it there. It rather reminded me of Santa Monica—a small but very vibrant city. More important, it would be a city where I had never lived.

Chapter Twenty

I don't remember precisely how much, but between cutting myself off from virtually everything that tied me to my old life and my move to Washington there was a fair period of time to reflect. I took advantage of it. It seemed to me that the only possible way for this phoenix to rise from the ashes was to get some handle on what had happened, and to work out a plan for how I wanted my new life to take shape. I didn't want it to be random chance. I didn't know how much, if anything, I could actually control, but I did at least want some intent behind my actions.

I listened to a lot of music as I pondered. It tended to be either the choral music of Heinrich Schütz or the instrumental music of Ralph Vaughan Williams. A particular favorite that seemed to ground me and put me in touch with my spiritual self was Vaughan Williams' "Fantasia on a Theme of Thomas Tallis."[30] I would sit and listen to it, breathe deeply, and remember. Particularly when I was feeling adrift, which was often, it helped bring me back.

Somewhere along the way came the Jewish High Holy Days, in particular Yom Kippur. Up to now, there were really only two key elements that had tied me to Judaism. The first was Passover and all it meant for how human beings treat each other. The second was setting justice as a personal compass, the star, if you will, by which to set my life's course. Not that every act will be just. We're human. But that we should always steer toward justice.

---

30   Not that there is any one "right" interpretation, but the one that has always deeply moved me was that of Sir John Barbirolli. A plus is that the recording includes some wonderful string music by Elgar.

These two were important guides for me, but they left a gaping hole, at least in my own life. How the heck do we get there?!! I now added Yom Kippur to make up a triad of Jewish practice. This triad by no means makes me a model Jew, but they have become the sustaining pillars of my life. Yom Kippur provides a time of deep reflection. We screw up. We all screw up. Some years are far more disastrous than others, but we all screw up. It's called being human. For me, Yom Kippur became not just an acknowledgement of my screwups and a time to try and right past wrongs, but also a time to reflect on doing better in the future—and how to go about it.

"This is who I am, today, Yom Kippur, this year. And this is what I hope to do tomorrow. Is the who I am today a person who can possibly accomplish the just life I hope for tomorrow? If not, then I need to change. And if I need to change, *what* needs to be changed?" At this Yom Kippur, realizing that my life was as messed up as it was, I knew that I couldn't possibly change everything at once. So I asked myself, what needs to be changed first? What in my life do I change this year that can move me a little further down the path I hope to walk?

If you're not Jewish, I should caution you that the Yom Kippur I celebrate is not necessarily one that most Jews celebrate, nor is it perhaps one that my beloved Rabbi Beerman would even recognize. But it has become foundational and truly important to me. I don't really celebrate Rosh Hashanah as the "New Year." But I do take the ten days between Rosh Hashanah and Yom Kippur to examine both who I am and what I've done (and left undone) and then either conclude this deep reflection with, "Yeah, I like this direction" or "Things have to change."

This year, as I prepared to uproot myself from Santa Monica and my life as I had known it and start anew somewhere north of Seattle, I knew there were a lot of changes needed. So it was time to take stock and think: what has to change now and what needs changing but can wait a year or two? The bottom line was, if I fall into the same old habits then it's the same old me, just in a new place.

One immediate change that I felt was needed was to stop clinging to her memory. She would want me to—I knew that. She would want me to be happy. That I hadn't moved on was my own doing, not hers. I needed to understand and accept that and to be open to meeting a new Ms. Right. The first step in healing must be to acknowledge that this was indeed true.

In many ways, I was very lucky in my timing. In the six years I had lived there, the house I had bought in Santa Monica had more than doubled in value. Once I sold it, I wouldn't need a mortgage for my new house. In fact, as long as I was careful, I figured I'd have enough to build my dream house. My dream house. How cool is that? Ok, what should my dream house look like to house the new me?

It would need to be big enough to house me, Ms. Right, and some kids. She might come with kids or maybe I would become a father. I'd be working at home, so I needed an office. I also wanted a room that would simply house books: a library, the most sacred room of my house. As you may remember, I can't visualize. I needed something concrete in order to picture myself as moving on. So, I went to an architect I knew to draw up a sketch of the house I wanted. Having that in hand made my new life feel more real than just dreaming about it.

My Independence Fund was fully funded. If I wasn't extravagant, and if I used only the money I received from the sale of the Santa Monica house for a new house, I would have enough for living expenses. I wouldn't need a job, at least not for several years. That meant I could last get back to the Roman novel. I could finish it and see if I could sell it. But in the meantime there was the matter of justice. I needed to *do*, not just proclaim. This crystallized for me that living a just life meant doing justice, not complaining about injustice. So I would need to get involved in my new community. What to do? That must be dictated by what the community needed, not me. Right now what was needed from me was a commitment.

I also needed a spiritual home, but this was going to be tricky. My study of myth, and praying with my Methodist friends, at least for those first two wonderful years, had opened my heart to the realization that there wasn't one "right" path to God—if indeed God was to be found. I didn't want to stop being Jewish, but I didn't want to worship only with Jews. "The family that prays together, stays together." How could the human family ever come together if praying together was "off the table"? I wanted to find a spiritual community where we could all be who we are and still participate respectfully in each other's traditions. I wanted to understand Christianity better. And I knew next to nothing about Buddhists or Muslims and so many others. Surely such a community existed—a community committed to justice and to a love for all of humanity that could bring us all together. So, when I moved to Washington, that must be one of my tasks. I must find these people, whoever they were, wherever they were, and join them.

One thing I had going for me was that with the exception of books and music, objects mean nothing to me and carry no emotional weight. Once the house my mom had lived in and I'd grown up in was sold, I never went back. Nor had I ever revisited the house of my childhood. I didn't miss them. I kept a couple of pieces of furniture that had been in the family for generations but otherwise got rid of pretty much everything else.

Did I want to get pets? That was a hard question. Pete and Phred had been so much more than just a responsibility to my mom, they had been a joy—two endlessly loving fur-balls. They were very different from one another. Pete was the epitome of calm; curious, energetic and loving but also completely unflappable. Phred, on the other hand, was a bundle of emotions. When Mom was in her last months, I would know exactly what kind of day she was having when I came to visit by how Phred met me at the door. Pete was always Pete. But if Mom was having a bad day, Phred met me at the door with his head low and his tail between his legs. If it was a good day, Phred was a bouncing bundle of joy, tail wagging a mile a minute. After Mom died, Phred wandered about the house night after night, whimpering. Pete simply went to bed as always and slept soundly.

What their differences showed was to remind me that Pete and Phred were sentient beings, with minds and emotions. I felt an obligation to care for them and love them. There was no way to "turn them loose" to live free, but to *buy* an animal, to *own* another animal, felt wrong. If you are thinking, "Oh come on, dogs sentient? Really?" Let me share a story of our first dog, Frosty. I was there. I saw it.

Dad had decided to teach Frosty to fetch. Frosty already had an idea of games and chasing after something that was thrown, as he enjoyed playing touch football with me and my friends, but now Dad picked up a stick and showed it to Frosty. Then, he threw the stick across the yard. Frosty immediately grasped what the game was. He dashed across the yard, grabbed the stick and happily brought it back to my Dad. Game over. No. Dad now threw the stick again, and Frosty didn't move.

It would be foolish and arrogant for me to pretend I know what Frosty was thinking. What *is* clear is that Frosty was indeed thinking. Frosty looked to where the stick had landed and then back at my father. He stared at my father for a few moments more, then turned and walked away. To my knowledge, Frosty never fetched another stick or anything else Dad threw for him. A dog capable of fetching a stick once and then deciding not to a second time is sentient. I had been convinced that Frosty thought things through before. Now I had proof. So, when Pete and Phred also thought about things it came as no surprise. That their personalities were different also came as no surprise.

I will confess that for the longest time I dreamed of living on the ocean and making friends with a wild dolphin. But owning an animal is contrary to who I am. This respect for animals also entered into the way I looked at farming and how I dealt with food.

I had already given up eating mammals. Lambs, pigs, cattle, are all from the same family as we are! I stopped eating them in my twenties. I had loved bacon, as well as a good steak, but had given them up. Now I wanted to go further. I resolved to become a vegetarian though it would take me another ten years to make it—almost. Today I eat fish perhaps twice a month, for my health. I also will eat organic, free range chicken soup to help me recover if I've been quite ill. Otherwise, it's all grains, fruits and veggies. I also kept and still keep a large glass jar in my house for the express purpose of capturing and evicting spiders. I admire those who strive to kill neither animal nor insect but I haven't been able to go that far. I will still kill ants and cockroaches if I find them in the house. And while I will first try to encourage a fly to leave the house, if it won't I'm not above swatting. But that's pretty much it.

Still, I realized that how I ate was a distraction, which is why it went to the back burner for several years. Most important, I needed to heal. I repeated to myself that I had to let go of her. I joined a dating service that I believe was called Great Expectations, and actually went out on a few dates even before I moved. None of the dates went anywhere. But it was a start. And my membership was transferable to the Seattle area.

I also needed to start getting out of the blasted house. I began going to a place that I believe was called Verdi's. As I recall, the waitresses and waiters were all aspiring opera singers. If memory serves, once an hour they'd stop waiting tables and sing. I was still watching my outflow and it was too expensive to eat dinner there. But I would go to the bar and have a couple of drinks and listen to some music, more to get out than anything else. And I did learn something intriguing about how my body was aging now that I was in my mid to late thirties.

Up until then, my metabolism had always seemed on overdrive. Not only could I eat anything I wanted to and never gain an ounce, but I could also drink any amount of booze and never feel it. But now, at Verdi's and in my thirties, I learned the hard way that my metabolism had changed. On a whim I ordered something called a Mozart Zombie that had, I think, three different rums, one of them extremely high proof. I drank one Zombie, but couldn't quite finish the second. I went to the men's room to freshen up before listening to one last set.

When I returned to the table the waitress was aghast. She thought I'd left, and she'd taken the not-quite-finished zombie away. I told her it was no problem, but she quickly returned with another zombie, and being much too polite, I felt I had to drink it. Not a good idea. I made it home VERY slowly, driving only back streets. Things seemed ok until I lay down. Then the room began to spin madly, followed by, well, if you've ever been drunk, you know what followed. From that day on, I decided that I had a two-drink limit and stuck with it. I also realized that now if I ate a carton of ice cream, the calories, um, stayed with me. Metabolisms change! Good to know. Also, I was in fact capable of getting drunk. Also good to know. The last lesson was that I didn't like at all the feeling of being drunk. I like a clear mind. I didn't like racing to the bathroom with the room spinning.

After Pete died, I put the house up for sale, but it didn't sell fast enough for me. I wanted my new life and I wanted to begin it *now*. So I made a quick trip up to Edmonds, Washington, and found an apartment that would suit me. I also found a bank that seemed friendly (as I recall they called themselves The Neighborhood Bank). I decided that the realtor could sell my house without me present and left for Edmonds to start my new life.

Chapter Twenty-One

I moved to Edmonds, Washington, in January of 1989. The date is fixed in my memory for two wildly different reasons. The first is almost comical. I moved the second week of January, not on January first, so the state of California decided that I owed it income tax for January. That had never occurred to me, so I didn't file in California and thus incurred not only a tax but also a penalty and interest. Bureaucracy can be fun. The second reason this is fixed in my mind is far more important and tragic.

Just a few months after I had moved, and as I was settling in, a student-led movement in China occupied Tiananmen Square in Beijing. Watching the demonstrators exercise their voices and their rights was spectacular and so wonderful. It filled me with such hope as well as joy. They occupied the square for about seven weeks, demanding such things as free speech, a free press, and if not specifically democracy then certainly the fruits of it. I had cable in those days and was glued to my television. Could they pull it off? Could they? It looked like it. I was watching history unfold on my TV, and it felt so much like a modern-day Passover. People were claiming their right to be free, to live free. Imagine, a bloodless revolution in China! I dared to dream of what this might mean not just for the Chinese but for the world.

Then the government sent in the troops. They massacred the students and anyone who supported them. The movement was ended with an avalanche of bullets and bucket upon bucket of blood. Dream over—replaced by heartache. Thugs still ran China, and thugs do to this day. But the goals, the bravery and the fierce desire to be free evidenced by the students and their supporters was truly inspiring. Watching their story unfold had pushed a "pause" button on my life. But now it was time to move ahead, though to this day, as difficult as it is since so much is made there, I still try hard to find alternatives to buying anything "Made in China."

I searched for a lot to build my house, and as I did I began to rewire my life. I had always heard of people giving blood, but had never gotten around to it. Such a *simple* thing, but I'd never done it. Now I began to visit my local blood bank regularly and give. It turned out I had A+ blood, which for this very much of a B student was quite amusing. Such a simple but important way to help others: giving blood. One change down. I signed up as an "organ donor" on my driver's license. Another change down.

I went to Great Expectations and started using it for dating. That didn't seem to work out all that well, so I took out an ad in the Singles section of a weekly, rather liberal Seattle paper. I met some very interesting people through that. Intriguingly, at least to me, everyone I met through Great Expectations was a thundering dud. Everyone I met through the weekly paper was a really nice person—in the end not a good fit for me, but a truly nice person.

The biggest cultural shock was that for the first time in my life I was not simply visiting but actually living in a city where there weren't very many Jews. I recall showing my driver's license to a shop clerk as ID for a check I had written. He looked at the name. "Greenebaum. That's Jewish, isn't it?" That had never happened to me before. I was taken aback and said something brilliant like "Yeah." But the next comment floored me: "So why don't you wear that funny hat?" While seeming weird, that didn't bother me all that much. But a week or so later I was in a parking lot and saw a woman, slumped over her steering wheel, sobbing. Then my eyes took in the area near the trunk of her car, where someone had written in the accumulated dust "Jew bitch." I started to get out of my own car to go over to her, but at that moment she drove away.

What kind of a place have I moved to? I wondered. I decided it was time I learned what most Jews had to put up with all their lives. Besides, the scenery was beautiful. I realized that I'd been sheltered by living in the Los Angeles area, where Jews, while very much still a minority, are also very much a fixed part of the cultural landscape. Here, clearly, they weren't. Happily, these experiences weren't repeated with much frequency—though I quickly learned that it saved a lot of awkward moments to mention I was Jewish sooner than later when dating someone new.

But in point of fact, the residents seemed far more antagonistic to Californians than they were to Jews. I had been warned to switch license plates as soon as possible, but it wasn't soon enough. I got the finger and some rather pointed shouts from people as I passed in my car. The gestures and shouting ended the moment I got my Washington State license plate. There was a popular columnist at *The Seattle Times* who referred to anyone who moved from California to Seattle as a "Californicator." People all over the world are all the same. Here, prices for homes were going up, trees disappearing, and it had to be someone's fault. So Emmet Watson and his followers blamed anyone and everyone from California.

However, I soon learned that there was a more basic underlying problem. It lay with housing codes stacked in favor of maximum profit for builders and little or no regard for such minor things as nature, trees, traffic, sewers, whatever. The future seemed irrelevant to the builders and the politicians they owned. While transplants from California had indeed helped to drive up prices, they were more of a convenient scapegoat than a cause. Sound familiar?

"If it's green, pave it" seemed to be the slogan. Thanks to really bad planning, the whole area around Seattle seemed on the road to becoming another over-built, smog-infested and overly congested Los Angeles. So I became involved.

The most straightforward part was finding a lot and building a house that would be constructed using good building practices. I found a lovely lot on a bluff that overlooked the Puget Sound. I found an architect who was in tune with what I wanted to build (an English Tudor-style two-story home) and, most important, a builder who would respect my wishes for an ecologically oriented house (well, as best as 1990 had and I could afford). Important, we didn't cut into the land and left the trees standing (besides planting a redwood of my own). The most unusual part of the house construction didn't hit me until later. The builder, Ryan Payne, and I made the deal on a handshake. Skeptics notwithstanding, the house was built beautifully and on budget. Ryan was not only an excellent builder but scrupulously honest. It never occurred to me I needed anything more from him than a handshake and I never did.

There was one hugely awkward moment as the house was being built. But that wasn't Ryan's fault. One thing I'd always dreamed of was having a hearth in my kitchen—a large, inviting, wood-burning hearth. Ryan hired a mason who specialized in such things and the result was truly beautiful. It was just what I had wanted, almost storybook, with a large kettle poised over the logs. Ryan, the mason, and I were there to admire the finished work. Then, it happened.

"Big enough to roast Jews!" the mason beamed.

I was stunned into complete silence. Ryan took the mason aside, and I could see them talking. I never learned what they said, but I've always guessed that Ryan asked the mason if he ever wanted to work for him again. Whatever the reason, the mason came over to me and apologized. That ended it. I never saw the mason again. Ryan and I remained friends.

By 1991, I had a beautiful new house. It was large enough for a family, should I ever acquire one, and gave me a true home. I'd designed it (and a dedicated architect named Karen Weisman had taken my "designs" and turned them into something that would actually work!). The mason notwithstanding, I loved sitting in the kitchen near the hearth, reading a book or listening to music. I truly felt rooted and it felt amazing. Now, just two years into my move, I felt comfortable and ready to do—what?

I became aware of and decided to join Seattle's Early Music Guild. As you may recall, Renaissance and Baroque music, particularly choral music, had been a favorite of mine. Here was a chance to expand my knowledge and GET OUT OF THE HOUSE as well as meet people! So I not only went to EMG concerts but became part of the guild itself—and was immediately made chair of the publicity committee. I did that for one year before being asked to become president. Me? Ok then.

The executive director was Maria Coldwell, who was a consummate professional and quickly became a friend as well. Still, me, president of the Early Music Guild. That's getting out of the house with a vengeance!! I think I lasted three years on the job before deciding I really needed to move on. But in the interim, I heard a lot of wonderful music and met a lot of great people. It was working. My new life was working.

Sort of.

My attempts at dating hadn't gone particularly well. My dates hadn't led to romance, but I did make some new friends through my efforts: particularly Kim and Cheryl. Both became rather important to me in very different and unfortunately tragic ways.

I met Kim at an otherwise rather dull party and we immediately hit it off. I asked her out and she hesitated. Then she rather calmly told me she was dying and that romance just wasn't in the cards. Still, we quickly became good friends. We tended to talk about rather deep subjects. Kim called me her *My Dinner with Andre* friend, a reference to a movie we had both enjoyed. I think she was rather taken aback but also pleased that I was willing to put the time and effort into a friendship with no romance in the cards and the end a forgone conclusion. In a nutshell, her doctors had blown it. Her initial surgery wasn't completely successful, and the recurrence of her cancer hadn't been caught in time. As I recall, a second surgery had bought her some extra time but that was all.

I think I was a good companion for her, until close to the end. She and I saw a lot of each other and we talked our way through an amazing number of things. Then, at the very end, I blew it. Kim needed me up and positive, and during those last few days of her life I was down and rather somber. NOT a good companion for someone who is dying. Kim, quite rightly, gave me the boot the day before she died. It hurt at the time, but she was right. She didn't need someone mourning her before she was gone, for crying out loud! I learned a lot from this. I've been able to help others as they prepared for death since then, but I was no help to Kim in her last days.

It didn't dawn on me until long after Kim's death why it had been so important to me to stay with her those final months. Yes, we were friends, but my motivation was deeper and less pure than that. Twenty years before, I hadn't been able to be there. I hadn't been able to comfort the single most important person in my life. She'd died alone. This was my chance to be there for a friend going through what has to be among the hardest passages we humans make.

A second friend I made and kept for some time was Cheryl. We dated at first. But there was no use to it. I liked her and she liked me, but there was no spark. We were meant to be friends and, happily, agreed on that. For a while we saw each other frequently, and by that I mean perhaps once a month or so for lunch. We chatted about a host of things. But over time we drifted apart and saw each other perhaps twice a year. Then, one day I found out that she had gotten into her car, fixed it so that her exhaust would re-enter her car and then turned on the ignition. She had killed herself. I had never had a friend kill him–or herself before. It was devastating.

At first, I was mad at her for not reaching out to me. Why on earth didn't she call? Then I became even more furious with myself. I replayed in my head our last lunch together and our last phone call, and now saw everything she had said and done as an "indicator" that she was unhappy. Why hadn't I picked up on it? Why hadn't I seen this coming? Good grief, I told myself, you only see her a couple of times a year, how could you know? Yes, I felt I should have known. I was her friend. I should have been able to do something. I carried that intense feeling of guilt for months.

That the suicide of someone I was friends with but not particularly close to could affect me so strongly was a huge lesson for me. How huge is for later.

In the meantime, while my love life was not going anywhere, my activity in environmental politics was. Soon, it wasn't just environmental politics. In late 1991, Senator Paul Tsongas was running for president. Up to that moment, I always registered independent or, as California listed it, "Decline to state." But here was Tsongas preaching fiscal conservatism as well as social liberalism. His point had always been mine: we need to help one another, and we need especially to help those who are struggling to make it. We also need to be honest about the costs, and we need to pay for it—and not with a credit card. This was the first time I'd heard a Democrat talk like that. I decided not only to support Tsongas but also to become active in the Democratic Party.

This would involve REALLY getting out of the house!

Chapter Twenty-Two

I was all ready to join the Tsongas campaign in my area. The only problem was that there wasn't a Tsongas campaign in my area. So why doesn't someone—oh, crap. Fine. I organized one. This was even harder than I thought it would be as the Tsongas Washington campaign seemed, well, screwy. In the course of flailing around trying to figure out what to do, I met James Arima, who lived in Tacoma and was having similar difficulties. We helped each other survive, and get our efforts moving. We became good friends.

This was my first presidential campaign in the state of Washington. Washington has a caucus system rather than a primary for the nominating of candidates for president. People backing the Democrats met in one place, Republicans in another. I gave a short speech in favor of Tsongas. The next thing I knew I'd been elected a delegate to the state convention. Then I was elected as a delegate to the national convention. Me! So was my friend James. It was really rather surprising, but also rather exciting and fun—mostly.

The national convention in New York was a spiritual eye-opener. There are people who enjoy power. They enjoy the recognition, but even more they enjoy exercising their will over others, and they seem to get high on it. As I got deeper into politics over the next several years this trait was confirmed for me. At first it was only a hunch, but it seemed to me that the best people in politics were at the grassroots. And the higher up the food chain you got, the more likely you were to meet corrupted, self-absorbed, power-mad creatures, with little of their humanity left.

One simple example, as this is a spiritual memoir, not a book on politics. A prominent member of our delegation, let's call her Angela, came to us before the first vote at the convention and told us that for the sake of unity we needed to vote for Bill Clinton. I rebelled. The people who had voted for me as their representative had voted for me as a Tsongas delegate. If and when Tsongas lost in the balloting, sure, I'd vote for the winner, undoubtedly Bill Clinton, so that the final vote could be unanimous. But I owed Paul Tsongas and the people who voted for me to represent them to vote for Tsongas on the first ballot. As it turned out, I brought some other delegates with me. In the end, unable to hand over a unanimous Washington delegation to Clinton as she had evidently promised someone, Angela backed down. When that first vote came, all of us, including Angela, voted for Tsongas.

After the vote, Angela angrily screamed at me that I'd never go anywhere in politics. More than that, my friend James told me that after the convention she'd met with Tsongas and bragged that she'd held us all together for him for the first ballot. Such is the nature of politics and the people who are drawn to it.

When I got home, I got involved in a local campaign. As the campaign manager became ill, I ended up running a part of the campaign—under the firm direction of the ill campaign manager. In one year, I had gotten a rather thorough immersion into politics.

One of the things I realized, working on the local campaign, was that there wasn't a handbook for new people to follow that would help them as they got involved. So, I set about writing one. In so doing, I met a woman I'll call Kate.

Kate was a firebrand, a force of nature. As we worked together on the handbook, she kept inviting me into her life. And I kept wondering if I was ready. Kate, in some ways, reminded me of her. Kate was not given to convention. She was passionate about her belief in justice. And, well, she took the first bold steps of turning our friendship into something more.

It was now, after 20 years, that I at last stopped saying "her." I said Maria's name out loud. I told Kate about her. We began to become much closer. We became intimate. Not unreasonably, Kate wanted to know if I could commit to her. I wasn't sure. I needed a few days to think about it.

I took those days, and in the end decided I really was ready to move on. I felt ready to commit to someone other than Maria. I could do this. Hallelujah! I could do this! What a wonderful feeling it was. I had my new life, my new house and my new love. There really are second chances in life. There really are! I called Kate, we met, and everything fell apart.

Kate informed me that she hadn't been able to wait for me to decide. There was someone else in her life, and she was committed to him. Sorry.

I was stupefied and started to weep—in a public coffee house. She told me to "man up." Ok then. We parted company—in every conceivable way.

I went home, my spirit completely demolished. A part of me already knew that Kate wasn't right for me. I mean, good grief, if she wanted to commit to me one day but just a few days later was in love with someone else, we were *not* right for each other. So there I was, with my entire life seemingly thrown in my face.

There were no second chances. That was the lesson. That's what was clear. This new life I was so excited about—it was all an illusion. I don't know if I can possibly describe the hurt, the sense of uselessness and the overwhelming sense of the futility of my continuing to live that now took hold of me. What was the point? There was none. There was no point to anything, and surely there was no point to living a life this painful day after day after day. It was time to stop. It was time for the hurting to end.

After perhaps a week of a downward spiral, I went about putting things in order. I wanted the hurt to be over, but I didn't want to leave a mess behind. I hadn't written a poem in quite some time, but now I felt called to it. I wrote it, typed it up and printed it. It would be my goodbye. Except for changing the names, this is the poem as I wrote it.

No Second Chance

It sits there, etched upon my mind,
In vivid, uncompromising colors.
The when, and how, and who,
All these, but never why.
For that there is no answer;
Only the empty echo of some demon's giggle.
I remember all as if yesterday.
But, of course, it wasn't.
The years have ambled by
Casually, en masse,
Like autumned leaves,
Drifting without form
In a light, unyielding wind.
Persistent.

Adamant.
Untouched.
And yet, tonight, the thoughts are not of yesteryear
But yesterday.
For once again the door was opened.
On hinges badly rusted, that I thought quite immobile,
You swung it wide sweet Kate.
And now that it's slammed shut again,
The dark reminds an aching soul
Of what it is to feel,
To hope,
To lose.
I find myself at war,
For part of me,
From some misguided habit,
Wishes to continue on. Still: on.
But much of me retreats
To images and thoughts and happenings
That though they unwound years ago
Remain for me the most dear of all experiences.

Maria,
It seems we both died years ago.
I merely went on breathing.
Such a waste of air.

I put the poem on the table and went downstairs. I left the garage door closed and got into my car. I got my key out and placed it in the ignition. Then I stopped. My friend Cheryl had taken her own life some five or six months before this. It suddenly flashed in my mind what I would be doing to my friends if I took my life. Yes, I hurt. I hurt horribly, but how could I inflict that kind of pain on my friends, whose only sin was to care about me? Was I really that far gone? Was I truly that selfish? No, I decided. I wasn't. I withdrew my key, got out of the car and went back upstairs. Now what? If I was going to continue living, now what? First, sleep on it! Then some heavy-duty work was in order.

The next morning things seemed clearer. I needed a plan. I needed a concrete, doable plan—and the first order of business was both to ac-knowledge that I hurt and that it was ok to hurt. One thing our insane culture teaches us is that we're supposed to be happy. Always! And if we're not happy we're to pop a pill or buy somebody's product to make us feel better. But some days are just rotten. They are. Some experiences are freaking terrible. When that happens, it's not simply "ok" to feel bad, it's very un-ok not to. So, my first step in survival was to give myself permission to be unhappy. A day. A week. A year. Whatever. My immediate goal was to stay alive and not hurt my friends, and that meant allowing myself the "luxury" of feeling truly miserable if indeed that's how I felt.

As I thought about this, I realized just how human but hugely wrong I'd been in beating myself up over not somehow knowing that Cheryl was in trouble. I don't remember who, but I know I talked to at least two friends that day I had decided to end the hurting. Neither one of them picked up anything. Beat themselves up all they wanted, they would never have been truly able to understand what I was going through that day—because there was no way to express it.

I had been in an emotional black hole, with everything bending in-ward—nothing escaping. I didn't call out for help because I didn't want help. I didn't want help, and I didn't want reassurance. All I wanted was for the pain to stop, and there seemed only one answer to that. Obviously, a part of me still wanted to live, or I wouldn't have been able to break free from that single thought and realize how much hurt I would cause. So, I was lucky.

I also thought it would be important to stay in touch with my feel-ings. For 20 years I'd denied my feelings, and doing so had brought me to the very brink of suicide. So, I would chronicle my healing. I would try to write a poem a week, if not more often. Stay in touch with who you are, I told myself. Don't lose yourself again. I wrote poems from January through September. I won't inflict them all on the reader, but a few might show some insight, so a select few along the way. The first two were written just days later. The second one, "Boom," was written with an eye toward push-ing a smile back onto my face.

SLAM

When they speak of second chances,
Be careful of the door.
For it may close with blinding speed
That you're not ready for.

BOOM

My candle burns at both its ends,
For I've no time to diddle.
But damn you, you've just blown apart
My well protected middle!

The next poem was written ten days later. I was beginning to pick up my life again. Slowly. Very slowly. I wasn't hurting so much these days as simply not feeling.

QUESTION

It's a strangely quiet sensation
When the heart shuts down.
Cool, and dry and white;
But without brightness.
The mind works well enough,
But nothing inside feels.
And little outside matters.
Curiosity remains though.
Detached.
Aloof.

Numb, yet curious —
An oddball combination
For an oddball time.
I ponder the time it takes to heal,
And question if every mood's a "stage,"
And idly, without vested interest,
Like some lab tech with his petri dish,
Wonder how long it takes
To trust again;
For never's far too pat an answer.

It wasn't that all thoughts of suicide had vanished. They hadn't. But now I was better prepared for them.

DARKNESS

A thick and starless ink inspects me
Unblinking through my window.

And I stare back as best I can.
Toe to toe.

Tequila helps,
Though not as much as yesterday.
Time has disappeared,
In lime and salt and cactus.
Not the ache.
Just time.

But after a month of this I was feeling well enough to stick it to myself.
I had put so much of my life on one roll of the dice: Kate. When it came up
snake eyes, I'd crumbled. It was time for a little humor at my own expense.

SO?

So.
No one else has ever had his
Heart handed back to him
Minced upon a platter –
A sprig of parsley on the side
For color.

So.
You're the only person
Who ever had a friend who wasn't,
Who ever trusted inopportunely,
Who played by rules others ignored.
Tragic.

So.
You fucked up, fella.
Now what?
You've forty years to go,
Or more,
Unless you slit your throat.
Messy!

So.

Ok. Partly In response to the question "so?" I felt I needed to do something more specific to help myself. What? I decided on a mantra, something I could repeat every day, something to remind me to keep looking ahead, not behind. I again took my cue from Greek mythology, the story of the phoenix that rises from its own ashes to be reborn. I had truly crashed and burned. This time I hoped for a true rebirth. The mantra would be "Out of the ashes, hope." To help it feel special, I wanted the mantra to be in Greek, not English. So, I asked a Greek friend for help. "Apo tis stahtes, elpis." I repeated it every day; sometimes many, many times. And it helped. I really don't know why, but it helped a lot.

This was my year. I worked my way through it. Once I was no longer feeling pain, I was feeling anger. Then, come September, I realized I was truly back.

AWAKENING

The anger has long abated.
And depression is at last
Evicted from its parasitic lair.
Soul intact,
I begin to look about
And notice: life.
Intriguing.

Finally, finally, I was ready to move on with my life. I began to re-engage with the world, and in particular the world of environmental politics. The rape of the land was proceeding, and I felt I could be of use.

Healing still took time, but now I was taking active steps to actually get there. One of the things I did was start to talk to my friends about Maria. My friend Candy took it particularly hard. Why did I shut her out? she wanted to know. How could I have kept this from her—for more than 20 years? I not only told my close friends but all friends, and then it seemed once I started talking about it I couldn't stop. It was almost, "How do you do. My name is Steven. Let me tell you about Maria." Happily, that stage ended, and the healing continued.

The big moment came when I started to think of myself not as a man who'd lost the woman he hoped to marry, but as a widower. Ok, we hadn't actually married, but we had intended to. For reasons that only a psychologist can answer, it was once I considered myself a widower that I was truly able to move on. I remembered my Uncle Jerry (the hugger!). He loved his first wife Dorothy. He loved her deeply. There was never any doubt of that. Yet a year after she had suddenly died, Jerry found another wonderful woman, Elizabeth, and married her. Dorothy and Elizabeth were both fantastic people, and Jerry loved them both. I so envied him that. Two great women in one life! Somehow, it was the fact of Maria and I having an unresolved relationship that seemed to make things so hard for me. Thinking of myself as a widower somehow truly gave me permission to move on without feeling that I was being unfaithful.

It took me more than 25 years to get there, and I don't recommend it. The truth of it is that a person can't will him or herself to heal, no matter how strong or independent they think they are. I have shared this in such detail because I urge you, the reader, to get help if you experience a loss (for most of us it's not so much "if" but "when"), I would urge you to seek and get help. Professional help. Don't let it take more than twenty-five years to begin to heal. That's too long. And life's too short.

Steven Greenebaum

Chapter Twenty-Three

One of the most important parts of re-engaging was contacting friends. Some were friends from Oxy that I'd lost touch with over the years. In particular that meant reconnecting with three good friends—Faye, Nancy and Elaine—whom I'd let disappear from my life. Then there were friends from my choral conducting days at First Church, particularly Ken and Marian and another Elaine. My friends Dennis and Maryel remained close, as did Tom and Candy. The same with Jim and Barbara, from my days singing at the Santa Monica Methodist Church. Don and Vicki also remained close, and Vicki and I became even closer after Don died. Indeed, Vicki became not only my closest friend but also my confidante. "Just don't make me your surrogate mom," she cautioned me. I never did. But we talked at least once a week on the phone, and Vicki became my sounding board for any new thought.

What all of this meant was that I was at last breaking free of my decades-old, self-imposed exile. Not only was I making new friends, but also warmly inviting my old friends back into my life. It felt wonderful.

As I was re-engaging with the world, I became active again in the Democratic Party in my area and was soon the vice chair of our local district. I had briefly flirted with the idea of running for office before my implosion, but those thoughts were gone. Instead I decided to take on the Democratic Party in Washington State! My friend James brought me up to speed about an incident in Spokane that, as I recall, had taken place roughly a year before. There had been a Democratic function where a modestly high-ranking Democrat had publicly uttered an ethnic slur. Stuff happens, as they say. The slur was real and frankly rather disgusting, but for me the bigger problem was how people who should have known better reacted to it.

Rather than apologize or deal with the person who had uttered the ethnic slur, the Democratic Party, including its Washington State chair, had been busy covering it up—the classic ostrich approach, sticking its head in the sand and believing that if we ignore a problem it will just go away. This felt crazy to me as well as bigoted and I began talking about it at Democratic meetings. But most people wanted to pretend it never happened and "move on." I frequently found myself booed.

So, I wrote an article about it for a local Democratic paper. The article was reprinted in the *Northwest Asian Weekly*. Then I managed to bring the issue before a dedicated woman named Lois Clements, the chair of the Washington Democratic district organizations. I introduced her to James, who laid out for her the whole disquieting mess. Lois listened and cared. More than that, she was in a position to get things done! Soon the issue became unavoidable and eventually, thanks to the tenacity of James, Lois and several other stalwarts, the state party at long last apologized. What this whole thing confirmed for me once more was that our political parties, both of them, at least at the top, house people who like and value power far more than they actually want to change or better the world.

This was confirmed for me yet again the following year as I was suddenly hip-deep in environmental issues. In Snohomish County, where I live, environmental protection seemed extremely weak. We lacked building codes that considered the effect our "build, build, build" world was having both on the environment and people's lives. I felt I needed to be involved. So, I did my homework and soon found myself making presentations at Democrat meetings and testifying in front of the county council.

Then, I got a phone call from someone I had met at one of the Democrat meetings. One of the most obstinately pro-development county council members was a Democrat, Swede Johnson. An environmentalist named Dave Somers wanted to challenge Swede in the primary, but the Democratic establishment was rallying around Swede. Dave needed a campaign manager. Me? Oh, good grief! But, if you're not going to leap in, then what's the point? So I met with Dave and said Yes.

There were some spiritual learnings that have a place here.

First, it was quickly confirmed that I was asked out of desperation. No one else wanted the job. Worse, whoever took on trying to defeat a sitting Democrat in a Democratic primary was going to be toast in the party. But

Swede really was NOT a friend of the environment and "somebody" had to take on the job. So, I stayed and got down to work.

The truth is, I had some wonderful people working with me. Again, proof that it's at the grassroots where you meet the people who truly warm your heart. I want to mention three of them by name: Meredith Mechling, Kay McDonald, and C.J. Heirman. There were many others who helped, who were crucial to the campaign, who contributed time, money, and knowledge—indeed there was an entire organization involved in helping, called Washington Conservation Voters—but these three women brought such energy and dedication to the campaign and such joy into my life. I want to thank them. Meredith's husband Marc was also of great help,[31] as was C.J.'s husband Bob but it was these three women who worked with me so tirelessly.

We got organized and outmaneuvered both the party brass and Swede's people at a Democratic organization meeting, where we got the grassroots, active Democrats to endorse insurgent Dave Somers for county council. Then came the campaign itself.

The Republicans threw their support to Swede, but we out-hustled, out-thought and out-campaigned him. We trounced him in the primary, even with his Republican support. This meant that after the primary there was no Republican running! Of course, a "write-in" Republican candidate appeared, but we trounced her too.

My next lesson came after the election, when I thought Dave was going to name me his administrative assistant. Instead, I was politely but firmly shown the door. Ok then, moving right along. One door closes....

It seemed to me that we'd had to work much too hard to raise money for Dave's campaign. The organized money was on the other side. The Master Builders and so on. So I now founded an environmental Political Action Committee, to raise money and support candidates for office in our county who believed in leaving something for the children to enjoy. It became known as CER-PAC, or Citizens for Environmental Responsibility-Political Action Committee. This was also a huge learning experience as I'd never done anything like it before. But within a year we had raised enough money to become a major player in Snohomish County. Cool.

The learning here came in the form of people who previously could not have been bothered to give me the time of day, but who suddenly now stopped me in the Snohomish County Courthouse to ask how I was and

---

31   Marc's dedication to good government, open government, would later lead him to run for a seat on Monroe's city council. I was pleased be able to help him chart his campaign.

pass the time. People in politics in the area answered all my phone calls. I could meet with anyone I wanted to—all because I was successful in raising money. I only lasted two, maybe three years before I resigned in disgust. What amazed me was the astonishment so many folks expressed when I resigned. I had power. I had a good deal of power. How could I just walk away?

How could I walk away? Because politics proved to be about money and power and only that. Our politics is sick, perhaps terminally ill. There may be multiple cancers afflicting our politics today, but certainly two of the deadliest are money and an attraction to power. Most of our politicians,[32] Democrats and Republicans, are addicted to dollars—and like any addict, they will betray themselves, their families and all who believe in them in search of the next fix. I couldn't do this. I couldn't be a part of this corrupt, disgusting system, even in the name of a good cause. I'd been taught by my father, and so many others, "What you do really well, you like. And what you like, you'll do really well." Not true. For whatever reason, I was very, very good at politics though I found them loathsome. There was no way I could respect myself if I stayed involved, so I walked away.

This gave me time to get back to work on my Roman novel. I spent a lot of time on it. Up to now, I'd only written when I could find the time. Now I spent another two years writing it, full time. The book was well over a thousand pages long before I realized I really wasn't capable of doing the topic justice. At least not yet. And as I was coming to this realization, I needed to focus my attention on my father—so I put the book away.

Dad's health had been deteriorating slowly. Now it was deteriorating quickly. Again, I didn't much like my dad, but I did love him. He was my father. More than that, I knew that he had lived the best life he could. He was scrupulously honest and did his best to instill that honesty in me. He was an avid reader and had passed that curiosity and love of learning along to me as well. He had not only been a Scoutmaster, but the (volunteer) president of the Reiss-Davis Clinic for Child Guidance (dedicated to helping troubled youth), teaching me that supporting a charity meant being active as well as writing checks. His wholehearted embrace of patriarchy, and how that had impacted Mom, had built a wall between us that would never crumble. But that did not blind me to the good he had tried to do with his life. I could not and would not turn my back on him.

I was taking train trips down to Los Angeles to visit him at least twice a year. Once I had to make a quick trip down because he needed an opera-

---

32 Not all, by some miracle, but most.

tion and there was a blood shortage. Dad and I had the same blood type, so I went down and donated.

Dad realized he wouldn't be alive a lot longer, and that weighed on him. For one thing, he wanted me to be the executor of his estate when he died. I firmly told him no. I refused him several more times before it became clear that it was my duty as his son to do this for him. Dad was afraid that after his death my sister would go after his second wife, Jean. He had no one else he thought he could turn to, so I relented.

I don't recall all the ins and outs, but I think Dad and Jean divided up the estate long before Dad died. As I recall, Dad turned half of all he owned over to Jean while he was still alive. This meant that when he died, what remained would go to pay his debts and his charitable bequests, and then the residue would be split between my sister and me. A part of this seemed like self-protection by Jean.

My father had cherished the time in his life when he was quite well off and had rubbed shoulders with the rich and famous at the Beverly Hills Country Club. But half of what he had went to Mom in the divorce. Then he ran into business problems and money got tight. And then half of what little remained had gone to Jean even before his death. Dad became increasingly frantic to regain his wealth and dumped money into a number of schemes in hopes of becoming rich again. Instead, he became even less wealthy. For a man like my father, losing wealth and position like this was humiliating.

Then dementia crept in—and I mean it *crept* in. Dad knew it was happening, and we talked about it on at least one of my visits. I truly felt sorry for him. For my father, a man for whom emotions were only a sign of weakness, his mind was all he ever really had, the one thing he relied on and valued. As he felt his mind slipping away from him, he felt his value as a human being slipping away, too. Meanwhile, he had something I believe was called "smoldering leukemia" that was slowly taking his life even as dementia was taking his mind.

For reasons I can no longer recall, when it became clear that Dad needed to be in a place that could care for him around the clock, Jean found him a place in San Jose, not Los Angeles, where they lived. She moved Dad up there and then started preparing to move up herself. For several weeks if not a few months, Dad was in a home in San Jose while Jean was tying up loose ends in Los Angeles, 340 miles to the south. I decided to take the train down to San Jose and try to fill at least a little of the void.

I got down to San Jose and had a good visit with Dad on that first day. My friend Richard, the same friend who had put his practice on hold when my mother died, lived in nearby Santa Cruz and acted as my chauffeur. I spent the night at Richard's but the next morning we got a call. Dad had died. The rest is a bit fuzzy. I remember Jean coming up to San Jose. There was a memorial service. Then I was back on the train home.

My duties as executor were quite straightforward this time. With the exception of a lot of credit-card debt, most of Dad's affairs had been put in order when he went to the home. As I'd surmised, he had pretty much blown through his wealth. There was very little left. It did not take long to sort things out. I was exceedingly careful as I knew I'd come under scrutiny from my sister. I also knew that she and my father had had virtually no relationship for years so it might well have come as news to her that there wasn't going to be much for her to inherit.

As it turned out, this finished the rupture between my sister and me. She couldn't believe Dad had so little to leave her. She wanted an independent auditor to examine everything I had done as executor. The audit was done. I was found to have acted with complete honesty and was able to account for every penny. That ended the audit, and I have not spoken with my sister since. I do not wish her ill—indeed, I hope she is happy. She's still family. As long as she is not a part of my life, I truly wish her all the best.

Yet, this was hardly the biggest conflict. To this day, it seems strange to me that it was my father's death that proved to be the final spiritual straw for me. Perhaps this is because Dad's death angered rather than saddened me. My deepest emotions were pretty much under control. Perhaps that's why things at long last came to a head between God and me.

I had been devastated by Maria's death, which had thrown my life into complete turmoil. Here was this wonderful young woman, preparing to spend her life in the service of humanity, snatched away in an instant. Here was the woman I had intended to be with the rest of my life, annihilated in a damned traffic accident. One minute there, the next gone forever.

I had been totally thrown by my mother's death as well. The injustice of it was so stark. Mom had finally put her life together and was truly enjoying it when cancer struck her down. Not without a fight—she beat it back twice before finally succumbing. Here was the mother I had always dreamed of, becoming the person I had always dreamed she could be, and barely had I had the chance to get to know her when she too was gone.

With my father's death, there was far less emotional baggage. Perhaps that's why I processed it so differently. Still, the injustice of it hit me hard.

Here was a repressed man who really had nothing going for him but his mind. So how did he die? Little by little, slowly enough so he knew exactly what was happening, his mind was taken from him. That was the final straw.

I told a few close friends, but mostly this was something I uttered in the privacy of my own home. There's a God? Really?? There's some kind of divine plan? Really?? For several months, I would mutter at least once almost every day, "God, if you're there—you want to send me to hell? Fine. Send me to hell! But first I want five minutes, and I want some answers!"

At the beginning of this book, I mentioned that there were five truly transformative spiritual events in my life. Thus far I've described four. Two from my childhood: first, learning of the Shoah and second, hearing what I believed to be the voice of God and thinking I had rejected it. The third was the death of Maria and my reaction to it, and the fourth, the death of my mom. Now, when I demanded five minutes with God and some answers, came the fifth event.

Steven Greenebaum

Part Three: One Family: Indivisible

Steven Greenebaum

Chapter Twenty-Four

Five or six months later I was walking down the stairs of my house, yet again muttering my angry message to God: "If you're there, do with me what you like afterward, but I want five minutes, and I want answers!" Now, after a silence of almost 40 years, the still small voice that I'd heard once before back when I was about 12 returned. "Get a pen," I heard clearly in my head. "Get some paper. Write." So, I got the pen and some paper, and then, well, I took dictation. It had never happened to me before nor has it happened since. Below is what I wrote, with one word changed that I'll explain later.

Religion is but a language for speaking to Me. Think ye that arbol *is "better" than* tree? *Was old English a "false language" because you now speak modern English?*

You have misconstrued hell and heaven. Those who separate themselves from Me in life will be separated from Me in death. No more. No less.

Go ye into all the world and preach MY gospel to every creature—not Matthew's, not Mark's, Luke's, John's or Paul's.

I have imbued every religion with truth. You have imbued every religion with magic.

Jesus did not die for your sins. He died of your sins.

Cleanse yourselves. Jesus, Moses, Muhammad, the Buddha—they all can provide you soap. But yours is the responsibility for cleansing yourself.

Jesus was a teacher I sent you. I loved him as a son, but I am God.

You cannot value wealth and love Me. You cannot worship power and be welcome in My home.

Lift a hand against another, and you lift your hand against Me.

Separate the criminal from you, but lift not your hand against him except to defend yourself. Vengeance is Mine. Protect yourselves from harm, but seek not revenge. If you would love Me, love my creation.

Open your hearts to those in need. Think ye that I cannot see? Think ye a phrase muttered in church or mosque or synagogue can hide from Me the truth of your heart?

Yours is not to judge! Yours is to love and help one another.

You have made my creation a sewer and worshipped wealth. Your greed condemns you.

You cannot live forever. But you can be with Me forever. Time is your measure, not Mine.

The mind is not the soul. Nor is the body. Sometimes, the mind decays or the body writhes with pain before the soul has left it. That is indeed a tragedy. Weep, but do not despair.

Love life. Cherish it. Seek to make life better for all within your ability to do so. But life is only a beginning. You but crawl. Do not despise yourselves for crawling. But never fear or forget that as a loving parent I hope one day to walk with you.

Many have spoken for Me. They were righteous, and they did carry My words. But I am not human, and you are not God. Language can be a barrier between us as well as yourselves that can be all but impossible to breach.

Seek truth in the commonality of religions—which are but the languages of speaking to Me. Worship not the grammar.

Think ye I prize green eyes over blue? Brown hair over blond? How can you say I would favor one gender over the other, or hold one race as special unto Me and in the same breath pretend you love Me? To hate My creation is to hate Me. To despise My creation is to despise Me.

My children are My children and I love them all. How dare you think I would choose between them?

THIS is My commandment. Seek none harm. Love the diversity of your brothers and sisters.

This above all. For so long as you put yourself before others, so long will you lose yourself and your way and increase the distance between us.

That which breathes has a soul. Think ye you understand the space wherein I live? Your universe fills not my fist...nor I it.

Ye who seek to live forever shall die. Ye who seek to live well shall crumble. Ye who seek to live in harmony with all shall know what it is to be blessed.

You cannot love Me and hate your neighbor.

I speak not to command, but so you may know.

Ok then. Prayer answered. Ball in my court. *Now what?*

The one word that I changed, I changed several years later—and the fact that the word needed changing taught me a lot. The word is "magic." When I first wrote it down, the word I wrote was "mysticism." Why? Because at the time I believe I drew no distinction between mysticism and magic. It wasn't until I met a deeply profound and wonderful mystic, one of my teachers at seminary, Sister Alexandra Kovats, that I realized there was a profound difference between the words, and that what I should have written was "magic."

What this tells me is that we can only hear words in relationship to what we already know and believe. When we look at sacred Scripture and indeed what others have written, it is important to remember that they and I can only write within the context of what we know. So, assuming that indeed God communicated with the ancients, be they Hebrews, Greeks, Romans, Indians, Chinese, African, New World, whomever, God can only communicate in ways that we can grasp. To look upon the Scripture that is then assembled as unchangeable is a mistake. God's message of love does not change, but we do!

Along that same line, the punctuation is all mine. I take full responsibility. It's my interpretation of what I heard. If someone later reads this and gets hung up on the punctuation, good grief! It's *me*. All I could do was interpret as best as I could what was communicated to me. Could I have gotten something wrong? *Yes*. I clearly got the word "mystic" wrong. As I began to understand and come to grips with this, I better understood how our approach to Scripture and any other sacred text needs to be carefully practiced.

Another thing the dictation taught me was that the way I hear God clearly comes out of Jewish Scripture as I learned it. I do not speak in Thee's and Ye's, but that's how I heard the dictation. Why? I can only guess. But my guess is that this was how I expected God to speak, and God met me where I lived. Along the same line, why was the example of the Spanish word *arbol* used? I can only suggest that it is because I know Spanish. Indeed, Spanish is the only language other than English that I have ever mastered. So, the example of a different language *had* to be from Spanish, or I wouldn't have understood it.

There is also the matter of *creation*. "To hate My creation is to hate Me." There are other examples of the word *creation* as well. What to make of that? I don't know; that's the honest answer. I think science is science, and right now the "Big Bang" and evolution appear to be the best scientific answers to how we've come to be here. I have long perceived and related to God as Cosmic Conscience, not a "hands-on" creator. I've never been one to take *Genesis* literally, so what to do with "To hate My creation is to hate Me" is something of a mystery to me—a mystery I'm willing to live with. Perhaps God was being metaphorical; perhaps not. Sometimes, I think, it is better to live with a mystery than to try to impose an answer to it based on what is admittedly limited knowledge.

Most of these understandings came later, as I lived with and pondered the dictation. What happened that afternoon was that I wrote what I heard and then read and reread it—again and again. What leapt out at me was that the questions that most oppressed my mind at that moment didn't even come up in the dictation until halfway through: "The mind is not the soul. Nor is the body. Sometimes the mind decays or the body writhes with pain before the soul has left it. That is indeed a tragedy. Weep, but do not despair."

"Weep, but do not despair." Simple words, but they were hugely comforting to me.

"But life is only a beginning. You but crawl. Do not despise yourselves for crawling. But never fear or forget that as a loving parent I hope one day to walk with you."

This, too, was hugely comforting.

Even so, most of the dictation concerned subjects I realized I hadn't been ready to deal with when I was a child. Now, it seemed, I was. And clearly it was aimed at an audience larger than myself. The question became, what do I do about it? Some of it felt like "old news." Some of it was startlingly new, but once I heard it, it made perfect sense. Some of it took a lot of living with to understand. Beyond the question of "creation," there remains this: "Think ye you understand the space wherein I live? Your universe fills not my fist—nor I it." For me, that still needs some pondering.

But what should I do? It's one thing to ask for guidance. It's another to actually get it!

I wanted to tell Vicki but couldn't at first. Once I recovered from the shock of receiving the dictation, the only person I felt I could share it with was my friend and mentor Rev. Wes Yamaka, the Methodist minister. I made a special trip to Oregon to see him. I showed him the dictation, and he read it. I wanted to see his reaction. Did he think I was nuts? Did he find it of value?

Wes read it carefully and then looked up at me. "So, what are you going to do with this?"

"I don't know," I told him.

"Do you think you should sit on it?" he asked me.

"No," I replied.

Then, he smiled at me. "So, how do you intend to share it?" I just looked at him. "Tell you what," he said, "once you've written the book, if you feel like it, I'd love to read it."

"It's going to take some time to process this," I told him.

"You have time," Wes told me with a big grin.

As it turned out, I not only had time but would soon, and quite unexpectedly, get a new job to help keep me active and involved as I pondered what to do, and how to write a book that could share what I had learned.

First, I had to come to terms with what I had been given and what I felt I was expected to do. "They are killing each other in my name. Stop it." Ok. Now I understood that I hadn't been asked to end all war, a job that was totally impossible for anyone, let alone me. Gandhi couldn't do it. King couldn't do it. How on earth was someone like me supposed to? It was impossible. And now I understood that that wasn't the task I'd been given.

"Religion is but a language for speaking to me." That was my call, to frame and share this important realization. I still realized I was wholly inadequate to the task. All I could do was start the ball rolling. So, I made a "deal" with God. I would give it my best shot. I would give it everything I had. I could not and would not guarantee success. All I could promise is that I would try.

So, what to *do*? How could I share the learning I had been granted? I had no clue. I did know it was going to take time and effort. And that effort is what I have dedicated my life to since the dictation. But at this point it seemed overwhelming. Good grief, how do I start?

"You have made my creation a sewer" tugged at my heart. I had moved up to this beautiful area, only to watch open spaces being trashed and development running amok with little or no thought to anything other than the quick buck. So why doesn't somebody—oh yeah. Right. Ok. This would definitely give me something positive to work on while I tried to determine how to even begin to chart my course ahead.

Before I knew it, I was testifying before the Snohomish County Planning Commission, pleading not for an end to development but for some thought going into it! A man named Kurt Munnich, one of the commissioners, was particularly sympathetic. More about Kurt later. Quickly, I realized that the planning commission wasn't the real problem. To have any significant effect on policy, I needed to bone up on my information and start addressing the Snohomish County Council again. Swell. More research.

I never saw it coming and never intended it, but my decision to become involved in local environmental politics set my course for me. By starting to speak regularly in front of the county council, I unknowingly pressed the accelerator not only on my spiritual development but also on something I had no plans at all for at that point—ministry. It began innocuously enough with a chance meeting.

Chapter Twenty-Five

I met Anne Robison in the county council chambers while we were both waiting to testify. Anne was almost 80 but still firing on all cylinders. We were both going to speak regarding the hot topic of "growth management," and from differing perspectives we were both going to be supporting what was increasingly being referred to as "smart growth." Given a lot of dead time, we chatted. I found out that she loved Bach and played the organ. She found out that I had a degree in music and in a former life had been a choir director.

As it turned out, the spiritual community where Anne played organ was the Evergreen Unitarian Universalist Fellowship in Marysville. The fellowship was experiencing some difficult times. The choir was no longer active. An interim minister, Reverend Alex Holt, was serving for a year while the fellowship searched for a new minister. Alex thought it would be good to bring the choir back so the fellowship was looking for a choir director.

I still had a rather bad taste in my mouth from my previous choir-directing days. I told Anne I wasn't interested. By the way, I asked, what on earth is a Unitarian Universalist? Anne was a certified force of nature and in the end I agreed to come and direct the choir for one service, the Christmas service. And so began what would turn out to be a 10-year relationship with Evergreen and the beginning of my relationship with Unitarian Universalism.

The choir and I bonded immediately, which was delightful. I immediately realized just how much I had missed directing. Yet there was also an early warning shot that I probably should have paid more attention to.

I was informed with a smile that the "J" word was not to be used and the "G" word was to be avoided. It didn't take a rocket scientist to realize those words were Jesus and God. We were going to celebrate Christmas but not mention Jesus or God? Who *were* these people?? I decided that the Christmas service would be my first and last.

However, it was so much fun directing again that I hesitated a little. I turned in my key but was immediately asked to come back in a few months to direct the Easter service. This struck me as quite strange. I had by now discerned that the most active members of the choir, and thus probably the congregation, were Atheists. Those who weren't were mostly either from Buddhist or Jewish backgrounds, or had been badly scarred by the Christian church in some way. There was some antagonism toward the idea of God, but the real hostility was saved for Christianity. Yet, I had just directed their Christmas service and now been asked back for Easter?

I was confused, to say the least. At Christmas, one could get away with being rather "holidayish" and not too terribly sacred, but how on earth could we have an Easter service and not talk about resurrection? I got in trouble speaking up for Christianity several times during my tenure at Evergreen. I believe what saved me, at least until the end, was that I was Jewish. My arguments came from a desire to respect Christianity, not proselytize. As it turned out, I stumbled upon a weakness. Evergreen was virtually all white, quite liberal, and suffered acutely from white guilt. That knowledge showed me the path to sneak in some respectful Easter music. Black spirituals! They couldn't say no.

After Easter, I was asked to finish the year as the choir director. It was so much fun, I couldn't say no. Then, I was hired for the succeeding year. After the second year, I was made the director of music.

I think it was my second Christmas when the you-know-what hit the fan. The service was very disrespectful of Christianity.[33] I told the new minister and whatever committee I was dealing with that as a Jew I felt no need whatsoever to celebrate the birth of Jesus, but if we were going to celebrate Christmas we ought to do it respectfully. We needed to honor Jesus. Again, being Jewish saved me, and some actually seemed to get the point. I felt heard. Meanwhile, the choir grew and was becoming an important glue for the fellowship. However, there was one other tweak I felt early on that I needed to address.

When I first started directing the choir, my name was printed in the Order of Service as the party responsible for the music. I asked that my

---

33   Elvis was one of the "Kings" at the manger.

name be removed and replaced by "Evergreen Choir." I didn't want it to be my show. It felt important that the choir be recognized, not me. To my surprise there was resistance, but in the end the Order of Service was changed.

Then, I talked the administrative powers into allowing the choir to perform a concert once a year. When I first took the reins of the choir, there was little confidence amongst its members. I felt that a successful concert would be a great confidence builder, and it was. The choir continued to grow and I continued to have more and more fun.

In the meantime, I was finding out more about Unitarian Universalists. There was a certain pride in welcoming people of whatever faith. This felt good. I hadn't found the spiritual community that I'd been searching for, one that celebrated the diverse spiritual paths of humanity, but the UUs, as they called themselves, seemed to be on the right track. Maybe.... but how "welcoming" can you be when you're overtly hostile to Christianity?

Mostly what I enjoyed, and what kept me there, were the people. I met a lot of terrific folks. What I loved about so many of them was how active they were in the community, how dedicated they were to living lives of justice. If I started naming names, I know I'd inadvertently leave people out, so no names. Well, just a few. It was definitely fun that Kurt Munnich, the very sympathetic member of the planning commission, sang tenor in the choir. And I would like to memorialize two amazing people who were examples to me of how to live and indeed die with grace. One was Don Chamberlin; the other was Linda Moon. Both had been quite ill from before I became the choir director. But both loved choir, contributed to it, and doggedly kept on singing for as long as they were physically able to do so.

Don was a tall bass and a fine, well-educated musician. He suffered from terminal prostate cancer but had somehow outlived his prognosis by years. I watched him as he struggled but would not give in. He needed help standing and staying upright, but still would not quit. We got him a stool that kept him high enough that standing was easier, though he still needed to lean on a nearby chair. But he never once complained, and stayed with us as long as he possibly could.

Linda suffered from Lou Gehrig's disease. Even as her body slowly betrayed her, as her pain increased and her ability to move disappeared, she too stayed with the choir as long as she could still muster enough breath to sing. Her lungs were slowly shutting down, so this took real effort. Months before she left the choir, Linda could no longer stand, so she sat and sang.

She sang at services. She sang in concerts. What was so amazing about Linda was her good cheer, her wonderful attitude. Also, as sometimes happens, it seemed as if I had known Linda forever. She felt the same way about me, and from time to time we speculated about our past lives.

I was privileged to visit and, I hope, be of some service to both Don and Linda, even after they had left choir and still later after they were confined to bed. I had learned from my missteps with Kim years before. Linda and I had some great visits. So did Don and I. Strangely enough, visiting Don got me in some trouble with a new interim minister at Evergreen, let's call her Edna. Don's family made it clear that they were very happy to have me come and visit with him. But they specifically and firmly asked Edna to stay away. Edna was not pleased about this and actually ordered me to stop visiting Don if I wanted to keep my job. By this time I loved my job, but I wasn't about to desert Don. For me, that's the spiritual lesson in all of this. And it was an easy choice. I told Edna to do whatever she needed to: I would visit Don.

The most important calling for all of us, it seems to me, is to help others whenever it is in our power to do so. The emotionally immobile me had been unable to help Anna when she had reached out to me. But happily I was no longer that wounded person. I was able to be a calm, compassionate presence for Don, and we discussed many things including, of course, music. I saw him frequently toward the end. And in the end, Edna backed down. I remained the choir director.

I had eight wonderful years at Evergreen. Unfortunately, I stayed there ten years, but that's for later. Still, for eight years it was a total delight, and gave me the time and space to put my spiritual house in order.

The minister I served before Edna, who had followed Alex Holt as Evergreen's full-time minister, was Reverend Alicia Grace. Alicia was a delight. She not only gave me support but room to grow. I had an idea for a service built around music, a "Service of Song." Still, it needed a sermon, albeit a short one, and Alicia encouraged me to give it. Me? It would be my first sermon. I've put it in the Appendices.[34] I found I enjoyed sharing a message with the congregation. And to my pleasant surprise I seemed to be able to hold people's attention. Evergreen always seemed just too small a pond for Alicia, and indeed she left after a few years to serve in a larger church. But while she was there, working with her was a complete joy.

One bump in the road came when a good friend from college, I'll call him Peter, called. As we were catching up on each other's lives, he men-

---

34   Service of Song, Appendex 1

tioned that he'd really wanted to buy something, I no longer remember what, but it was just too expensive. Peter then explained, "I Jewed him down and got a good price." My jaw dropped. I was all too aware of the stereotype of Jews as money-hungry, but was unfamiliar with "to Jew" being used as a verb—especially by a friend. "I Jewed him down"? I was shocked. Baffled. And yes, hurt.

A week or so later, I got another call. Peter apologized. The people he ran with used the word and he had "somehow" picked it up without thinking about it. He now swore not only never to use "Jew" as a verb again, but to correct any associates who did.

Peter meant it. I forgave him, we moved on and have remained close friends to this day. Heck, we all screw up. There have been things that escaped my mouth over my lifetime that I'd give anything to have back. I knew this really wasn't the way he normally talked. Peter was and is a good man, not a bigot. But it was a reminder to me of how easily any of us can fall into verbal traps and end up saying things that are hurtful. Most of us know that what we say matters. This was a reminder that what we hear others say matters too. It was something to think about.

Still, my thoughts were returning more and more to writing. Having lived with and pondered my dictation for several years, I began to envision how I might put what I had learned into a book. The working title was *Spiritually Thinking*. But it took a lot of time and many drafts. I didn't have the words just yet to communicate well what I felt needed to be shared. Meanwhile, three things happened almost concurrently that helped me to see the way forward.

Evergreen had yet another new minister, the fourth I had served: Reverend Bruce Davis. Bruce was very supportive when I told him I was thinking that ministry might be where I needed to go. Maybe I could coax Unitarian Universalists into a more broadly respectful and diverse welcoming of our world's spiritual paths. Bruce cautioned me that it would be a difficult road, but he also thought it a worthwhile effort.

Meanwhile, I had concluded that a second Ms. Right was just not in the offing, and if I ever did meet her and she had children, they would all be grown up by now. So I didn't need a house as big as the one I lived in. The house was beautiful, the view of the Puget Sound was beautiful, and I truly enjoyed it. But it seemed simply too big a footprint for one person to make. If I believed in what I preached, I needed to leave this lovely house, this house of my dreams, and live more simply in a much smaller house. So I decided to put the house up for sale.

And now that the house was up for sale, it became clear that I would have plenty of money to go to seminary and become a minister. For various reasons, not the least of which was that it was both nearby and Bruce strongly recommended it, I determined to go to Seattle University. SU, as most refer to it, is technically not a seminary. Their School of Theology and Ministry is "simply" a school for ministers. It was also hugely expensive; around $25,000 a year!

Once again my timing was perfect, for the real estate market was in overdrive. In the ten years I'd lived in my dream house, its value had yet again doubled. Real estate, of all things, had made me financially independent. Who could have guessed?

I realized that selling the house was not only going to give me the cash I needed to pay for my schooling at Seattle University, it would also be my retirement fund. So, most of the money that didn't go into paying for what would now be my third master's degree was carefully invested. Still, I did withhold a bundle of cash and put it in a money market account.

One small bit of wisdom from years of carefully watching the dollars come and go. I realized that once I became a minister and knew where I was going to live, I'd want a house. That would be at least three and perhaps four or even five years in the future. At any given moment, stocks can tank. The market can suck. If you know you're going to need money for something in less than five years, keep it liquid, as in an insured money market account. Never place yourself in the position of having to sell stocks at a specific moment. You can lose your shirt.

End of investment lesson. Time for that third and final master's degree.

Chapter Twenty-Six

I went to an orientation meeting, filled out a bunch of forms, submitted some rather ancient college transcripts, and then was interviewed by a staff member before being accepted into Seattle University's master's program. Afterward I again asked myself, do I really want to do this? Is ministry really where I feel called? Me? Yes. Writing the book wouldn't be enough. I had to live my beliefs, not just write about them. But back to school, good grief, back to school *again?* "Education is lifelong." Fine!

Having made the decision to attend SU's School of Theology and Ministry (STM), I determined to let no grass grow under my feet. I enrolled for the first session I could enter, which was that summer, and was bowled over by my teachers. Father John Heagle and Sister Fran Ferder taught one class. Sister Alexandra Kovats taught the other. All three were superb, but for me Alexandra and John had the most profound impact. This is not the place to chronicle all my classes at Seattle University. But I do think it may be worthwhile to point out some important spiritual observations as well as teachings along the way.

In a sense, having John and Alexandra as my first teachers at Seattle University spoiled me. These were not just teachers, they were master teachers. Yet their influence was far greater than that. Yes, their classes were interesting and informative, but both John and Alexandra taught most strongly by the example of who they were and how they lived. They number (along with Rabbi Leonard Beerman and Reverend Wesley Yamaka) among the most inspiring and deeply spiritual people I have known. The most important thing I learned from both of them, or at least that I have aspired to learn from them, was how to create safe, sacred space.

Simply by being who they were, when they walked into a room they made me feel it was safe for me to be me—and therefore safe for me to explore who I am and my spiritual self. The value of this is incalculable. I could and did push myself to the limits because I knew I was completely safe in their hands. I owe both Alexandra and especially John a debt I cannot possibly ever repay.

A simple but powerful example of creating safe, sacred space comes from the very first day of my class with Father John Heagle. He began the class with a prayer, as he clearly always did. The prayer ended, as I recall, by John saying, "In Jesus' name, amen." This was also how he clearly ended every prayer. But now that the class had started, there was a time for all of us to introduce ourselves—to each other as well as to John and Sister Fran Ferder, with whom he co-taught. In introducing myself, I said that I was Jewish.

The next day, John again began the class with a prayer. But he no longer finished the prayer by saying "In Jesus' name." Instead, it was simply "amen." There was no announcement. He just did it. It was so low-key that I don't think it struck me until the third day. I was bowled over. And as I thought about it, I realized there were some important things to note here.

First, simply by changing how he ended his prayer, John had created safe, sacred space. I had been included, indeed welcomed. Second and just as important, John never talked to me about it. And as I pondered this, I realized what a gift it was. He didn't say, "Steven, I'm going to stop saying 'In Jesus' name' so you'll feel included." That would have been a patronizing exercise in ego: "Aren't I wonderful? See what I did for you?" But no ego was involved, and no patronizing of me by calling attention to it. He just did it! *That* is how you create safe, sacred space. *That* is how you ensure that all are included, quietly and without fanfare.

For very different reasons, I also learned a great deal from Father Mike Raschko and Father James Eblen. These were more traditional teachers, but their classes were excellent and helped me immeasurably.

The most important class that I took from Mike was "Christian Anthropology," where I was asked both to define God and then explore the implications of that definition. This was one of the very positive aspects of my study at the School of Theology and Ministry. I had all these thoughts, ideas, and beliefs floating about in my head and heart, as well as the dictation I was still grappling with. Now I learned a vocabulary for verbalizing them and organizing them into a coherent statement. That's a gift! Mike not only allowed but encouraged me to develop my own vocabulary—NOT about the one "right" definition of God, but rather about how I had experienced the divine. He was a true teacher, with no ulterior motives. With Mike, one of the humbling things to come to grips with was that while he gave you his all while you were his student, the moment you were no longer his student you disappeared from his mind—literally. Poof!

I have experienced God as Cosmic Conscience. This is the God of justice who calls both to me and upon me to act, paraphrasing the Prophet Micah, with justice, compassion and humility in the world. One thing I appreciated and enjoyed about my classes with Mike was listening to differing people relate (or not) to God. This reinforced for me that we all experience the divine differently. This is far more important than it may sound. Regardless of how we "define" the divine, and even if we agree on that definition, we still experience the divine differently. We *experience* the divine differently. Once we understand and appreciate that truth, to try to come up with one "right" answer, seems rather foolish. In Mike's class no one was encouraged to come up with the one "right" answer to God. Rather we were encouraged to strive to articulate how we had experienced God. Truly empowering stuff.

Another mind-opening course was "Hebrew Scripture," taught by Father James Eblen. I always felt the course mistitled; it should have been called "The Skill of Close Reading of Scripture." Yes, we used Hebrew Scripture as our foundation for reading. But what James magnificently led us through was how much we have learned to "see" in Scripture that actually isn't there! We are taught to *expect* certain things and, being human, more often than not when we expect to see something, we do. Now we were asked to get rid of those glosses and get back to reading what was actually in Scripture—albeit in translation.

Where this was of enormous spiritual help was when we were tasked with closely reading a single passage in Hebrew Scripture and then writing a paper about it. I chose the passage that had vexed and haunted me from the time I had first encountered it as a youth: Abraham's near-sacrifice of his son Isaac. Abraham stands up to God when it comes to Sodom and Gomorrah but then meekly obeys God's instruction to murder (sorry, but that's how I saw it) his own son. I'd had to willfully put these concerns aside as I embraced Judaism. The God I believed in was the God of justice that Abraham could argue with, the God of justice that Moses could argue with. The God I believed in demanded justice, and no call to kill, *ever*, even if I think it came from God, was to be obeyed without vigorous discussion and argument.

I believed and believe that we are called to use both our minds and our hearts neither separated from the other and never to mindlessly move in obedience to any authority, even God's. Israel. He who wrestles with God. This was the Cosmic Conscience that called to me. I believed in a Moses who would challenge God atop Mount Sinai and a God who would listen. This had required my turning away from Abraham's willingness to kill Isaac. Now, at last, I was going to face it; and frankly I didn't have a clue where it would take me.

One of the things James had taught us was that when the word God appears in our English translation, the word in Hebrew is *Elohim*. When the word *Lord* appears, the word in Hebrew is *Yahweh*. Two different words, two very specifically different words. This triggered memories from when I'd first studied Scripture as an undergraduate in college.

According to most Biblical scholars, Hebrew Scripture was not the work of one hand. It had at least four main and distinct sources. The first two were the Yahwist and Elohist sources (possibly from the southern and northern tribes, respectively). Later came the Deuteronomist source, and lastly the Priestly source, which may have been responsible for bringing it all together.[35] Hebrew Scripture, in translation at least, approaches the names of God as if they are like Richard and Dick; different, yet referring to the same entity. But one of the things to be learned about Hebrew history is that the tribes of Israel were a diverse bunch, perhaps far more diverse than most of us realize. The believers in Yahweh may have met the believers in Elohim and decided it's the same "one God," but, as we know from *Genesis*, there are at least two rather different creation stories.[36] What if the traditions of the nature of Yahweh and Elohim were not only distinct but actually quite different? This was the conclusion I was led to after I went back and closely read the story of Abraham and Isaac. It was not what I expected. Here is the story, as related in Scripture.

Elohim (God) comes to Abraham and says, "I want you to sacrifice your son to Me." Abraham packs up his son, and Elohim tells Abraham the location of the mountain where he wants the sacrifice to take place. Then,

---

35   For anyone interested in following up on this, I strongly recommend the groundbreaking works of Norman Gottwald: *A Light to the Nations*, 1959, and *The Hebrew Bible*, 1989. Anthony Ceresko's book *Introduction to the Old Testament*, 2003, updates Gottwald's work and adds some interesting and worthwhile perspectives as well.

36   Mostly famously, man and woman created at the same time, both in the image of God on the sixth day (*Genesis*:1 27–28), and yet a few verses later we find Adam being created first and Eve created only after God created animals before deciding that Adam needed a better "helpmate" (*Genesis*: 2 18–24).

Elohim tells Abraham to take Isaac up the mountain, after which Elohim tells Abraham to bind Isaac and kill him. Then, the Angel of Yahweh (the Lord) says, "Stop! Sacrificing that ram over there will do just fine." Elohim has said, "You owe your first born as a sacrifice to me." Yahweh has said, "No, actually a ram is fine; let your first born live."

This led me to wonder, what if the tribes that followed Elohim believed in sacrificing their first born to God, but the tribes that followed Yahweh didn't? This sent me on a search through the Torah (the first five books of Hebrew Scripture). It certainly should not be considered exhaustive, but what I found was rather startling. I found ten instances where human sacrifice to God is mentioned. In two of them, Elohim is referenced and human sacrifice is expected. In eight of them, Yahweh is referenced and human sacrifice is rejected.[37]

Adding icing to the Scriptural cake, when Abraham argues with God about destroying Sodom and Gomorrah, it's Yahweh. When Moses argues with God about destroying the children of Israel after they've made the Golden Calf, it's Yahweh. Clearly, Yahweh is a God you can reason with. Elohim wants blind and sometimes bloody obedience. Fascinating!

Happily for Judaism, at least from my perspective, it was the call of Yahweh that won out. More personally, this at last resolved the tension I had long felt over what is traditionally called "The Binding of Isaac." It also reminded me about how fluid our sacred history can be, and how important it is to remember that our Scriptures are guidebooks to being better human beings and not histories.

Looking back at my papers at this time, I was still strongly focused on becoming a Unitarian Universalist minister. But the wheels now slowly began to come off that wagon. It started with a gentle bump during my class in UU history. My teacher, Reverend Gretchen Woods, was grand. But my paper was on orthodoxy in UU history. The Unitarians, like every other spiritual movement, have had their "right believers." Gretchen liked the paper, but a few of my fellow UUs in the class didn't. Not at all. That was the first gentle warning shot.

The next warning shot was not so gentle. As required, I met with Janine Larsen, the executive director of the UUs in the Northwest. Janine was extremely negative about Interfaith (capital "I") as it was evolving in my mind and what I wanted to do with it, and she challenged my UU commitment. Strangely, up until then my commitment to UU had been quite

---

strong, but this "you're either for us, or you're against us" mentality that she evidenced was one I had long rejected.

I call it the "Messala Complex" after a character in the movie (and novel) *Ben Hur*. Messala and Ben Hur had been friends from childhood, but t returning from Rome as a freshly minted tribune, Messala demands that Ben Hur support him 100 percent, including spying and reporting on his fellow Jews. "You're either for me or you're against me," Messala says.

Ben Hur replies, "If that is the choice, then I'm against you."

I've spoken about the spiritual bankruptcy of the Messala Complex many times. I feel this "you're either 100 percent for me or you're against me" is a deep illness that infects our politics as well as our religions. Now I felt I was hearing it from the executive director of the UUs. Definitely not encouraging.

I was disturbed enough by what Janine had said to drive down from my home north of Seattle to a city south of Portland in Oregon. This was where Gretchen Woods had her church. Gretchen reassured me that all was ok. She knew my work as a student. She felt that despite what Janine had said, I would make a good UU minister and Janine wouldn't stand in my way. I was only somewhat reassured, but put it away for now.

Then, another blow blindsided me. I had become good friends, or so I believed, with a fellow UU student I'll call Carla. I had met Carla at that first orientation meeting for prospective students, and we'd hit it off immediately. We shared most of the same classes. I had met her husband I think only once, but he seemed like a nice fellow, too.

Carla and I talked all the time about life as well as our classes, and we "covered" for each other whenever one of us had to be absent from a class by sharing our lecture notes. I thought everything was going swimmingly and looked forward to a long friendship. Then, it all exploded. There was a class we all took that was quite toxic. It tried to help people be more aware of what an inclusive ministry in the multicultural context of the United States should involve. The motives for the class were wonderful. Unfortunately, for many the class seemed toxic and it messed with a lot of minds.

I don't recall what the topic was, other than it concerned this class. Carla and I were having a spirited discussion as we frequently did. Then, Carla frowned at me and said that "You Jews" ("You Jews"?—huge alarm bells started going off), "You Jews need to get over the Holocaust and anti-Semitism." She then patronizingly reminded me that "everybody has problems." I was stunned. I knew Carla well enough to know she would never tell a person of color to "get over" slavery, Jim Crow and racism, and that "everybody has problems." So, what was this? "You Jews"?? It stung.

I waited for her to clarify, but she didn't. Days later, remembering my friend Peter, I was still hoping to hear from Carla—a phone call, an e-mail, *something*. But not only did I not hear from her, she now began avoiding me. Suddenly, we weren't speaking. Several months later, we happened to sit next to each other in a class and I thought, "Enough already." So, I turned to her and asked how she was. Her only response was a cold, "You're speaking to me?" The friendship died.

The next incident was quite baffling. This, too, began with that toxic class in multicultural ministry that messed with so many minds, including a friendly acquaintance I'll call Phil. As I recall, Phil had a Native American heritage. He'd written an angry paper for the class and had gotten into so much trouble over it that he'd been called before the dean.[38] Phil was in a bad place. Another friend, I'll call her Janice, and I were worried about him and wanted to cheer him up. A lot of e-mails went back and forth, trying to establish a time for all three of us to meet and talk this through, but our schedules just wouldn't match up.

Finally, in one e-mail, we'd all agreed to meet whenever and wherever Janice thought best. Janice wrote back something to the effect that we were two passive males. Thinking I was keeping things light, I wrote something like, "Ok. Just don't wear spiked heels." Janice took offense. HUGE offense. Her offense when she wrote back seemed so overblown that I mistakenly thought she was joking. But she wasn't. Then came an e-mail accusing me of sending her an e-mail about my wanting to put a camera in her bathroom to spy on her. What??? I had no clue where that came from. I had sent no such e-mail, nor any e-mail that could ever possibly have been misunderstood as "hinting" such a thing.

What made this something to ponder was I didn't believe Janice was the sort of person to make something like this up. So where on earth was it coming from? Again, I had no clue. And Janice made it clear that she didn't ever want to talk about it or to me. I mention all this because she was a good person, who as far as I know would never lie. Yet, this was totally untrue. Go figure that out! It was weird, and it baffled me.

Despite these exceptions, I did make some good friends in seminary. Some have remained friends long past our SU experience. Intriguingly, all the friends I've kept from SU are women. And no, no romance involved with any of them. They're just really good people and good friends.

---

38 I don't think I ever read the paper, so I won't characterize it other than angry, which is how Phil characterized it.

Steven Greenebaum

Chapter Twenty-Seven

Then, for a blink of an eye, I was almost famous. This book is a spiritual memoir, not a political manifesto, but this was a moment where for me politics and spiritual integrity intersected with a vengeance. After 9/11, I had gone against my more left-leaning friends and supported bombing Afghanistan when the leaders there gave shelter to Bin Laden. This to me was rather straightforward self-protection, one of the few times when violence was justified. On the other hand, I had been strongly against invading Iraq, going against my more right-leaning friends.

What bothered me most was that after invading Iraq the Bush administration was going around the country proclaiming how much safer the invasion had made us. Safer? I didn't think so. Indeed, in every way I felt we were much less safe. Iraq had been Iran's one natural enemy in the area, and now who was going to put the brake on Iran? Not to mention that the work in Afghanistan had been left unfinished and the situation there left to fester. Or the poppy crop in Afghanistan, and the drugs it had produced, which had been all but eliminated but was now back and flourishing, in no small part because the U.S. had moved its attention to Iraq. I could go on. What bugged me was that the Democrats were essentially silent. I kept wondering, even as I studied for ministry, is no one going to call the Bush administration on this?

Yeah, I know, I'm someone. But good grief what could I do? Yet, still there was silence. So, I wrote a response to what the Bush administration was saying. Again, I respect that the reader may disagree with me, but I felt that going into Iraq, leaving Afghanistan unfinished with no one to balance Iran, had left us exceedingly unsafe. Not to mention, and few people had, that putting the war on a credit card had vastly increased our national debt and put Social Security at risk. Yet once I'd written up what I felt needed to be said, then what? At last I felt I had no choice. I either had to stop saying, "Why doesn't someone say something?" or I had to say it myself. So, I took out a full-page advertisement in the two Seattle daily papers, *The Seattle Times* and the *Seattle Post-Intelligencer*. I didn't know, so you may not, that such an ad cost roughly the equivalent of a full year's tuition at Seattle University. Gulp! But it seems to me that there are times when you either live by what you believe or you stop pretending that you really believe it. So, I raided my savings and wrote a check.

Interestingly, that didn't end it. As the day of the ad's publication approached, I began to become more and more fearful. What would be the response? The Bush administration had very successfully made it seem like anyone who disagreed with them was unpatriotic. That had worked on most of the Democrats and seemingly all of the major newspapers, who'd stayed silent. Would I get hate mail? Would I get a rock through my window? Would it get worse than that? If so, how much worse? The kind person at *The Seattle Times* knew how deeply I was dipping into my savings and gave me a deadline before which I could call the whole thing off and get a refund. I let the deadline pass. Again, you either believe in what you proclaim or you don't. I have to admit, I was scared. What would happen?

One of the spiritual things this experience taught me was at least a partial answer to a question I'd long pondered about people not speaking up. No, this was not in any way Nazi Germany nor even the United States during the McCarthy era. Nonetheless I was learning not only how expensive speaking up can be but also the toll it takes on our spiritual selves, the stress of speaking up when those in power are willing to point the finger at you and proclaim you traitor. As I'm sure is abundantly clear, I have many, many faults, but happily, I know who I am and am willing to stand up for it. Still, on the day the ad was published I was a stressed-out puddle of conflicting emotions—aka, a mental wreck.

A local television reporter, Essex Porter, saw my ad. He called and wanted to interview me. I said yes but was still so scared that I told him I didn't want him showing up at my house in a vehicle that marked him as a reporter. When he saw a menorah in my house, he asked if I was Jewish. I said yes but asked him not to mention that in his report. Mr. Porter must have thought me a complete wacko, but he was very kind, a real gentleman as well as a fine reporter. He reported the story while respecting my wishes. I owe him.

By the next day, things were better. There had been no car bombs. There were a LOT of phone calls (I had been required to include my phone number in the ad). Happily, most of them were positive, thanking me for saying what I'd said. That was rewarding. A few calls were quite negative. I was accused of being a communist, among other things. No big deal. And by the third day, when I got my first really threatening call, it rolled off my back. I was fine. I'd gotten my balance back. I knew the caller was a nut. I didn't bother calling the police.

At the end of the week, I was called by a different television station. They wanted me to come down and be interviewed. If they'd called on the first day I probably would have declined, but now I said sure. I was interviewed by Kathi Goertzen and received some gentle but firm pushback from her on why I'd written the ad. I'm pretty sure I held my own. I had a radio interview as well with a local talk-show host, Dave Ross. In addition, one person took the ad and paid for it to be reprinted in an Eastside (Bellevue?) newspaper. But I was still leery enough that I unjustly chastised the poor fellow for using my name and personal information in the ad when all he was trying to do was give me credit.

That was it. In another week it was as if it had never happened.

Frankly, I was rather surprised. No national television news had picked up the story. Nor had any national or local radio news, including National Public Radio. I had mixed feelings. In part I was just as glad to be finished with it. But also, as I thought about it, I was taken aback about how little interest there was in a single citizen feeling strongly enough about something to take out a full-page ad in the newspaper. Then again, being ignored was undoubtedly why I hadn't suffered the onslaught of negativity that I'd anticipated.

Still, the big teacher in all this was the psychic (not to mention the dollar) cost of putting myself out there. It was a reminder to me of what Edmund Burke is reputed to have said; that "All that is necessary for evil to flourish if for good men to do nothing," and how easy, even tempting it is to do nothing. And how hard it is to do what you believe is right when the prevailing wind is in the other direction. As Nietzsche said, "What doesn't kill us, makes us stronger." I am stronger for having gone through the experience. But it was a lesson in just how much strength is sometimes necessary. Nonetheless, the important thing for me was that I could look at myself in the mirror. I'd done what I could and what I believed in. The rest wasn't up to me.

Steven Greenebaum

Chapter Twenty-Eight

My first drafts of this chapter talked about how my life now underwent a complete change of course. But the truth of it is, I remained on a steady course. I just didn't know it. Indeed, I had no clear idea of the course I was truly on, and had been all along, until the last few months of my Seattle U experience. Even then, it took a series of seemingly unrelated experiences to break through to me. Let's start with the positive ones.

One of the requirements for study at Seattle University's School of Theology and Ministry was a class called MTI, which as I recall stood for Ministry/Theological Integration. The year-long class required that a student intern at a church. The class itself met as a seminar to help students adjust to the real world of ministry. I had been wondering where I should do my UU internship when I came across a wonderful small church in Ballard, just north of Seattle, called (at that time) the Interfaith Community Church.[39]

I was still director of music at Evergreen UU, and Rev. Bruce Davis, my boss, had recommended that I meet a man named Jamal Rahman. Bruce thought that given my interfaith proclivities, I'd enjoy talking to Jamal. He was right. Jamal and I had coffee, and a long chat. As it turned out, I did more than simply enjoy meeting him. Jamal, who is Sufi Muslim as well as a grand human being, told me about his work as a minister at the Interfaith Community Church. What luck! It sounded like the perfect place to intern. Jamal then put me in touch with Karen Lindquist, who was not only a minister at the church but also pretty much ran the place. After meeting with Karen, also a truly remarkable and open human being, I was sold. But

---

39   It's now called the Interfaith Community Sanctuary.

to be sold on me, Karen needed one more meeting. She included a friend of hers whom she wanted to come and look me over. I passed muster and it was settled. So instead of interning at a UU church, I interned at Interfaith Community Church, where there were three clergy serving: Jamal, Karen and Debra Lajimodiere, whose heritage is Native American. While all three were people I could definitely learn a lot from, Karen would be my mentor/supervisor.

My internship turned out to be both a joy and a virtually seamless transition. Just a month after beginning at the Interfaith Community Church I was given one Sunday a month to lead the service. I put together a five-part series called "The Gift of Living Interfaith," which was not only well received but would eventually become the name of the church I would one day found.

What was truly weird was that this internship, this foray into "real-life ministry," was supposed to be stressful. It wasn't. Karen was one of most thoughtful, caring and compassionate mentors I could ever have hoped to have. What *was* stressful was the seminar class given to help "ease" my way into ministry! This was a symptom of a growing problem I would have at the School of Theology and Ministry. The school prided itself on what it called "formation," but it reminded me of the movie *The Paper Chase*, in which Professor Kingsfield tells the new law students something like, "You enter here with a head full of mush, and you leave thinking like lawyers." STM's formation concept presupposed students with heads full of mush and was intended to get us thinking like ministers. I found it to be an exceedingly arrogant and unhelpful approach.

I want to be fair. I do recall being stunned by how many students were there who seemed to be at the school to find out who they were. It may even have been the majority of students. For them, the STM formation process might indeed be very helpful. I do recall that in the MTI class I took, our professor, Richard Cunningham, was both sensitive and very helpful to at least one student who was going through a full-blown spiritual crisis.

For me, however, Dick Cunningham was no help at all. Indeed, he was the cause of my recurring stress throughout the year. Dick had his own idea of what a minister should look like, including how a minister should express him/herself, and I didn't fit his mold. He kept trying to change me, and I kept declining his kind offer. I knew who I was, and I knew what I wanted to accomplish. I'm sure Dick found me frustratingly uncooperative. I would vent to Karen at the Interfaith Church about the stresses of my class—the class that was supposed to help me overcome my problems dealing with her! It was a rather amusing turnabout.

As my internship was drawing to a close, there seemed a genuine sorrow on all sides. The folks at Interfaith Community Church didn't seem to want me to go, and I certainly didn't want to leave. As the end approached, it left a very positive if bittersweet feeling.

Another positive experience came as a result of the stresses mentioned above. I decided I should take a required psychological exam during my second year of study. The exam, a battery of psychological tests as well as a daylong interview with a qualified psychologist to see if a person is psychologically fit and ready to become a minister, was traditionally administered after the second year. Since Dick Cunningham had made it clear he was convinced I was at best unready and perhaps unfit and I disagreed, it was time to hear from an impartial third party.

I took the written tests and then went through my daylong exam. I was asked a lot of pointed and sometimes pointless questions, or so it seemed at the time. Upon reflection, I realized that the person examining me was trying to push my buttons to see how I would react. He seemed pleased, for once it was all over I received a strong, unequivocal endorsement of my readiness for ministry. Ok. That question resolved.

Then it felt as if the universe stepped up, grabbed me by the lapels and said rather clearly, "Wake up! UU is NOT your calling."

I took my second class specifically focused on Unitarian Universalism. This one was taught by Reverend Jon Luopa. Jon is a good man, a deep thinker and a dedicated minister. I not only enjoyed his class, but also liked him. Yet while it was friendly enough, he and I had a strong parting of the ways. I talked to Jon about my Interfaith beliefs and he told me firmly and flatly that they were incompatible with UU. "There's such a thing as too big a tent," he told me. There wasn't room for our diverse spiritual paths and beliefs under one tent. Jon was and is a serious man to be taken seriously. He reinforced what the executive director had told me.

It was clear that if I wanted to continue on and become a UU minister I would truly have my work cut out for me. And a part of the equation, at least for me, was that I was no spring chicken. I will also admit that echoing in my memory was the story of my personal hero of the Unitarian movement, Theodore Parker. Parker, a Unitarian minister as well as dedicated abolitionist before the Civil War, had seriously rocked the "take no sides" Unitarian boat. As a result, as he was dying of tuberculosis, an angry assembly of Unitarian ministers refused a request to pray for him. And at age sixty I was going to join the ranks of UU ministers with the intent of rock-ing the boat? Time to reflect. Was I on the wrong course? But if so, then good grief—what was the *right* course??

Another helpful experience was being asked to give a guest sermon at a UU church in Bellingham, Washington. I stayed overnight with a lovely couple (Bellingham was too far away to drive up for a Sunday morning ser-mon). I gave a sermon on, who could have guessed, respecting rather than tolerating or even ignoring our diverse spiritual traditions. The reactions I received afterward were another indicator of trouble down the road should I stay on the path of UU ministry. Publicly, I was told by several people that I was "preaching to the choir," that this was what UU was all about. Then, privately, several people took me aside and with heartfelt emotion thanked me for talking about what for them was a very sore subject. They felt dis-respected in their own congregation. Most, perhaps all, of these people were Christians, who for whatever reason (these were only brief conver-sations) felt they had needed to leave their specific denomination. They had left their denomination behind, not their Christianity, and had sought refuge in UU only to feel themselves tolerated but not respected in their new spiritual home.

That, for me, remains both the call of Interfaith and the reason I have put so much work into it. I wanted and want there to be safe sacred space for people of good will from all our spiritual paths to come together and share; a place not simply to "feel heard," but to truly be respected. This came later. At the time, what I began to realize that I was not only being pushed away from UU but also being pulled toward something else. Some-thing *else*. Ok, fine. But what? Hello? A clue would be helpful.

It would seem that the universe decided that a clue wouldn't be enough. I required a strong whack on the side of my head. It came in the form of a letter that arrived in my mailbox one Friday. The letter was from Sharon Callahan, the Associate Dean for Academic Programs and Student Life. I can quote from the letter because I've not only kept but framed it. I keep it in my office. This was one cold letter, informing me that I would not be advanced to candidacy for the Master of Divinity degree.

"This may come as a surprise, since you have a very adequate grade point.[40] I remind you, however, that from the time of your student orien-tation, you have been aware of our stated ministerial competencies. You were reminded again of these when the candidacy process was initiated in January 2007, and your Ministerial and Theological Integration faculty has

---

40   I suppose a nearly A average might be considered "very adequate."

reviewed these with you within the course as well as through written and oral feedback."

Sharon's letter continued, telling me to contact her "as soon as you receive this letter" and make an appointment to see both her and Mark Taylor, the Interim Dean at STM. I was stunned, to say the least. I was also frustrated that the letter arrived on a Friday. By the time I got home from classes to see my mail, the school offices were closed. So, I couldn't call to make an appointment until Monday, in spite of being instructed to contact Sharon as soon as I received the letter.

What was I to do? That weekend was to say the least extremely difficult. To be ordained a UU minister, I needed to have the Master of Divinity degree. The letter later spoke of working with me to address my "deficiencies." My deficiencies. So what did I need to do?

I count as one of the great blessings of my life that when I called first thing Monday morning I was informed that the "earliest" Sharon and Mark "could possibly" meet with me was in four weeks. Four weeks??!!! I had been instructed to call as soon as I received the letter, and now was told I would have to wait four weeks!

Again, what a wonderful stroke of luck. Had I met with Sharon and Mark that Monday, I was still so committed to my current course that it's possible I might have given in to whatever they demanded. But having four weeks gave me plenty of time to decompress and think things through. I'd taken two classes from Sharon and knew she had no great liking for me. And I knew Dick Cunningham, who as my MTI instructor had direct input into this decision, resented my rejection of his attempts to "form" me into the kind of minister he wanted to see emerging from his classes. And it hit me, "Déjà vu all over again." Once again, people were trying to throw me out of a graduate school. It had happened when I got my M.A. in Myth. It had happened again when I got my M.A. in Music. Now it was happening a third time, and I needed to apply the same principle. If these people wouldn't help me, I needed to get them out of my way.

Ok then, this door was closing. So, what door could I kick open? Once I framed the question that way, the answer seemed obvious. Ok universe, I get it!

I went to the Interfaith Community Church and talked with Karen, Jamal, and Debra, but most particularly with Karen, as she had worked most closely with me. People don't normally stay with and get ordained at the church where s/he intern, so we hadn't ever considered it. But the congregation still seemed to love me and I very much still loved them. What if I didn't leave? Would the Interfaith Community Church be interested in ordaining me and having me serve not as an intern but as an associate minister? The answer was yes. Ok then, what do I do about my meeting with Sharon and Mark at STM?

The Master of Divinity degree was the crown jewel, but there were other degrees that the School of Theology and Ministry offered. One was an M.A. in Pastoral Studies. I had taken two very full years of classes (year-long, as I was there both summers). I had more than fulfilled the requirements for an M.A. in Pastoral Studies. Ok then. I was armed and ready for my meeting with Mark and Sharon.

I walked in the door not the quaking, fear-filled student they expected but very sure of what I wanted to accomplish. I listened carefully to their complaints about my formation. I did so not only with interest and sincerity but also with pen and paper in hand. If they had some worthwhile criticism of my work, something helpful to share with me, I very much wanted to listen and learn from it. I'd be a fool not to. It turned out, though, they had nothing helpful to offer. Nothing. So I sprang on them that I had decided to switch to an M.A. in Pastoral Studies and wanted to graduate in June (it was already May). In fact, I insisted on it.

Happily, I took Mark and Sharon completely by surprise. When they found that I had no intention of backing down, they switched gears and suggested that we let a third party decide—an impartial arbitrator, so to speak. They suggested that I take the psychological tests that they clearly didn't realize I'd already taken. The offer they made to me was this: if the psychologist said I was ready to be a minister, then they would advance me to candidacy for my MDIV: but if the psychologist said I wasn't ready, I would need to agree to work with them before I would be advanced to candidacy.

I told them no. I was no longer interested in the MDIV—oh, and by the way I'd already taken those psychological tests and the conclusion was that I was quite ready for ministry. So they agreed that I would graduate in June with my M.A. in Pastoral Studies. Just for punctuation, I gave Mark a copy of the complete psychological evaluation to read.

What a blessing this entire mess turned out to be! I was already coming to the conclusion that UU and I weren't a good fit. But I hadn't seen a way out. Now it seemed that God or the universe had not simply pointed the way out to me, but virtually shoved me through the flaming door. That September I was ordained and joined my friends Debra, Karen and Jamal at the Interfaith Community Church as an associate minister.

Meanwhile, I had to inform both Rev. Bruce Davis as well as the Evergreen choir that circumstances had changed. I had thought I'd be leaving Evergreen and the choir in a year's time (it would have taken that much longer to finish the MDIV).[41] I would then have interned for a year at a UU church. That was the usual path to becoming a UU minister. But I had now put aside UU ministry. And as I would be one of four ministers at the Interfaith Community Church, I would be able to continue as the quarter-time director of music. I thought it was great news. It was for many, but not all.

I didn't understand until I processed it later, but I think some in the choir may have taken my decision not to pursue UU ministry as my rejecting Unitarian Universalism and, by extension, them. I should have been more aware of this, but wasn't. I was just so happy to be able to stay at Evergreen and continue with the joy of leading the choir.

Along with this came a warning I did see. For reasons I didn't understand, it became clear to me that Bruce wasn't all that easy with my decision. Ok. This needed to be talked through. I met with him and told him that I'd been at Evergreen for seven wonderful years. I had led everyone, including Bruce, into believing I would be leaving after eight. Now I wasn't leaving. I made it as clear as I possibly could that if he wanted me to move on, or simply felt it best for Evergreen, I would resign at the end of the year. I was ok with that. It wasn't my preference, but I would understand and really was ok with it. Bruce shook his head no. He didn't want me to leave, he told me, and neither did he think it would it be good for the fellowship. I was still uncomfortable. I felt that I'd heard clear warning bells, though again I had no idea why. So, I pressed it. I repeated that the end of the year would be the perfect time for me to resign if it would be best for Evergreen. Bruce as emphatically yet again declined my offer. So, I stayed. I've never been as good a "people reader" as perhaps I ought to be. I would pay for that.

---

41   Another reason to be grateful to Sharon and Mark. By not attending STM that extra year I saved about twenty-five thousand dollars! Nearly the same amount I spent on my full-page ad about Iraq.

Chapter Twenty-Nine

Never underestimate the siren call of ruts. I put the warning bells out of my mind as I settled into my new life, and the next two years were very happy. I enjoyed my work with the Evergreen choir (which also paid enough to put food on the table). I enjoyed my work as an unpaid minister at the Interfaith Community Church (none of the ministers are paid—it's an all-volunteer community). Most important, I felt I had at last developed the vocabulary I needed to write my book the way I wanted to. I not only began to rewrite it, but changed the working title from *Spiritually Thinking* to *The Interfaith Alternative*. One small setback came from a discussion with Karen.

I shared with Karen that I was coming to see interfaith as much more than a way of describing dialogue. I was beginning to see it as a faith. Not interfaith, but Interfaith. I was still grappling with it, and writing as I grappled, but it seemed to me that truly embracing all of our spiritual paths as potentially righteous paths to the sacred involved, well, *faith*. "Religions are languages for speaking to Me. Worship not the grammar." The more I reflected on it, the more I realized that I now truly took as an article of faith that there is no one "right" way to approach God, or nature, or whatever it is that we hold as sacred. Karen told me that she and others at the church had considered Interfaith as a faith but rejected it. This was not something that the Interfaith Community Church (ICC) wanted to deal with.

I continued to work on the book as well as live with the dictation. As I did it at last dawned on me that Interfaith as a faith had become the core of who I am. I began to self-identify by saying, "My faith is Interfaith. My spiritual path is Judaism. My tribe is humanity." This was how I felt. This was who I had become. My faith was Interfaith. My faith is in the under-standing that religions are languages for seeking and speaking about the sacred. As there is no hierarchy among languages, there is no hierarchy amongst religions. My spiritual path remains Judaism. I still walk that path. I still cleave to it. Judaism helps me to steer by the star of justice. What I have left behind is any thought or belief that my path is the "best" path, let alone the "right" path. It is simply but crucially the right path for me. Lastly, my tribe is humanity. I accept no divisions. I see no group within my human family as inherently better or worse. What kind of human being we will be is up to each of us individually.

With these thoughts more and more clearly etched into my thoughts and beliefs, I felt I needed to talk to Karen again, I was rebuffed again. At the same time, a misunderstanding became evident. When Karen and I had discussed my becoming a minister at ICC, we also discussed my be-coming a full minister at some point in the future. I had been thinking in terms of a few years. Karen was thinking rather longer. For me, Karen's opinion settled the issue. I was very much the junior partner here. It had been Karen, Jamal and Debra who had founded the church. They were en-titled to decide how long they wanted it to be before I was no longer con-sidered an associate minister. I wasn't about to argue. If they didn't want to embrace Interfaith as a faith, who was I as the new kid on the block to push it?

This was truly a small bump. While we disagreed about a few things, my admiration for Karen, Jamal and Debra was undiminished, as was my joy in directing the Evergreen UU choir. I was about to enter my sixties and feeling very comfortable. Looking back, I realize I was at that moment fully content to run out the clock as an associate minister and choir director. Almost two years passed, and I was even more comfortable. But I did hit a snag in writing my book. I couldn't figure out how to finish it. I decided to put the book aside for a while, but really wasn't bothered. I was comfort-able and very happy.

In the meantime, I had begun attending an annual interfaith confer-ence at Camp Brotherhood, a lovely retreat about an hour north of me. I met some amazing people there. One of them was Dilara Hafiz, an inter-faith force of nature who lived in Bellingham with her husband and chil-dren. We became friends and kept in contact. I also made good friends at ICC, among them Steve Crawford, who very much enjoyed pondering spiritual matters along with environmental activism. This was a fun crowd to "run with."

Indeed, now that it seemed certain that this was what I would be doing until I retired, I decided to take the plunge and buy a house. It was the middle of the housing slump. By the time I was through "fixing it up" it still took every penny I had put aside, but I was able to buy a split-level foreclosed house in Lynnwood. The location was no coincidence. Lynnwood is just about halfway between Ballard, where ICC was located, and Marysville, where the UU choir sang. Had there been no intervention, I'm pretty sure this is how things would have stayed.

No sooner had I closed escrow on my new house than I was informed that because of financial considerations Evergreen was going to eliminate the position of director of music. What? This was May. It was flaming May at the end of nine years now at Evergreen! The change would be effective in June. If Evergreen had informed me of this in February or March, I never would have bought the house. Had I not bought the house, who knows what course my life would have taken? But I had. So now what?

I knew there was at least one person at Evergreen who was out for my scalp. You don't work anywhere for nearly nine years and not make at least a few people unhappy. This person was *exceedingly* unhappy. But I couldn't believe that one person alone could get the board to eliminate my position. My thoughts went back to the alarm bells that went off when I'd first told Bruce that I wasn't leaving. Ok then. My offer to resign was being accepted a few years later and with only a few weeks' notice. Not the friendliest way of doing things, but clearly it was time for me to move on.

I had some hurt feelings. There's no getting around that. The way this was handled really sucked. It had seemed like a done deal. This was the hand I'd been dealt. So again, what now?

Did I really want to live in Lynnwood, no longer working in Marysville and with no work except my once-a-month responsibility as an associate minister in Ballard? Not really. But I'd just closed escrow! I was stuck. Ok, but was I really ready to retire? And if not, *what* was I going to *do*? What occurred to me rather quickly was that I was most definitely *not* ready to retire.

I puzzled over this for at least a week or so. One door closes, another door can be kicked open. What? Where? Then it came to me. It made sense. It was the next logical step along my spiritual path. But good flaming grief! This wasn't just a step, it was a giant leap into the unknown, even for me. I called my dear friend Vicki Nagel in Los Angeles. We had yet another long talk. I ran what I saw as my options by her. Bless her, she had a few heartwarmingly choice words describing both Bruce and the person out for my scalp, but otherwise Vicki was hugely supportive. This was jumping out of that proverbial plane without a parachute, I said. Why not? Vicki asked me. Has that ever stopped you before? Good point.

The bottom line was this; I wasn't ready to retire. So, what was I going to do? Karen had ruled out Interfaith as a faith at ICC. Though I embraced it as long as I stayed at ICC I knew this must remain out of reach. I would be a quarter-time associate minister there for the foreseeable future. Could I move? Sure. But where? Good question! There wasn't a church or congregation anywhere, at least none that I knew of, that embraced Interfaith as a faith. If I wanted to be a part of one, I'd have to start my own. I'd have to start my own!

Ok then. Fine! That, surely, was going to be a full-time job. No retirement in my future.

In all honesty, it felt very much as if a power a whole lot bigger than me had taken me by the lapels again and said, "Stop taking the easy way out. Get off your posterior. Do what you're supposed to." But start a church? Me? Start a church??! Oy, gevalt!

Yet once I made the decision to "do what I'm supposed to" everything became so amazingly clear. I realized why I'd put away the book I'd been working on. The only logical conclusion to it was what I had thus far carefully avoided: the actual practice of Interfaith as a faith. More than that, it meant people from differing spiritual paths coming together in safe sacred space, the kind that John and Alexandra had taught me to create, and sharing our spiritual selves with one another. Ok then, it was time to talk to Karen.

When I'd been ordained, I had promised to stay at ICC at least three years, and frankly had intended to spend the rest of my life there. Now, after just two years, I was asking Karen to be released from that promise. I wanted to start my own Interfaith church, based on Interfaith as a faith. After I explained what had happened at Evergreen, Karen was exceedingly gracious. She not only gave me her blessing but asked how she could help. I thanked her and told her I'd let her know. First, I also had to attend the annual meeting at Evergreen. The board could only recommend to the membership that my position be eliminated. Perhaps the choir or congregation would object. Doubtful, but possible.

For my part, I didn't ask anyone to do anything. I didn't complain to Bruce, I didn't petition the board, and I didn't speak to the choir, as a choir or individually. I didn't feel it was up to me. Either people would object or they wouldn't. I had a hunch that as this was supposedly being done to save money that Evergreen simply didn't have to spend, the board recommendation would pass. And quite frankly, at this point I was ready to move on. Actually I was more than ready—in my mind I had already moved on. I attended the meeting out of curiosity as I wanted to see how things would play out. Still, I was not only fully prepared to empty my office after the meeting, but in point of fact had already done my packing. Everything was boxed and ready to go.

Then came the day of the meeting. I sat at the very back. I was there to observe. I'm talking about it here because all this led to a rather large and costly mistake on my part.

To make a drawn-out process reasonably short, the board said the cut was necessary and no one disagreed. But then a member of the Evergreen Fellowship, Jackie Swyer, volunteered to fund my position for a year from her own savings. The board panicked (they were seated at the front of the sanctuary, facing the congregation, so the panic was there for all to see). It was quickly decided that Jackie's offer couldn't be accepted. This was fascinating! Then, after much squabbling, it was decided to put it to a vote of the entire congregation. The congregation voted to accept Jackie's offer. A member of the board immediately objected and demanded a revote! A revote? Really? Wow. Meanwhile, Bruce sat to the side and said nothing, even when the board decided to throw democracy out the window and start over. That's what confirmed for me what I'd suspected all along.

As things descended into chaos, I went over to talk to Jackie. I told her it was clear that neither Bruce nor the board wanted me to stay. If somehow the congregation overruled this, I wanted her to know that I would stay one more year to try to protect the choir but under no circumstances would I stay any longer than that. And I asked her, was she really that big a choir fan? She told me no, she wasn't, but she really liked my sermons! Over the past few years, Bruce had turned the pulpit over to me several times. Wow. Jackie's reasoning was flattering and hugely unexpected. Despite my gentle urging she did not retract her offer.

I wondered in my mind just how many sermons Bruce would allow me the next year. But things moved ahead and the congregation voted a second time to accept Jackie's offer and fund my position for one more year. This time there was no getting around it. I was asked if I would accept the position and made the mistake of saying yes. Bottom line, I thought the choir deserved better than a few weeks' notice that they were going out of business.

I had hoped to begin work on starting my Interfaith church. As I thought about it, I realized I could still move forward. It would just have to be more slowly. Bottom line, I felt that after nine years together I owed it to the choir to stay. My motives were the best, but with benefit of hindsight it was incredibly foolish. I had the feeling that if I didn't stay, the choir I'd helped to build would melt away. Surely, by staying one more year I could help Evergreen figure out a way for the choir to continue, even without a director of music, but by deciding to stay in such a toxic situation, I now experienced one of my most spiritually difficult years since my mother's death.

Bruce did what he could to make both me and the choir irrelevant, to the point that when a young woman who had sung in choir died tragically, he cut the choir out and went elsewhere for music, when previously the choir had usually sung at a memorial for any member of the congregation, let alone a former choir member. Beyond this, the chair of the music committee was encouraged to form a musical mini-group separate from the choir. Suddenly, I was no longer being informed about music committee meetings, meetings that as director of music I was supposed to attend. Ok.

Contrary to Jackie's hopes, Bruce didn't let me into the pulpit any more than absolutely necessary. I haven't speculated as to what Bruce's problems were because, frankly, I don't know. I have some pretty good hunches, but that's gossip, not knowledge. I can speak to his actions, not his motives. Still, our friendship died.

The truly horrific time came that December—my December from hell. I've mentioned before three good friends. A quick review. Marc Mechling I'd helped with his city council race. He was the husband of Meredith Mechling, with whom I'd worked some fifteen years before in the Dave Somers campaign. I enjoyed and valued them both. Faye Phelan was a dear friend I'd kept since college, now nearly forty years in the past. How closely we stayed in touch can perhaps best be exemplified by the time she called me in panic: Faye still in the Los Angeles area, me up in Edmonds, north of Seattle. Faye, you may recall, played the harp. She had a gig and couldn't find her music. Not knowing where else to turn, she called me! Like I'm supposed to know? Yet somehow I knew immediately where the music was. I told her it was under her bed. It was, and Faye happily drove off to play her gig. Lastly there was Vicki Nagel, my one-time junior high teacher who had become a lifelong friend—over fifty years and counting. While all three of these lovely people were good friends, I was the closest to Vicki. We spoke almost every week. Indeed, now that I understood my path and had started writing my Interfaith book again, Vicki was the first person I'd sent a draft to ask: does this make sense?

Then, in less than two horrific weeks, all three were dead. Marc's death was the only one that I knew was coming. He had bravely been battling brain cancer. Along with other friends, I'd paid him a last visit not long before. Still, knowing someone is going to die doesn't make it much easier to accept when it happens. Then Faye died. I knew she'd had health issues—as one example, she had steadfastly refused to give up smoking, but I hadn't realized how bad things had gotten. Now, suddenly, she too was gone. The hammer blow came with Vicki. She'd just returned home from a trip to Europe with friends. We'd chatted over the phone about the sights she'd seen and how much fun she'd had. She also mentioned that she just couldn't shake the jet lag this time. Maybe it was the flu, she thought. Vicki went to see her doctor, who ran a few tests and then immediately had her hospitalized—from the doctor's office straight to the hospital. I was able to talk to her once more while she was in the hospital. She had leukemia. The question, it seemed, was how virulent was it? They were running tests. Hours later she was moved to intensive care, where no phone calls were allowed. The next day she was dead. From possible jet lag to dead from leukemia in three, maybe four days.

All three of these beautiful friends, two of them lifelong, gone in less than two weeks. I was shell-shocked. I went early to the next choir rehearsal knowing I'd need some quiet time to center myself, but I didn't get it. I was still the director of music, but I hadn't been told that the music committee chair had scheduled a rehearsal of his mini-group immediately before choir. My time to center myself had vanished. With tragedy pressing hard on me, I couldn't think, let alone gather myself, and rehearsal would begin in twenty minutes! I snatched up my materials, abandoned the rehearsal area, and stalked out into a hallway to get some silence and pull myself together. I was not a happy camper. My space had been invaded with no warning. Calm down, concentrate, breathe. You have a rehearsal. You have responsibilities. Breathe!

Immediately after the choir rehearsal I got a phone call from one of the mini-group members, telling me that I owed her and everyone else in the group an apology for not respecting them. What? What on earth?! As I listened it became clear that she and the others had observed that I was anything but happy that night. Their immediate conclusion: I was mad that they had formed this mini-group and was not respecting them.

It took a while to figure that one out. Most of us, when we see someone we know who is really upset, will go over and ask, what's wrong? That hadn't happened. Instead of support in my time of crisis or even just a friendly, "Are you ok?" these folks had *evidently assumed* I was upset with them. When they saw me upset and reeling, their reaction was not "Steven's upset, let's find out what's wrong." Their reaction was, "Steven's upset, it's obviously because he doesn't like what we're doing." I have my suspicions but don't know who primed them to think that way. This brought home to me just how toxic the situation had become.

So, why bring all this up? Because I believe there's an important lesson here. My head had been telling me that there was something wrong at Evergreen for some time. My heart wanted to do everything I could to support the choir that I so loved. In all things, we need balance. The head should listen to the heart. But the heart should also listen to the head. The one good part of all of this is that I struggled like mad to keep my personal problems from becoming a choir problem. I sought to shield the choir, which, after all, was going through its own mourning, knowing that this was their final year. I recently talked to one of the choir members and discovered that I had been at least partially successful. He'd had no idea what was happening, but told me he was glad for and had indeed enjoyed that final year. That was some positive reinforcement.

While this was indeed the December from hell, and a December I'm not likely to forget any year soon, things were already in motion for founding the Interfaith church. That is a *much* happier story!

Chapter Thirty

Start a church. Right. For "some reason" they don't teach classes in seminary on starting a new church, let alone founding a new spiritual tradition. This was going to be an adventure. I chronicled the adventure in detail in *Practical Interfaith*. But beyond the challenge of putting a church together there were other spiritual aspects that may have some relevance.

Once I sat with the shock of it, I realized that founding the Living Interfaith church was the logical and indeed necessary outgrowth of The *Interfaith Alternative*. This first book, as yet unpublished, was my attempt to put onto paper the combination of my life experience and what I began to refer to, at least to myself, as an "afternoon's dictation."[42] Fundamental to the book and to my spiritual blossoming was the revelation that religion is a language for speaking to and about God. More than that, there was the groundbreaking revelation that we shouldn't worship the grammar.

Grammar supplies the rules by which a language works and is therefore crucial to it. Grammar is more than important; it is fundamental. Grammar will tell us whether we should use an adjective before the noun (English: *a beautiful house*) or after the noun (Spanish: *una casa bonita*). Without grammar, a language is just a collection of words. Grammar orders a language and makes it comprehensible. So, grammar is vital. To deny that would be foolish.

---

42   My friend and mentor Rev. Wesley Yamaka, to whom I had first shown the dictation, not only read a late draft of the book but then wrote an affirming comment for inclusion on the back cover. Father John Heagle, who was so instrumental in teaching me how to create safe sacred space, also read a late draft of the book and wrote an affirming comment for the back cover. That truly warmed my heart.

All the same, in spite of its importance, grammar carries no intrinsic meaning. This includes the grammar of our diverse spiritual paths. Whether or not we cover our heads when we pray, or what direction we face, or whether or not we cross ourselves—these diverse rituals and many others are all important markers of our spiritual traditions. They can help to focus us, to ground us, but as important as they are, in the end the rituals that order our spiritual paths and give them such a wonderful richness and individuality are simply grammar.

So much became clear to me once I truly understood the implications of religion being a language, rather than a repository of sacred rules. That's a simple sentence, but the truth of it is that it took me nearly ten years truly to understand and internalize those implications.

Once we understand and embrace that our religions are languages for dealing with the sacred, their ethnic roots and differences not only become clearer but far more understandable. Different languages develop in different countries that experience differing cultures. Most of us are most comfortable with the language of our birth, but that doesn't make our language "the one true language." With religion, as with language, what is important is what we *say*, not the language we use to say it. Just as there have been great and profound writers in all of our languages, so have there been writers of pornography. People have written great and profound things as well as pornography in every religion as well—Malala Yousafzai as opposed to the leaders of Daesh (ISIS), is but one example from Islam.

Once the cultural roots of our religious languages became clear to me, the need to become multilingual took on even more importance than it already had. So, how do we learn each other's spiritual/religious languages? One important way that I had discovered in my years of choir-directing was by worshiping together.

Worshipping together. For me, that meant moving from interfaith dialogue to Interfaith congregations. But could it be done? It hadn't been done yet, at least not to my knowledge. But if I was going to urge Interfaith congregations in my book, I had to know it was possible! That meant starting my own spiritual community. This, along with at long last having a house of worship where I truly felt at home, was what motivated me to found the Living Interfaith church.

Found a church? Me? Found a church? Good flaming grief! But, to paraphrase Hillel, if not me, who? And if not now, *when*? I was over sixty years old and my health has never been spectacular. "Time limited" is a phrase that came to mind more than once. Yes indeed, if not now, when? Ok. Fine. Question One: How on earth do I start?

One immense help in putting my spiritual house in order was my spiritual director, Suzanne Seaton. Seeing a spiritual director had been a requirement while I studied at SU. Their role is to help a person sort through his or her spiritual issues. As with any other field, some spiritual directors are exceedingly helpful and some not. Thanks to the recommendation of my good friend Jill Komura, I had sought out Suzanne.

Throughout my assorted difficulties at SU, Suzanne had always been there for me, helping me sort through the ups as well as the downs. One qualm I'd had from the very first time she and I discussed my future as a minister, was how many ministers are perceived. My guides for ministry were two very different, yet amazingly similar men: Wesley Yamaka, a Methodist minister, and Leonard Beerman, a Reform rabbi. The differences in their religious beliefs seemed unimportant to me. What *was* important was that both men led by example, not by "the power vested in me" sort of thing. They were towering examples of living a life of justice, coupled with a life of humility. In fact, the more I thought about it the more the two seemed to go together—justice and humility. That in itself was an important life lesson.

"Do as I say, not as I do" is not only a bad joke about parenting from my childhood, but can also be one of the more grating aspects of ministry that I've witnessed. I have long believed that ministers should be examples— not of perfection (we're all human, for crying out loud) but of striving to live the life that Micah called us to. Act with justice, love compassion and walk humbly. It dawned on me that these are not separate traits. They are interlocked aspects of a life lived in concert with spirit—however we define spirit. Justice requires both compassion and humility. I don't look upon clergy as men or women of God. I see clergy as fellow humans striving to live just, compassionate and humble lives, who are called to be of service to others striving to live just, compassionate and humble lives.

One thing I set out to do with focused intent was to be sure than no one ever mistook me for a "pastor." I have no flock. I am not a shepherd. I serve, not from any God-given authority but because I find myself in a position of being able to serve. At a service I wear a jacket and tie because I want people to know that I take the service seriously. I wear a stole that carries a multitude of spiritual symbols because I want everyone to be able to see that I represent no one faith. But I purposefully put the stole on moments before the service and take it off the moment the service is over because whatever spiritual "authority" may be present during the service is not my possession. It is not me.

Making sure that Interfaith and not the persona known as Steven Greenebaum was the focus of what our congregation was about was possibly the most intentional of my actions as we began. Not that I didn't make mistakes. I made plenty. Starting a new faith and starting a new congregation were never on my radar until I was faced with them. But one of the great advantages of this whole thing being about Interfaith and not me was that none of my mistakes were fatal to the congregation. I admitted them and we moved forward.[43]

One of the other conscious things I did was resolve not to officiate at weddings. I have several minister friends who love officiating at weddings. We're all different, and I would never call them wrong. But for me, weddings ought to be civil ceremonies. I never want to utter the words, "By the power vested in me by the state of Washington..." I'm a minister. I don't believe the state of Washington should be vesting me with any civil power. I deeply believe that the wall between church and state should be unclimbable. Gay or straight, whatever your spiritual path, a marriage is a contract between two loving individuals. A contract! Religion should keep out of it—or so I feel. For me the clincher is that the state allows clergy to marry people, but only a judge can grant a divorce. If only a judge can grant a divorce, this seems yet another signal that only a judge should officiate at a wedding.

Not that I wouldn't be honored and happy to officiate at an Interfaith *celebration* of a wedding, or an Interfaith renewal of vows. That's an entirely different matter.

I'm also very much disposed to putting as much power as possible in the congregation's hands and as little as possible in the minister's. I've never liked power. I don't like to wield it myself, and I confess I like it even less when others wield it. Lord Acton was right—on every level: political, social, religious, you name it. Power corrupts, and absolute power corrupts absolutely.

But to my huge joy, relief and, I'll admit it, immense pleasure, Living Interfaith got launched. It was most definitely launched as a team effort. Now, at long last, I could finish writing *The Interfaith Alternative*, the book that took ten years to write even after the afternoon's dictation. But with the book written, now what? Would anyone publish it?

---

43 One example being that I needed to write my sermons down—and then rewrite them several times. Some of my early Living Interfaith sermons were extemporaneous and—well, not helpful.

Drawing on my stunted career as a writer, I bought a book that listed agents and their specialties/interests. I then wrote to a number of agents, trying to find one who would work with me to find a publisher. Most agents never bothered to reply. Most of those who did reply sent the typical form rejection ("Dear Author ..."). I think I got two written replies, one saying my book sounded interesting but she didn't know how to market it. Interfaith as a faith? It hasn't been done, if it hasn't been done, she felt no one in the publishing world would want to be first.

Ok. The agent door was closed. For every door that closes, there's one that can be kicked open. Fine. Where??!

The answer came in a book that my friend Rebecca Alder had mentioned a few years before. Rebecca had sung in the choir I led while I was the associate minister at the Interfaith Community Church. She is very much justice oriented. It's one reason (besides music) why we bonded. The book was called *The Better World Shopping Guide*. She thought I might like it and she was right. The book fit me like the proverbial glove.

Since my early college years I had subscribed to *Consumer Reports*. But then, I think it was in my mid to late forties, I stopped. I found myself turned off by *Consumer Reports*. The magazine tells us which products are cheapest, last the longest and are the best value. Why did that turn me off? Because what the magazine doesn't tell us is the human cost of a product. Is slave labor involved? Is that why the product is so cheap? Does the process of manufacturing pollute the air or the ground? If I'm shopping somewhere, does a cheap price reflect employees of the store not getting a living wage?

I wanted to live my beliefs, not simply proclaim them. I was already driving a Toyota Prius hybrid to cut down on the amount of gas I used. While I didn't have the kind of control I had when I'd actually had a house built for me, one of the things I did immediately upon buying my house in Lynnwood was to have all the single-pane windows replaced with double panes. I also began what turned out to be a five-year process of having solar panels installed on my roof. I couldn't afford the full array at once, and didn't want to take out a loan, so I had the panels installed in stages. Today I'm energy neutral: the panels produce more power than I need during the late spring, summer and early fall, and less than I need during the winter. Yes, it was expensive, and no, my solar panels won't save the world. But they seem a good step in the right direction of contributing toward combating climate change. And that seemed far more important to me than the drag on my Independence Fund.

One of my largest gripes about our society is how we are fed from birth the doctrine that we alone are important. WE are where we need to focus. We are to think of ourselves and only ourselves. Forget everyone else. By now I've given more than a few sermons on what I believe to be the high cost of cheap, as well as the exorbitant cost to others of our thinking only of our own well-being. *Consumer Reports* feeds that. I'd written to them several times, pleading with them to broaden the scope of their interests, and they'd never written back. But now Rebecca pointed me at *The Better World Shopping Guide*. This book focuses precisely on the social and environmental costs of what we buy. It rates products and stores from "A" to "F," not by how cheap or tasty or useful the products may be or how low their prices are but rather what buying that product costs the rest of the world. I refuse to live my life ignoring the impact it has on others. This book was just what I had wanted.

I'd just purchased the most recent edition (it's updated every few years because the world is NOT static!). And in thumbing through it, I came upon the publisher page. New Society Publishers. They were dedicated to helping build a better world for all humanity. My kind of people! I thought: well, forget agents. Maybe I should be looking for a publisher who views the world the same way I do. *That's* the door to kick open. So, I wrote to New Society.

Long story short, I was soon in contact with a wonderful editor, Ingrid Witvoet. A year later, the book was published. Ingrid went out on quite a limb for me and my message. To my knowledge, New Society had never before published a book on sacred matters, but Ingrid, like me, felt that we were seeking to change the world in a similar way, a way that helped all of humanity, not just the selected few; whoever they might be.

I felt so validated. My book was going to be published, and it would be published by a publisher that cared more about changing the world than it did bestsellers! I was flying high. Living Interfaith church was holding regular services. The wonderful board of Living Interfaith took guidance from me but never orders. We did everything by consensus. Now I'd kept my "deal" with God. The dictation that I had received had at last been turned into a book, and the book was about to be published.

What brought me down was cancer.

Chapter Thirty-One

In the several years before my diagnosis I'd had some bouts with what's called prostatitis. It's a prostate infection. The first experience was the most difficult, and fortunately friends were visiting who could take me to urgent care. After that I learned to spot the symptoms early on and it was no big deal, other than it meant that I now had an urologist and he was keeping track of something called my PSA numbers. I'd had two biopsies over those years, and both came back negative. It seemed I was a good candidate for prostate cancer, but so far, so good. But then my numbers rocketed up and I had yet another biopsy.

It's probably not shocking to learn, but there is a galaxy of distance between knowing you may have cancer (which is why the biopsy) and knowing that you DO have cancer.

I found out that I did indeed have cancer on a Tuesday. My first reaction was a form of denial. "Fine. I knew that. No big deal. Let's just get on with life." That reaction lasted most of the day. But that night, when I turned out the lights and went to bed, it morphed into, "Oh shit! I have CANCER. How far has it gotten? How much has the doctor told me? Is it treatable? If so how debilitating might the treatment be? And what if it's not treatable?"

Toward the middle of the night a moment of clarity came. I realized that I'd done the really important things. I'd written the book. And by this time I'd gone over it with the copy editor, who had been very generous with his praise for my use of English. The book would be out in a few months. And, I thought, I'm sixty-three, not twenty-three. So in that sense I'm really pretty lucky. I've had the time to do what I needed to do. But oh, shit! I have CANCER! It was neither a good nor a happy night.

But by the next morning things were better. My mind began to reclaim me from my fears. Ok. I have cancer. But it's prostate cancer, and the doctor really did seem hopeful that it was early and hadn't spread. Time to breathe and figure out what to do. Part of "what to do" was how much to tell the congregation. My ministry is based on openness. I didn't want to hide anything. But I also didn't want to dump my troubles onto people with plenty of their own.

By coincidence, that morning I had an appointment scheduled with Suzanne, my spiritual director. I had expected to be talking about something completely different, but instead we talked about my cancer and more important my reaction to it. I had come to the conclusion that I would tell the congregation all, but not until I had both a firmer grip on my emotions and a clear plan for how I would treat the cancer. My urologist had recommended surgery, but I wanted to explore my options.

I have two dear, longtime friends, Liz and Bill Hawkins, whom I met when I first got involved in things political around 1992. I'd told them about the cancer, and that night we met for dinner. Bill's a very thorough man so I shouldn't have been as surprised as I was at dinner when he presented me with two books. Bill had been to the bookstore and spent quite some time looking through several books on prostate cancer before buying the two he thought particularly helpful. He handed them to me.

I remain grateful. It hadn't occurred to me to do this kind of research. I had just thought of talking to people, but now that I had the books, I read them carefully. Everyone's different. Every situation is different. But it seemed clear that for me surgery wasn't the best option. Instead, I decided to go with what are called radioactive "seeds." I made appointments with two different specialists before deciding on whom to have do the procedure. Only when this was all taken care of did I inform the congregation that 1) I had cancer, 2) it was treatable, 3) I was having an outpatient procedure, and 4) assuming all went well, I shouldn't have to miss work.

I had the procedure, and all indeed went well. I had a few days of intense discomfort, but then things seemed to calm down. I backed off the pain pills and thought, enough of babying yourself. Time to get back to work!

A few months after the procedure, my book was published. I was hugely aware of what kind of chance Ingrid was taking in publishing the book. I wanted to support her in every way possible. So, in those months before the book was published, and for a few months after I set about arranging a book tour. I arranged it rather than the publisher because, as it turns out, book tours just aren't done that much anymore unless the book is a potential bestseller. So, I had to make all the arrangements as well as pay for my transportation and hotel costs. Still, I was more than willing to do what I considered my part. New Society was taking a big gamble on me, and I wasn't trying to get rich. I was trying to spread what I believed to be an important message.

My ears still prevent me from flying, so mine would be a train trip. I spent those next several months lining up train schedules with bookstores in cities around the country and even in Canada. It was hard work. I tired easily and frequently felt frustrated with myself. I couldn't figure out why putting a book tour together felt so blasted overwhelming. It didn't dawn on me until well after the tour that having just gone through radiation treatment, my body probably needed a little downtime. Well, duh! But at the time my focus was: the book is about to be published and I have work to do. It couldn't wait. Still, I continued to be frustrated and even disappointed in myself for feeling overwhelmed by everything. Such a wuss! Was I really that old? Good flaming grief! These days sixty-three is not that old. Get off your butt and concentrate! I fought my way through the fog and was able to put the tour together.

The publicist for New Society was supportive and arranged for me to have radio interviews along the way. The trip was by train down the West Coast, across the country and then up the East Coast to Canada and across Canada back to Seattle. Lots of stops and lots of talks—mostly at bookstores. Toronto proved to be one of the highlights. Paul McKenna, of the Scarboro Missions just outside Toronto, had contacted me before the trip. He had read my book and really liked it, which meant a lot to me. Paul has spent much of his adult life not only working for interfaith dialogue but also putting together a wonderful chart of the Golden Rule as it appears around the world.[44] I had a lovely chat with him in the gardens of the missions, and then had a good chat with an interesting roundtable of individuals he had brought together to hear me talk about my book.

By the time I got back home I was completely exhausted. Just getting up was a trial. Fortunately, I had a lot of help with Living Interfaith from Steve Crawford, who had been in on things from the beginning. Since our church met in the cafeteria of a middle school (and would until September

---

44 scarboromissions.ca/golden-rule

of 2014),[45] we had to create the sacred space every time we met. Sunday after Sunday, Steve would come over and not simply help but do a lot of the heavy lifting. I don't know what I would have done without him. But with him, the church continued to thrive. We remained small, but we thrived. And I began to work on my second book.

There was a brief health hesitation. Steve had noticed that my breathing was somewhat labored whenever we "packed the church" into my car to take it to the middle school cafeteria on Sunday. Was I still recovering from the radiation therapy? Now that Steve had mentioned it, I was forced to consider that there did seem to be some difficulties that might indicate—heart problems? Oh swell! After putting it off for a while I at last went to a cardiologist, who took one look at me and said I was fine. He then scheduled me for a treadmill test to be sure, but told me that he was certain it would come out negative. It did. My heart was healthy. Ok. I could concentrate on writing my follow-up Interfaith book.

One question had been asked of me repeatedly on my book tour. It came from those who liked the idea of Interfaith as a faith. While they liked it, they also doubted that it was practical. After several thousand years of humans dividing themselves into righteous (and much too frequently self-righteous) pockets of differing spiritual beliefs and practices, could Interfaith possibly work? This made clear to me that what the second book needed to focus on was the practical side of Interfaith. Indeed, *Practical Interfaith* became the title. The point of the book would be to show not only how Living Interfaith had started but how it worked, on a day-to-day basis. In many ways it's a book on how to start an Interfaith congregation. I wanted to be of concrete help to others who might wish to follow the path of bringing people together.

But even as I was writing the book, I wondered if it would see the light of day. My first book was still selling, but not hugely. It had still not yet earned enough back for me to see a dime more than my original advance. I also knew that New Society was going through some financial difficulties. Even if they wanted to, how could they possibly afford to publish my second book? I'd mentioned to Ingrid that I was going to work on a follow-up book as soon as I got back from the book tour and had processed the ques-

---

45   At that date we moved to a beautiful sacred facility, the Good Shepherd Baptist church. My dear friend Reverend Christopher Boyer is the minister there and invited us. Chris and I disagree just a bit from time to time about theology, but we are bonded by our mutual commitment to the path of love, justice and, while we will both freely admit our humanity and therefore our imperfections, lives of integrity. As Chris and his church are busy on Sunday mornings, our services moved to Saturdays.

tions I'd been asked. Ingrid's response had been a rather cool, "We'll see." I realized that my first book was anything but a money-maker for them and understood Ingrid's hesitation.

They were such truly wonderful people. How could I push them? As I was getting to the point where I had a readable draft of my new book, I wrote an apologetic e-mail to Ingrid. In it I told her I would understand completely if New Society didn't want to publish my second book, but by any chance did she at least want to see it? I heard nothing back. Not a peep. Ok then. But if the door at New Society had closed, was there any door I could possibly kick open?

By coincidence, some months before this quandary Sam Freedman, a writer on religion for *The New York Times*, had come out, witnessed one of the Living Interfaith services and written an article about us. I'd been introduced to Sam (through e-mail) by my friend Dilara Hafiz. Dilara had been instrumental in helping Living Interfaith get started. I had written Sam that I'd be in New York for my book tour, but we'd been unable to connect. Then, nearly a year later, he hadn't forgotten. He came out to Washington (I assume he had other business here as well), attended a service and wrote a rather nice article about us. Suddenly our little church and what we were trying to do to bring people together was in *The New York Times*.

There were some exceedingly negative reactions to the article from those whose approach to religion tended to be, "My way or God will send you to hell." Among those who read the article with a more positive attitude, however was Emily Wichland, an editor at Skylight Paths Publishing. Skylight Paths published the books of Jamal Rahman, one of my friends from the Interfaith Community Church where I had worked before starting Living Interfaith. Emily got my contact information from Jamal and wrote to ask me if by any chance I was intending to write another book. If so, she was interested in seeing it.

Wow! This was cool. Finally, a door I didn't have to kick open. This one opened all by itself! Is that great or what? I wrote back that indeed I was working on another book. I also told Emily that while I really liked my current publisher, books on religion really weren't their thing and I didn't think they were interested in publishing anything more of mine. Emily wanted to see what I had written and to make a long story short, she liked what she saw, and almost by return mail I had a book contract offer. I wrote a happy e-mail to Ingrid to tell her she was off the hook. That's when my emotional roof caved in.

Steven Greenebaum

Ingrid replied that she had no idea what I was talking about. My book hadn't been a drag on New Society. Yes, she had stuck her neck out for me but no one had lopped it off. What on earth was I talking about?

The tone seemed more one of hurt than anger. Frankly, it stung. What had I done? I wrote back and referenced my earlier e-mail. I think at this point we talked on the phone. Ingrid told me that there had been a glitch in their server and they'd lost a lot of e-mail over the past few months. She had evidently never seen my earlier e-mail asking if she might be interested. What now? What now indeed!

Lesson for the future. Don't assume. For crying out loud, don't ever assume. I should have called. 20/20 hindsight, I know, but when Ingrid didn't reply to my e-mail asking if she were interested in seeing my new book, I should have called, but I felt Ingrid had become more than just my editor. She was my friend. I didn't want to impose. That she didn't want to have to say "no" made far more sense to me than the thought that she'd never received the e-mail.

Most of the time, I think humility is a good thing. I very much find myself repelled by the "me, me, me!" world of today. I find self-promotion to be distasteful at best, and mostly pretty darn repulsive. This time, humility got in the way.

In the end, things worked out. Ingrid waved me off, and my book was published by Skylight Paths. People would have *Practical Interfaith* to refer to to help them not only find a path to Interfaith but also guide them in forming their own Interfaith congregations. There would be no need to reinvent the wheel.

Chapter Thirty-Two

Having begun Living Interfaith at age sixty, I knew I hadn't a prayer of retiring at sixty-five, but seventy was where I wanted to draw the line. There were several reasons for this. One was the practical reason that as the founder of Living Interfaith I felt if I stayed longer than ten years it would in all likelihood become "my" church. I didn't want that. At our very first meeting I told our newly formed board that I would stay ten years and no longer. I would need to be replaced after that. I wanted to plant this thought early. I never wanted anyone to think of me as the indispensable person. That's the road to a cult, not a faith.

I also had more personal reasons. I still very much hoped somehow, someday, to meet a second Ms. Right. Also, age seventy would in all likelihood be my last possible chance to put aside my full-time work at Living Interfaith and tour the world. I would really like to do that. Indeed, I harbor the breathtaking dream of circumnavigating the world by cruise ship (no planes, as you may recall). Ok, sure. The cost might be prohibitive, but one can still dream, right? And last there was my Roman novel.[46] It has been so many years, but I've never lost the desire to tell that story. Indeed, I believe it more relevant and important today—though I finally realize that as a person who cannot visualize, historical fiction is beyond me and I'll need a coauthor with a gift for description willing to share. With all of this, retiring at age seventy was not something I felt was negotiable.

---

46   OK, trilogy. One of the problems with the book when I first tried to write it was trying to cram too much story into one book. I now see it as three separate but very much related books—someday.

Some very caring people have asked me, won't it be hard to just walk away? For me the answer is a straightforward "No." It will, in fact, be as easy to walk away from leading Living Interfaith as it was to walk away from politics, even though I very much like one and dislike the other. Walking away from power or the appearance of power, and leadership or the appearance of leadership, goes back to something that forms the core of who I am. I mentioned much earlier that I have always seen pride and shame as two sides of the same corrupted coin. That's why it has been relatively easy for me to slough off appeals to my pride and/or vanity, as well as appeals to my shame.

To be sure, I frequently seek advice from people whose opinions I value and from books by authors I respect. To believe even for an instant that I always know best would be nothing but unbridled pride. But what I do believe is that, like Rommel, having gathered the best information I can, it's up to *me* to make the decisions in my life and then, having made them— well, move on. We're human. We make mistakes. But whatever happens, keep moving. I try to learn what I can from any and every experience, pleasant or not, and then move forward.

If you've read this book at all carefully, you'll know that from time to time I haven't always followed through with this. When I haven't, I've deeply regretted it. But I've always tried to make leaving both pride and shame in the dustbin a part of who I am. It's why I tend to let both praise and criticism roll off my back with equal indifference. I have long felt that praise and criticism have everything to do with the person giving it and very little to do with me. So I tend to ignore both.

In terms of Living Interfaith, I trust that being able to lovingly walk away is a sign that the church and the movement are not about me. I am not now and have never been the indispensable person. To be willing to walk away doesn't mean I don't care. I care deeply. Interfaith as a faith is my life's work. Of course I care! But walking away means that I trust the people I've worked with. When my work is done, it will be time for me to leave.

Another reason I felt good about walking away from Living Interfaith was that as I reached age sixty-five, a truly wonderful thing happened. A young woman who had been interested in Living Interfaith but then gotten too busy had re-engaged at the church. She was now attending regularly and wanted to be even more active. Cathy Merchant was bright, articulate and, most important, had clearly and firmly set her sights on living a life of justice in the world. I had Cathy and her husband over for dinner a couple of times. They are an interfaith couple; he is Muslim and Cathy is Buddhist. As we chatted, Cathy spoke of feeling a call to some kind of ministry. I could sense her calling as well. I broached the subject of her becoming an Interfaith minister. To her credit, though she liked the idea, she wanted to think about it. I liked that. This was something big and perhaps life-changing. It would have been foolish and immature for her to rush into it. She thought about it, and talked it over with her husband and her father (who is Christian). Everyone encouraged her.

Cathy then studied with me for nearly three years in preparation. We met nearly every week. The truth of it is, while there appear to be several interfaith theological schools, there are not as yet any Interfaith theological schools (that I'm aware of). So I created a curriculum for Cathy and she followed it assiduously, in spite of a very difficult pregnancy that happily resulted in a beautiful daughter: Inara.[47]

The plan was to have Cathy intern with me for a year after studying with me for three. After that, assuming the Living Interfaith board gave its approval, Cathy would be ordained an Interfaith minister. She and I would co-minister for one more year as I tried to make her transition to ministry as seamless as possible and then, God willing (*Inshallah*), I would retire.

It seemed a good plan but became more like an imperative in 2015. In February I was off to an interfaith conference near San Francisco called "The Big I" (for both Interfaith and Inter-spiritual). I presented about Interfaith as a faith, and my new book *Practical Interfaith*. All went well. But the day after I got home I had a heart attack.

Talk about foolhardy. I don't know how many public service ads I've heard in my lifetime about heart attacks. "Don't be dumb." "Don't ignore the symptoms." Easy enough until it happens! I woke up at around 3:00 AM with classic symptoms. My heart hurt. The pain was what woke me. And I also had an aching pain radiating down my left arm almost to my elbow. Was this a heart attack? Hell no. It couldn't be. I had been in for a heart exam not THAT long ago and the cardiologist had all but made fun of my concerns. So it wasn't a heart attack. But what? By 5:30 the pain still hadn't gone away. Hmm. But then, at last, I fell back asleep.

When I got up that morning I knew something wasn't right. So I waited patiently until 9:00 and called my primary care physician. I talked to the scheduler. But when I told him why I thought I should probably see the doctor that day he refused to make an appointment. "Hang up," he told me. "Call 911, and go to the emergency room." "Oh, come on. I just need to see the doctor." "Hang up. Call 911, and go to the emergency room."

---

47   See Appendix 3 for a suggested reading list/curriculum for Interfaith ministry.

We must have argued for close to ten minutes. He was polite, but also firm. He wouldn't give in. So, at last I did—sort of. I didn't call 911, instead I called a friend who lived nearby and asked her to drive me to the emergency room. It was a strange adventure. The moment I walked in I was given an EKG, but everything seemed fine. And I looked fine. Hah! I knew it. Still, the emergency room person said I should take a seat as some further tests needed to be run. About three hours later, I had my tests.

The doctor I met was a delightful and friendly woman. She took my history, looked at my EKG results and said it probably wasn't a heart attack. But she had some blood taken to be sure. Sometime later she returned a bit baffled. Evidently there's an enzyme that the heart produces when a person has had a heart attack. That enzyme was in my blood. So.... "Sorry, but a further test needs to be done and this one's a bit more invasive." I would have an angiogram of the arteries to my heart. But, she told me, it's probably nothing big. Not to worry.

All this changed when I recovered from the angiogram sedation and an ashen doctor told me that I couldn't go home. I would need to stay in the ER overnight for observation, and needed to see the cardiologist immediately. The three main arteries to my heart were all blocked. As it turned out, two were blocked about 99 percent. One was blocked "only" about 90 percent. Long story short, two days later I saw a heart surgeon. I was going to need triple bypass surgery. Ok then, this is serious stuff. For one thing, open heart surgery is nothing to take lightly. For another, the heart is very well protected by the ribs and sternum. Open heart surgery means the surgeon has to smash his or her way in just to get to the heart.

I still recall the surgeon's offhanded description. "We'll stop your heart. You'll be on a heart/lung machine for several hours. There are probably two arteries we can use from your chest. The third one we'll cut out of your leg. Don't worry, you won't miss it. We'll attach the new arteries, restart your heart, take you off the machine and that's it."

Sure. A piece of cake! Stop the heart. Start the heart. What could possibly go wrong?

From a spiritual point of view, this all turned out to be much easier for me to handle than the cancer. It was so completely out of my hands that it seemed beyond worrying. I'd go to sleep. If the surgery was successful, I'd wake up. If it wasn't, I wouldn't. What was there to worry about? It wasn't bravado. For reasons that still baffle me, I felt no fear, no anxiety.... Yet! Weirdly, fear would indeed come crashing down on me about ten days later.

There is a bit of Christian Scripture that I have made mine over the past ten years, and really longer than that—ever since I took the dictation and agreed to do my best. That was my "deal." I never agreed to succeed. I agreed to do my best. And from that time on, "Thy will, not mine" has truly governed how I have tried to live my life. I will do the best I can and get as much done as I can, for as long as I am able. That is my only obligation. Spiritually, it really does take the pressure off. As long as I do my best, the rest is not my call.

Over time, I have also developed and deeply cleave to the idea of nibbling at life's great issues. It seems to me that for much too long we have suffered under a debilitating meme that the only acceptable result in dealing with a problem, particularly a large one, is completely solving it. If we can't solve it, then why try? That seems to me so very foolish. Life is so much bigger than all of us. What I have many, many times urged the congregation I serve is to set their sights on nibbling at issues. Don't worry how big a problem is, let each of us do what we can. That, for me, is the sane approach. About a year ago, I learned that a rabbi of the second century CE said it much more elegantly (not to mention almost 2,000 years before I thought of it). Rabbi Tarfon, as recorded in the Jewish *Ethics of the Fathers*, told us that it is not our responsibility to finish the work—but neither are we free to avoid it.

I knew I hadn't avoided my work. I hadn't finished it, but neither had I avoided it. So I truly approached the surgery with no fear. I had a certain amount of curiosity, but no fear. And while the first four days after surgery taught me the true meaning of excruciating pain, I still felt no real fear (I am, however, so very grateful for morphine, as twice I had to be wrapped in blankets, shaking uncontrollably, as a nurse dashed in with a syringe of that wonderful painkiller).

Other than those few days of pain, and with the exception chronicled in the next chapter, all has gone pretty well. My heart appears to be doing fine, though even a year after the surgery my chest was still recovering from the violence done to it.

A few months later, Cathy and I had the honor of attending the Parliament of the World's Religions, where we made a joint presentation. This gathering in Salt Lake City, Utah, attracted almost ten thousand participants from across the globe. We spoke to a pretty full room of exceedingly interested people about Interfaith as a faith. I spoke of Cathy and me as "Interfaithers." For me, always, words matter. I didn't want us to be embracing an "ism." So no Interfaithism or Interfaithists; "-ist" connotes to me adherence to doctrine. Rather, as an Interfaither, I could state that my faith is Interfaith, my spiritual path is Judaism, my tribe is humanity. Cathy's faith is Interfaith, her spiritual path Buddhism, and her tribe humanity. As Interfaithers, there's no conflict. This is a way to acknowledge our common humanity while at the same time appreciating our diverse spiritual traditions. I think most of the people there got it.

After the presentation, three of the people attending walked down with me to the Skylight Paths booth where they bought my book. All three were very interested in starting their own Living Interfaith congregations in their own cities. When I got home, there was an e-mail waiting for me from yet another attendee. She is already an ordained minister but forming a Living Interfaith congregation is now what truly calls to her. I have also received e-mails from interested people in the UK, New Zealand and Italy. And I was contacted not long ago by e-mail and then spoke on the phone with an enthusiastic young Muslim who is studying Islamic Chaplaincy at the Hartford Seminary and wants to start an Interfaith church.

The truth is that we can change our world. Step by step, we can stop dividing ourselves and allowing ourselves to be divided into religious, ethnic, socioeconomic and gender tribes. One family: indivisible. We can live as the human community, on a healthy, sustainable planet, bathed in love, justice and community. The choice is ours. But we must make the choice. Nothing will happen if we just sit back and wait.

And we weren't sitting back. The movement was growing. My books would be available long after I wasn't. Just a few years in the future I would hand over my ministerial duties to Cathy. That was the plan. My hope was to continue from time to time to do some public speaking about Interfaith. Perhaps I could find a way to work that in as I cruised the world, found help to write my Roman trilogy and enjoyed my retirement. What was clear and hugely reassuring to me is that Interfaith as a faith will do just fine without me. And that, dear friends, is as spiritually rewarding as life gets. I felt so very grateful.

Then I got blindsided yet again. There is a glorious Yiddish proverb: "Man plans, God laughs." My lovely retirement plans went up in smoke.

Chapter Thirty-Three

I needed to power back a bit after the heart surgery. I tried to resume my activities and in many ways succeeded. But there were some things I just couldn't do any more. That's hard to acknowledge. Still, it's intriguing to me that it was easier to let go of what I couldn't do any more than to deal with the things I couldn't do *yet*. Can't do "yet"? Ok, then how soon? Next week? Next month? Next year? When?!—Patience. Patience!! It was hard for me to learn that—well, to be honest, I'm still working at it. I think it must be a lifelong effort.

Most enlightening to me was seeing how others reacted. I learned early on that I could best communicate my approach to my heart attack and surgery by not calling it that. I quickly began calling it my heart adventure. An adventure was what it was. Fascinating, as Spock would say. There were so many things to discover and unwrap, both about recovering from surgery and about myself. To be sure, not all of the discoveries were pleasant. Indeed, one was downright painful!

It was one of the few places where my surgeon's team let me down. I was transferred from the hospital to a cardiac rehab facility after four days. I had not yet had a bowel movement and only learned later that I should never have been released under those circumstances. Whatever, with all the pain meds I was taking, the fact that my plumbing was clogged should have surprised no one. The tension came from my being told repeatedly to be very, very careful when visiting the bathroom—that "exerting" myself could increase my blood pressure and cause a heart attack given the freshly attached arteries. Keeping my blood pressure low was crucial at this point in my recovery. Now, after almost two weeks with blocked bowels, I was in severe pain.

But what could they do? A saline enema was off the table as it would raise my blood pressure to dangerous levels. I was on every laxative they could throw at me, but nothing worked. For the first and only time during my heart adventure I found myself afraid. My overactive imagination got the better of me. Would I survive a heart attack and triple bypass only to die from over-exertion as a result of my plumbing being plugged? Good flaming grief, how ironic would *that* be?

Obviously, the problem got solved. At last I passed three baked-potato-sized brown concrete bricks. I mention this only because the truth of it is, we never know what will scare us and what won't. And none of us is immune to fear. The fun came when I showed my nurse what I'd just passed. She nodded absently and flushed the toilet. Like those concrete bricks were going anywhere! A maintenance crew was hurriedly called and worked for close to an hour to unplug the toilet. It cracked me up! My sense of humor had returned.

This one experience notwithstanding, it was and remained an adventure—as is all of life. I have tried to be gentle with those who express their sorrow or fear for me. If I were 30, it would still be an adventure though I would definitely see the grounds for some sorrow in that powering back after age 30 is rather different from powering back at age 67. But still, it's a great adventure. The creativity and the challenge for me is always, "Ok, these are my new cards. What can I do with them?"

The need for this was brought home for me when I later visited a beloved friend in his eighties who'd had a brain tumor removed and was facing new limitations. My friend had done much hard and worthwhile work over his lifetime to make the world community better, happier and more loving. Yet now, facing his new limitations, he was having trouble playing the cards he still had and was mourning the ones he had lost. I think his was a natural reaction. But I did try to help him to see just how much joy in life there could still be with his new cards if he would embrace them. I think I got through.

But then the tumor returned and was inoperable. Now my role changed dramatically, and I was accompanying my friend on his final journey. I mostly listened during what were now weekly and sometimes more frequent visits, being as helpful as I could. He died peacefully, and I felt humbled and hugely honored to be asked to be a part of his memorial service.

For myself, I found I had my own new hand to play. About a month after my heart surgery I developed a hacking cough. They stuck a needle in my back, drained the fluid and were done. That happened twice. But during one of my visits to the emergency room to take care of this, for a reason I don't recall, the doctors took an ultrasound not only of my lungs but also of my kidneys. The doctor found an "anomaly" on one kidney and suggested I check it out.

I've never been good at multi-tasking. I decided to wait until I felt pretty well recovered from my heart surgery before following up. Now, some eight months later, I had the anomaly examined. The result: "You have a kidney cancer. But we caught it early! The prognosis is good."

Kidney cancer? Good flaming grief! I have kidney cancer? Less than four years after prostate cancer and less than a year after my heart attack and triple bypass, now it's kidney cancer? Come on!

After a few "Give me a break!" moments, I pushed ahead. It truly became simply a new adventure. Yes, I would definitely have preferred to have avoided it! But we are born with two kidneys. Losing one, particularly at my age, just didn't seem that big a deal, the surgeon thought he might not need to take the entire kidney.

Getting pneumonia just two weeks before surgery, though, seemed a bit much. "My name's Steven, not Job. You know that, right?" My sense of humor had not deserted me.

I was put on antibiotics and an inhaler (happily it was bacterial, not viral, pneumonia, and possibly because I'd had a pneumonia vaccination it was easily treated). I recovered in time to have the surgery —a "partial nephrectomy"—as scheduled, and it was successful. Ok. What's next?

The first "what's next" was developing hand tremors a few days after surgery. When I got home I checked my copy of "Best Pills/Worst Pills" and discovered that the inhaler I was still on could cause tremors in older folks. I took myself off the inhaler and the tremors stopped. So much for mindlessly taking whatever my doctor prescribes.

I sometimes think of the old canard that "God never gives us more than we can handle." A part of me keeps thinking that the people who can't handle anything get off much too easily! But seeing my health difficulties as adventures has truly helped me spiritually along the way. To be sure, a person can get hurt or even killed on an adventure. Some adventures are *by far* more pleasant than others. But my mind responds far better to an adventure than a trial. Mostly.

Which brings me to my meltdown—the adventure I couldn't handle. Prostate cancer, a heart attack and triple bypass, and kidney cancer coupled with a small case of pneumonia on the side couldn't unhinge me. So, why did a fall from a ladder? I've pondered that one.

I recovered from my kidney surgery pretty quickly. I'd been instructed by my surgeon to wait six to eight weeks before attempting any real exercise. The timing seemed perfect. Almost exactly eight weeks later the pears on my lovely pear tree had ripened. Picking the low-hanging fruit was easy. Then I climbed a ladder and was some ten feet off the ground, happily plucking the last of the pears, when the ladder I was on collapsed. Gravity being what it is, not only did the ladder hit the ground with a thud but so did I. I was pretty banged up, but the only substantial injury appeared to be to my right leg. There was a rather nasty rip.

At first, things seemed ok. I cleaned the wound and carefully bandaged it. For a few days there wasn't a problem, then everything went downhill. Suddenly I was in a great deal of pain. What had happened? I wondered if my wound had become infected, and got an appointment to see a doctor. She examined the wound, said it looked fine, and sent me home. That was the beginning of the nightmare. The wound wasn't infected, beyond that the doctor didn't seem to care that it hurt, let alone show any interest in discovering why. The pain not only continued but got progressively worse.

A week later, I saw another doctor, who had an x-ray taken. It was negative. The doctor felt that this probably meant ligament damage and wrapped the leg. The next two days were excruciating, and I was put on very high doses of a painkiller. Still, no one seemed to know what the problem was. One thing clear: wrapping the leg made things worse, not better. So I unwrapped it, which helped. In order to function, as soon as I could I cut my pain meds in half during the day. I was now on crutches and learning that stairs are death traps for people on crutches; I learned to sit on the stairs and scooch myself up and down. So, I could function. Then, after about three weeks of 24/7 pain, I experienced a meltdown.

With a bit of perspective, perhaps it was just one setback too many, too soon. I'd recovered fine from the prostate cancer. But then came the heart attack and triple-bypass, then kidney cancer—and even before I could have surgery for the cancer I had the wracking cough and trouble breathing that comes with pneumonia. Barely had I recovered from the kidney surgery when I ripped up my leg, and no one could tell me when the pain would end or even what was wrong. I've left out the joy of my stomach suddenly churning out massive amounts of acid at about the time of the kidney cancer diagnosis. I not only needed major meds for that but experienced being over-medicated by a sloppy doctor. Bottom line, I just couldn't take any more. I'd reached the end of my ability to cope. I totally lost it. Thank God for friends.

Without a dear friend in Maine I don't know what would have happened. But I called Nancy and, bless her, she caringly listened to my long and painful rant. I may have freaked her out, as I think she could hear me weeping in despair. She was clearly worried. But it turned out just unloading my frustrations and fears to a loving ear appeared to do the trick. The pain was still there, but now the meltdown began to recede. A few days later I had an MRI that at last pinned down the problem, which also helped. It would seem there was no ligament damage, but thick fluid had been trapped, with no way to drain, in an area of my leg filled with nerves. This was why wrapping the leg was so NOT a good idea. Again, knowing what was wrong really, really helped.

My leg healed as the fluid was slowly reabsorbed, and I took a lesson. I think I was undone not so much by the injury nor even the pain but by weeks of pain without knowing the cause, made worse first by a doctor who didn't seem to give a damn and then by a doctor who couldn't figure it out until he saw the MRI. I also learned just how draining constant pain can be. Pain over several days is different from pain over several weeks—coupled with having no idea of when or if it will end. I mention all this because the truth of it is, we all have our limits. All of us.

Just as this pain was ebbing, I was hit with something new though this time it wasn't physical. With the truly nasty 2016 presidential contest, it was clear that the United States was becoming more and more polarized. Donald Trump had emboldened both racists and xenophobes to crawl out of their holes. Some of the hate and bigotry was aimed at women, some at Hispanics, Jews, blacks and gays. But the most spiteful and vicious venom was aimed at Muslims.

At the same time I was learning more and more about what was happening at Standing Rock in North Dakota. In brief, a huge corporation wanted to push an oil pipeline through the state. The original pipeline route was slated to cross the Missouri River ten miles north of Bismarck, North Dakota. The largely white residents of the city were worried that any pipeline leak just ten miles north of them would threaten their water supply. So, the route was changed so that it would cross the river south of Bismarck—just *half a mile north* of the Standing Rock Sioux Reservation. Now a leak would only threaten Native American access to clean water.

Steven Greenebaum

The state of North Dakota seemed not only surprised but indeed outraged that the Standing Rock Sioux protested. How uppity!

It felt like an ugly rerun of the 1960s civil rights struggles. There seemed little I could do about Trump's nationwide call to bigotry, but I felt there must be something I could do here. It had bothered me all of my adult life that I hadn't been able to march with Dr. King. I felt I needed to go to Standing Rock to show solidarity and *act*—not just proclaim my support for civil rights but *act* on it. Then, just as I was wondering how I could possibly manage this, Reverend John Floberg of the Standing Rock Episcopal Church put out a "clergy call" on social media. There was only a week's warning, but along with five hundred other clergy from across the country, I put my life on hold and came to Standing Rock. For me it was just a bit tricky as my leg still wasn't fully healed and my ears prevented me from flying. So that meant taking the train, then renting a car to get to Standing Rock.

My education on what Native Americans had experienced at the hands of the Europeans who had colonized the New World had come in dribbles over my lifetime. As a child, I had experienced the portrayal of the "savage" American Indians in movies and television and the "brave settlers" who simply sought to live in peace as they moved west to civilize this new land.

The truth of how the West was actually "won" had slowly seeped in. At some point, it at last dawned on me that the indigenous peoples of what was now called the United States of America had in so many ways become the New World's Jews. Most horrifically, they had experienced their own Shoah. Whole tribes had been slaughtered. The "Indian Problem" seemed to require a "Final Solution." No, there weren't gas chambers, and yes, it took place over more than a century. But it was no less than an attempt at genocide. And like the Jews who were shoved into ghettos, Native Americans who survived the genocide were enclosed in reservations. And if the land the reservations were on proved to be valuable, the reservation was moved (please web-search "Trail of Tears" if this is not familiar to you).

In 1870, the Fifteenth Amendment granted people of color the right to vote (though it was opposed and resisted well into the 1960s and in many places is still resisted). In 1920 the Nineteenth Amendment granted women the right to vote. It wasn't until 1924 that Congress passed "The Indian Citizenship Act" (no amendment) that at last granted Native Americans the right to vote. For so many reasons, I felt I needed to be at Standing Rock.

224

There were many deeply spiritual moments at Standing Rock, but for me two in particular stand out. The first was when (with the permission of the Standing Rock representatives) we burned a symbolic copy of the "Doctrine of Discovery" in the tribal fire. This fifteenth-century doctrine in essence gave the full sanction of the Christian Church for European Christians to do whatever they liked to any non-European land they discovered, giving the indigenous peoples who actually lived there no rights whatsoever—not even the right to live. The Doctrine of Discovery is a notorious and horrific as well as abhorrently arrogant document. It was not only burned but denounced by denomination after denomination. This was symbolism, but beautiful symbolism. I was so very glad to be present.

Far less important, but still a moment that gave me a feeling of deep spiritual fullness, was being asked to lead the gathered clergy in an interfaith prayer. I'd been asked to play a role in our support of the people of Standing Rock. Me! The whole trip took a lot out of me, though I did my best to hide it. It was disappointing, to put it mildly, that my declining health was imposing greater and greater restrictions on me. But that didn't diminish the high I got from being able to contribute. Indeed, it probably made it all the sweeter.

I returned home from Standing Rock just in time for the election. Trump and his anti-Islamic (as well as anti-Hispanic, anti-Jewish and anti-so-many-others) platform won. Among the many people affected by this purveyor of hate and intolerance, I noticed among my Muslim friends two very different reactions. Some were determined to stand their ground as American citizens and residents with rights, in spite of the increasingly blatant hate speech and threat of outright violence. Others feared not only for their own safety but that of their children. Echoes of the fate of the Jews who had refused to flee Nazi Germany until too late reverberated in my mind. There was no way I could fault any Muslim who decided to leave.

Cathy and her husband were among those who decided that they needed to move to Canada. I couldn't blame them. Cathy called me the day after the election to tell me that she and her family would be leaving, and what that meant for Living Interfaith. What it meant, of course, was that Cathy would not be replacing me as minister. She would be in Canada.

I will be honest. I not only felt so very badly for Cathy, her family and all my Muslim brothers and sisters but also for myself. With that phone call, all my carefully prepared plans for retirement were completely blown out of the water.

Chapter Thirty-Four

I'd poured everything I had into working with Cathy for nearly three years. Now what? For every door that closes, a door can be kicked open, right? Fine! For a while I was just numb. But as the dust settled I came to appreciate that Cathy's three years of study with me had not been wasted—for either of us.

Cathy is blooming. She is not only continuing her studies in Canada, working toward an MDIV (Master of Divinity), but has already started a Living Interfaith sanctuary in her new home of Vancouver. She will be a fine gardener for the Interfaith seed of community and love. It took me a while, but I see this now as a true blessing. The movement will spread. Cathy and others will help to spread it. In fact, Cathy has already been in contact with two other ministers who plan to start Living Interfaith congregations where they live, one in Canada and the other in the United States, in 2019-2020.

Yet, there was still that flaming door to kick open. I wanted, indeed needed to retire, but how could I if there wasn't someone with strong Interfaith shoulders to carry the load? I couldn't just walk away. It was important to hand off to someone I trusted and around whom the church could rally.

The answer came to me as I pondered the wonderful conclusion of "Part One" of a dream I'd had for Living Interfaith from our beginning. I wanted us to create an Interfaith Curriculum, a program that would help teachers introduce children to the bedrock similarities of our diverse spiritual paths (most particularly love, compassion and community) and to appreciate and discuss our many differences without resorting to hierarchy.

This seemed a crucial aid to answering that call to action I had received when I was a child: "They are killing each other in my name. Stop it." No, teaching children about our common beliefs while respecting our diverse spiritual approaches will most assuredly not bring us world peace. But it might become a truly crucial building block, and no such curriculum for teaching Interfaith yet existed. The Living Interfaith board agreed that this was an important contribution we could make to the world, and we were successful in raising the funds to begin our curriculum.

We then hired a good friend of mine from seminary. Marie Preftes Arenz had spent years curriculum-building in her own Lutheran church. She seemed an excellent choice. Happily, she agreed. We determined to create this curriculum in four parts. It took longer than expected, but Marie did a wonderful job on Part One (grades 1–3), and that curriculum is now available for free on the church website for all of good will who would wish to use it.[48] We then raised more funding and were ready for Marie to begin Part Two. That gave me the idea.

In writing Part One of the curriculum, Marie had come to appreciate Interfaith even more deeply. Might she be interested in Interfaith ministry? I took her to lunch and we discussed the possibility. Marie thought about it long and hard. We discussed it several times, over several lunches, and in the end she gave me an enthusiastic yes! I believe she will be a true gift, both to our congregation and to the faith of Interfaith.

But as this was progressing, I found myself facing yet another limitation. Under the Trump administration, things were not going well for my Sioux brothers and sisters at Standing Rock. I wanted to go back there, but I wasn't physically up to it. My strength had never fully returned. Ok. I can't return to Standing Rock and march. Then I had to face that I wasn't up even to driving to Seattle and marching in support of Standing Rock. Ok, then. So what cards *did* I have?

I organized a gathering and a short one-mile march from a park in my home town of Lynnwood to city hall. I had "We Stand with Standing Rock" signs made and also put together a petition to the city council and as well as a draft resolution of support based on a resolution passed by the city of Seattle (that I'd found online). At city hall we presented a sympathetic council member with our petition and draft resolution. I then went before the Lynnwood City Council to urge that they pass the resolution. It took some more nudging and several weeks, but the resolution was passed. I

---

48   See the "Education" tab at http://livinginterfaith.org/

got a copy of it from the city and mailed it to Rev. John Floberg at Standing Rock. John shared the resolution with the tribe.

Powering back also meant I couldn't march in support of the efforts to save our planet from what I believe to be President Trump's unconscionable withdrawal of the United States from the Paris Climate Accord. However, I could and did speak to the Lynnwood City Council and provide it and our mayor with the necessary information (also found online) for Lynnwood to do what other states and cities around the U.S. had done: namely go around Trump and pledge support of and to the accord. Our mayor is now a "Climate Mayor." Lynnwood has joined well over 350 cities across the United States as "Climate Cities."

I kept hoping that my energy might return but found myself staring at the reality of a new normal. Perhaps even more distressing, as I was adapting to this, the arthritis in my hands started getting worse, and then *much* worse. It is worst in my right hand, and I'm right-handed. So, I embarked upon the adventure of learning to use and rely on my left hand. Most recently there appear to be some new health issues as well. So, I've continued to grope with the challenge of figuring out just what cards I have left and how best to play them.

In the meantime, I've happily and with great joy passed the torch. Marie is now the minister at Living Interfaith in Lynnwood, as Cathy leads Living Interfaith in Vancouver. More to the point, the faith of Interfaith is in your hands now as well.

What to make of my climbing this mountain? I hope you'll remember that a budget is a spiritual document, and that when one door closes another can be kicked open. I hope you'll find comfort in recognizing that whatever our situation, and even if we don't have the cards we want, we always have cards to play. Most especially, I hope you'll not only take to heart the "afternoon's dictation", but most especially help to spread the word, gently and always with respect, that we are indeed one family: indivisible. For the sake of our children and their children, let this recognition that we are indeed but one family, no matter our differences, become a rallying cry for the human race. Each of us can make a difference. And together, we can make all the difference.

May your world be filled with love. And may you help to fill the world with love.

Appendices

Steven Greenebaum

Appendix 1
Reflection for Service of Song

Before there were space stations, palm organizers[49] and e-mail, before there were planes and cars, before there was a United States, before there was religion, even before there was language, there was song: the humming of a mother to her infant—of the gatherer at work—of the child at play.

We all sing—every race, every ethnicity on every continent. Few of us will sing at Carnegie Hall, or, for that matter, on American Idol—for which, I think, we may all be grateful.

But like the humpback whale, we sing. For singing, while very much a part of being human, is not exclusively a human endeavor. Indeed, we may be reminded of the phrase: let heaven and nature—sing.

And—one need not believe in God or the gods to feel the spiritual connection that forms when we sing together. I suppose that someday I'll attempt to rip off a well-known U.U. minister and writer, and pen the book: *Everything I Ever Needed to Know of Life I Learned in Choir.*

That every voice counts. That we are so much stronger when we sing together. That to sing in harmony with each other means that no one person, no one faction can take precedence or assume some mantle of supposed superiority. That we are equal—not merely because some philosopher says we are, but because to succeed we must be equal. And that in truth, we have a real and important stake not only in our own part, but in the success of the parts around us.

---

49   Ok, this was a few years ago! Today I would say "smart phones" instead of "palm organizers."

Our altos and tenors will confirm for you, just ask them, that all too often sopranos get the great melody, the basses get—well, the bass line— and the tenors and altos get whatever's left. Sometimes, when you hear just the alto line or just the tenor line, particularly if you're an alto or tenor, you cringe. That's music? And yet without that line, without those "other notes," the music falls flat. But with them—with them the music soars. The "grunge" notes, it turns out, are every bit as crucial as the melody. A good life lesson.

But is singing really that special? That—mystical? I think so. Consider what we say to the instrumentalist whose playing has truly moved us. What is the highest compliment, even beyond technical prowess, that we can give an instrumental musician? Ask. The highest compliment you can give is to say, "You made your instrument—sing."

What is so special about singing? No matter how magnificently Ted[50] plays his saxophone, and he plays magnificently, there is always inanimate metal and a reed and more between him and the music. No matter how superbly our accompanist Ruth "tickles the ivories," there are always keys, strings, metal and wood between her and the music. There is one and only one instance in which the instrument and the musician are one. When you sing, you don't "play" an instrument, you *are* the instrument. Think about it. In so many ways, each of us is the instrument of our lives.

Still, not every moment is harmony, not every song is one of joy. When the music of our lives seems to come apart in disappointment or loss, when our confidence is as a drop of water on a red-hot skillet and the notes just don't—seem to make sense anymore, the question becomes: what now? What now? It happens; it happens profoundly in our lives, and sometimes on Thursday nights in choir.

When it does, we can either stop the rehearsal and go home, or we can pick it up at measure 47 and start again. And, if necessary, start again. And sometimes, yet again. That's when the reality of choir kicks in. Because we *are* in this together. Because as a member of a group, even one as diverse as our Mighty Evergreen Choir, we are there for each other—and we know it. You catch the rhythm that I can't, I nail the note that eludes you. And in the end—in the end the song comes out stronger than ever.

I had the privilege of studying choral conducting with Howard Swan, a magnificent and inspiring teacher. Howard died several years ago. But I shall never forget what he shared with us during a seminar on choral con-

---

50   Ted was a fine musician and a member of the congregation.

ducting. I can no longer give you the exact words he used, but would like to share the essence of what he said.

Anybody, he said, can give voice to the right notes. But to sing, to truly sing, you have to be able and willing to pull your car to the side of the road and examine a flower you've never seen before, appreciate its beauty, partake of its scent. You must be able and willing to close your eyes when you're near a waterfall and listen to the rhythms of the water, and of the different sounds that water on water makes, as opposed to water on wood, and on rocks.

To sing, to truly sing, you must go to museums and appreciate the wealth of expression and emotion in the art that is housed there. You must look at the differing styles of buildings and see the beauty even as you see the differences. Most important, you must see the beauty not only in the world around you but in the people around you.

Music is not life. It is the breath of life. To truly sing, you must inhale deeply of all that lives or you will have nothing upon which to float your notes when you exhale. And if you would sing beautifully, you must always remember that harmony requires a balance of voices. If one voice dominates, the harmony dies.

Anyone can give voice to the right notes. But far too few of us learn to sing. So Howard taught us, and so I believe.

And while I love our choir, I will share with you a secret. You don't have to belong to the choir to sing. You don't even have to be able to carry a tune.

Let us all sing.

Appendix 2
Passages Regarding Human Sacrifice in Torah

(this is not intended as complete)

Human Sacrifice Expected/Required

Gen 22:1-10	Elohim	Abraham ordered to sacrifice his son
Exod 22:28-29	Elohim	Elohim is owed the first born as an offering

Prohibition, Negation or Mitigation of Sacrifice

Gen 22:11-13	YHWH	Abraham told "Do not raise your hand against the boy or do anything to him."
Exod 13:13	YHWH	You must redeem your first-born male
Exod 34:20	YHWH	You must redeem your first-born male
Lev 18:21	YHWH	Do not allow your offspring to be offered to Molech
Num 3:46	YHWH	Levites replace first born/if not enough Levites redeem with five shekels
Num 8:16-19	YHWH	Levites replace first born and perform rites
Num 18:13	YHWH	First born must be redeemed
Deut 12:31	YHWH	Child sacrifice is an abomination and prohibited

Steven Greenebaum

Appendix 3
An Interfaith Ministry
Curriculum/Reading List

As this is written, there appear to be a number of "interfaith" curriculums at various seminaries but no "Interfaith" curriculum. If you are seeking to become an Interfaith minister, look for a seminary experience that includes these subjects. The list of books is, of course, not exclusive. It's suggested. If you seek to study Interfaith on your own, here's a good way to start—with comments from Steven Greenebaum (who put the curriculum together) and Cathy Merchant (who has completed it). While the order of the subjects is important (first "Beginning," then "Mythology," then "Religion" and so forth), the order of the books within each subject (with the exception of "Mythology") should simply be taken as suggested and not written in stone.

Beginning:

The Interfaith Alternative by Steven Greenebaum
Let Your Life Speak by Parker Palmer
Man's Search for Meaning by Viktor Frankl

Steven: These are intended to set the tone for the study. Why Interfaith? Why listen to your deepest self? Why has meaning been so important to humanity?

Cathy: I definitely agree that it makes sense to start with these, since the topics discussed here are foundational to Interfaith study. *The Inter-*

faith Alternative makes a strong case for going beyond tolerance and judgment to embracing Interfaith as its own distinct spiritual path. *Let Your Life Speak* does an excellent job of helping the reader come to terms with his or her own inner calling, especially toward ministry. And I know *Man's Search for Meaning* is reportedly groundbreaking for a lot of people who say that it helps them put their own lives into perspective. For my part, I read it immediately after reading *Night* by Elie Weisel—which struggles with many of the same topics—so I don't think I was as influenced by it as I might otherwise have been. But I still agree that it is worthwhile and a good place to start one's study.

Mythology:

Singer of Tales by Albert Lord
Mythologies of the Ancient World, edited by Samuel Kramer
The Myth of the Eternal Return by Mercea Eliade
The Hero with a Thousand Faces by Joseph Campbell
Myth and Mythmaking, edited by Henry Murray

Steven: I strongly believe that myth should be studied before religion. Once we rid ourselves of the idea that "myth" means wrong, and are able to understand that myths reflect our sacred stories, understanding myth becomes foundational to understanding people and their beliefs.

Cathy: Until working with Steven, I'd never studied myth in conjunction with religion before, so I had no idea what to expect during this part of our program. But I actually thought it was quite eye-opening to see how myths evolve over time and how similar myths are shared by different groups of people around the world. My favorite of these five books was *The Myth of the Eternal Return*, as I found Eliade's thesis about Eastern and Western myths to be rather compelling. And I agree that this definitely helped pave the way for studying religions through a more noticeably "Interfaith lens," afterward.

Religion

A History of Religious Ideas by Mercea Eliade (volumes 1, 2 & 3)
A New Handbook of Living Religions, edited by John Hinnells
Divinity and Diversity by Marjorie Suchocki
No Religion is an Island, edited by Edward Bristow
The Battle for God by Karen Armstrong

Steven: This is NOT everything you ever wanted to know about religion! But I believe it can provide both a great breadth of understanding of our differing spiritual paths and also some of the difficulties that have been faced with as we attempt to understand each other, and perhaps even fill in a few blanks.

Cathy: I don't believe there is a single handful of religious books that could possibly cover them all or even go far in depth into any one of them, but as far as a general overview of the various teachings and challenges within most of the traditions, I think this is a good list. These are all useful and interesting in different ways, so I don't even know how to recommend any one over the others.

Interfaith

Practical Interfaith by Steven Greenebaum
Beyond Tolerance by Gustav Niebuhr
Getting to the Heart of Interfaith by MacKenzie, Falcon and Rahman
A New Religious America by Diana Eck (if you intend to minister in the United States)
Handbook of Denominations in the U.S., 11th edition, revised by Craig Atwood (again, if you intend to minister in the United States)

Steven: These can help set the foundation for Interfaith ministry. We need not only to be able to articulate Interfaith as a faith, but also understand the true breadth of our varying spiritual approaches.

Cathy: I quite enjoyed this subset of books because I was most interested in learning about Interfaith in action and how it is currently being understood and practiced (in various forms) in the United States (where I live). *Practical Interfaith* is the most useful if you are looking at starting your own Interfaith community. Otherwise, the subsequent four books go deeper into the backstory of Interfaith and interfaith dialogue and are good resources for all kinds of cross-cultural and Interfaith programs, not just overtly spiritual ones.

Deeper

Night by Elie Wiesel
Divided by Faith by Benjamin Kaplan
When Jesus Became God by Richard Rubenstein
Introduction to the Old Testament by Anthony Ceresko
Reading the Bible from the Margins by Miguel De La Torre

Justice Rising by John Heagle
The Heart of the Buddha's Teaching (Buddhism) by Thich Nhat Hanh
Gleanings from the Writings of Baha'u'llah (Baha'i) by Baha›u›llah
Approaching the Qur'an (Islam) by Michael Sells
A Stream of Light (Unitarian Universalism), edited by Conrad Wright
No Future Without Forgiveness by Desmond Tutu
Where Do We Go From Here? by Martin Luther King
Terror in the Mind of God by Mark Juergensmeyer

Steven: This list goes deeper in several ways. It tries to supplement an Interfaith minister's knowledge if s/he is not familiar with a particular spiritual path (Buddhist, Islamic, Baha'i, Unitarian Universalist). It also goes more deeply into the themes of justice and a more just world, as well as what we sometimes do to each other in the name of our spiritual path.

Cathy: I love that this list combines both social justice-oriented books with religious commentaries and spiritual guides, as I believe these things are all deeply intertwined and should not be pursued exclusive to one another. The first and the last three in this list all impacted me greatly, but I can't say that I necessarily prefer them to the others because they are all important in different ways.

Ministry

The Active Life by Parker Palmer
Facing the Fire by John Lee
Your Inner Child of the Past by Hugh Missildine
You Just Don't Understand by Deborah Tannen

Steven: These books more directly go to the life and challenges that humanity faces, and therefore a minister will face. They are intended to help a minister in day-to-day ministry. In all honesty, they would be as relevant in a Christian or Jewish or any other ministry as they would be in Interfaith ministry.

Cathy: I will even go farther than Steven and say that these would be useful to anyone, not just clergy. Learning how to lead a balanced life, safely address anger, heal from one's past wounds, and communicate effectively are skills every person should learn. Indeed, if we all followed through on the recommendations given in these books, the world would be a lot safer and healthier place for us all.

Supplemental Reading

Your Sexual Self by Ferder and Heagle
A Hidden Wholeness by Parker Palmer
America's Four Gods by Froese and Bader
Jewish-Christian Dialogue by Mary Boys
Encountering God by Diana Eck
The Miracle of Mindfulness by Thich Nhat Hanh
Rediscovering Values by Jim Wallis

Steven: This is NOT intended to be the end-all, but there's only so long a list can be! I think these books can be exceedingly helpful in broadening a minister's outlook. But there are a lot of wonderful books out there. Let this be the *beginning* of supplemental reading, not the end point!

Cathy: I agree with Steven that these books are helpful, although I preferred the others that were listed earlier. In my opinion, you really can't go wrong with books by Parker Palmer, Diana Eck, Thich Nhat Hanh and Jim Wallis, as they seem to me to be some of the great sages of our time. I do think that one of Wallis' more recent books—*On God's Side, The (Un)Common Good, or America's Original Sin*—would be a better choice than *Rediscovering Values*, because that book was written in the midst of the Great Recession and seems somewhat outdated to me now. I also would add *A History of God* by Karen Armstrong, *The Places That Scare You* by Pema Chodron and *The Seven Storey Mountain* by Thomas Merton to the list.

Select MSI Books

Foreign Language & Culture

Managing Cognitive Distortions & Mitigating Affective Dissonance (Leaver)

Road to Damascus (E. Imady)

Syrian Folktales (M. Imady)

The E&L Construct: Supercharging Language Learning Success One Mind at a Time (Leaver)

The Rise and Fall of Muslim Civil Society (O. Imady)

The Subversive Utopia: Louis Kahn and the Question of National Jewish Style in Jerusalem (Sakr)

Thoughts without a Title (Henderson)

When You're Shoved from the Right, Look to Your Left (O. Imady)

Health & Fitness

108 Yoga and Self-Care Practices for Busy Mommas (Gentile)

Girl, You Got This! (Renz)

Living Well with Chronic Illness (Charnas)

Survival of the Caregiver (Snyder)

The Optimistic Food Addict (Fisanick)

Humor

How My Cat Made Me a Better Man (Feig)

Mommy Poisoned Our House Guest (S. Leaver)

Soccer Is Fun without Parents (Jonas)

The Musings of a Carolina Yankee (Amidon)

Inspirational and Religious Books

A Believer-in-Waiting's First Encounters with God (Mahlou)

A Guide to Bliss: Transforming Your Life through Mind Expansion (Tubali)

Christmas at the Mission: A Cat's View of Catholic Beliefs and Customs (Sula)

Easter at the Mission: A Cat's Observation of the Paschal Mystery (Sula)

El Poder de lo Transpersonal (Ustman)

Everybody's Little Book of Everyday Prayers (MacGregor)

How to Argue with an Atheist: How to Win the Argument without Losing the Person (Brink)

Intrepid: Fearless Immigrant from Jordan to America (Leaver & Leaver)

Introductory Lectures on Religious Philosophy (Sabzevary)

Jesus Is Still Passing By (Easterling)/*Study Guide edition*

Joshuanism (Tosto)

Living in Blue Sky Mind: Basic Buddhist Teachings for a Happy Life (Diedrichs)

Overcoming the Odds (C. Leaver)

Puertas a la Eternidad (Ustman)

RV Oopsies (MacDonald)

Saints I know (Sula)

Surviving Cancer, Healing People: One Cat's Story (Sula)

Tale of a Mission Cat (Sula)

Memoirs

57 Steps to Paradise: Finding Love in Midlife and Beyond (Lorenz)

Blest Atheist (Mahlou)

Forget the Goal, the Journey Counts . . . 71 Jobs Later (Stites)

From Deep Within: A Forensic and Clinical Psychologist's Journey (Lewis)

Good Blood: A Journey of Healing (Schaffer)

Healing from Incest: Intimate Conversations with My Therapist (Henderson & Emerton)

It Only Hurts When I Can't Run: One Girl's Story (Parker)

Las Historias de Mi Vida (Ustman)

Of God, Rattlesnakes, and Okra (Easterling)

Tucker and Me (Harvey)

Parenting & Teaching

365 Teacher Secrets for Parents: Fun Ways to Help Your Child in Elementary School (McKinley & Trombly)

How to Be a Good Mommy When You're Sick (Graves)

Lessons of Labor (Aziz)

Noah's New Puppy (Rice & Henderson)

Understanding the Challenge of "No" for Children with Autism (McNeil)

Psychology & Philosophy

Anger Anonymous: The Big Book on Anger Addiction (Ortman)

Anxiety Anonymous: The Big Book on Anxiety Addiction (Ortman)

Awesome Couple Communication (Pickett)

Depression Anonymous: The Big Book on Depression Addiction (Ortman)

El Poder de lo Transpersonal (Ustman)

How to Live from Your Heart (Hucknall)

Road Map to Power (Husain & Husain)

The Marriage Whisperer: How to Improve Your Relationship Overnight (Pickett)

The Rose and the Sword: How to Balance Your Feminine and Masculine Energies (Bach & Hucknall)

The Seven Wisdoms of Life (Tubali)

Understanding the Analyst: Socionics in Everyday Life (Quinelle)

Understanding the Critic: Socionics in Everyday Life (Quinelle)

Understanding the Entrepreneur: Socionics in Everyday Life (Quinelle)

Understanding the People around You: An Introduction to Socionics (Filatova)

Understanding the Seeker: Socionics in Everyday Life (Quinelle)

Self-Help Books

100 Tips and Tools for Managing Chronic Illness (Charnas)

A Woman's Guide to Self-Nurturing (Romer)

Creative Aging: A Baby Boomer's Guide to Successful Living (Vassiliadis & Romer)

Divorced! Survival Techniques for Singles over Forty (Romer)

Helping the Disabled Veteran (Romer)

How to Get Happy and Stay That Way: Practical Techniques for Putting Joy into Your Life (Romer)

How to Live from Your Heart (Hucknall) *(Book of the Year Finalist)*

Life after Losing a Child (Young & Romer)

Publishing for Smarties: Finding a Publisher (Ham)

Recovering from Domestic Violence, Abuse, and Stalking (Romer)

The Widower's Guide to a New Life (Romer)*(Book of the Year Finalist)*

Widow: A Survival Guide for the First Year (Romer)

Widow: How to Survive (and Thrive!) in Your 2d, 3d, and 4th Years (Romer)

CPSIA information can be obtained
at www.ICGtesting.com
Printed in the USA
LVHW031747021019
632974LV00009B/636